Aspects of Near East Society

Aspects of
Near East Society

by Moshe Zeltzer

COLLEGE AND UNIVERSITY PRESS
New Haven, Connecticut

FOR I. U.-Z.

Preface

The task originally envisaged in this book was to trace the evolution of the main aspects of Near East society, country by country. I soon realized that this was a Sisyphean task and confined myself to those countries where the problems are most acute, or of greater consequence.

The plan of chronicling the main political events had to be dropped, though not for fear of taking sides. An analyst is not above interpretation. Bertrand Russell, in his *History as An Art*, regards one-sidedness in a historian as a natural attitude: Let them beat one another, that the truth may emerge. Bernard Lewis admits the feasibility of forming one's opinion, in historical writing on the Middle East, by studying dispassionately, to the best of one's ability, all the evidence and its interpretations.[*] But the inadequacy of source material, hence the difficulty to establish "bare facts," cannot be compensated for by the best of intentions. Moreover, even if all the hidden material could be laid bare, there is still an arduous task to detect the motives of attitudes and activities, to tell strategy from tactical moves, and to glean the real meaning of speeches and other utterances. Granting intellectual integrity, the limitations of objectivity lie in personal, imaginative and ideological commitment—in the very order of presentation, which ultimately reflects preference on a personal level.

Compilations treading on the fence of objectivity, with no access to inside material and no attempt to sound the workings of the self-ruler's mind, are no more satisfactory. The historical narrative dealing with the *coup d'état* is designed only to illustrate the nature of this phenomenon, in itself a mark of social impasse, as a vehicle of political warfare.

One of the problems, evidently underestimated, is the position of minorities in the nation-states of the Near East. In the survey

[*] *Middle East Forum,* June 1958.

of minorities in Iraq and Syria attention is called to social background. The Kurdish minority may prove a decisive factor in shaping the destinies of the whole region. The chapter on Lebanon—that unique state composed of minorities—is in some respects complementary to this survey.

In two chapters the problem of large landownership is dealt with extensively. The present generation became keenly aware of the impact of this problem on society, and this largely accounts for the political upheavals in these countries. Warnings of its ill effects went unheeded. Within six years the monstrous system of landownership has been abolished in Egypt, Syria, and Iraq. From lists of the landowners affected by the land reform laws in Syria and Iraq it is easy to see how great was their influence on the affairs of government. The ability to implement these laws and make constructive use of them remains the crucial question.

I have been guided by the consideration that the involvements in pacts, dictated by reasons of oil and cold-war strategy, have been ephemeral and of minor importance. Against this, the underlying human factors may prove decisive in their effects. The interplay of tradition and rebellion, colored by local background, is what matters most. Here lie the deeper levels of motivation in politics. Concepts from West and East, seen against the background of politics in the world, are translated into practice and theory in a peculiar way. Again and again, special blends of authoritarianism win the day. One has only to confront the Egyptian brand of neutralism with the ideological type of Indian neutralism. But this book has to stop short of an attempt to touch deeper recesses of human problems.

Governments and regimes are fast disintegrating, and yet the pattern of events seems to have come full circle. With all its limitations, some of them self-imposed, this book attempts to provide, through a composite approach, some clue toward more intimate understanding of the scene in the Near East.

Mention can be made here of only a few of the many who have lent me their support. I wish to acknowledge my indebtedness to the Lucius N. Littauer Foundation whose generous grant made the publication of this book possible. Mr. Harry Starr, President of the Foundation, has taken a kind interest in my work. Dr. Manasseh G. Serag and Mr. Kegham A. Mississyan were most helpful in furnishing data on the Armenians.

For technical reasons the diacritical points had to be omitted. The license in transliteration of some Arabic words is well-intentioned.

M. Z.

Contents

Part One

MAJORITY VERSUS MINORITY

Chapter One

Minorities in Iraq and Syria

No hard and exhaustive rules can be set forth for distinguishing minorities in this region.[1] Even in the West, opinions differ about exactly what constitutes a national entity, and with the establishment of multilingual and multiracial India, Pakistan, and Indonesia, the criteria have become much more confused. Successive waves of immigration, caused by invasions and infiltrations, and religious ferment, have left behind them both national and confessional or sectarian minorities. These minorities differ from one another both in their bonds of unity and the strength of these bonds, that is, in the degree of their historical consciousness or of their attachment to a particular language. Some of them occupy an intermediary stage between nation and community. They also differ in their trends of development. The following classification, therefore, will do no more than throw a certain light on this matter.

1. National, linguistic, and territorial minorities: Kurds (Iraq and Syria), Turkomans (Iraq), Circassians (Syria).
2. Religious, linguistic, and territorial minorities: Yazīdis.
3. National, religious, and linguistic minorities: Armenians.
4. Religious and territorial minorities: 'Alawis, Druzes.
5. Confessional and linguistic minorities: Syrian Orthodox, Syrian Catholics and Chaldeans (that is, those sections that still use an Aramaic dialect).
6. Confessional minorities: Greek Orthodox, Greek Catholics, Syrian Orthodox, Syrian Catholics, Protestants, etc.

There are at least four main factors which have brought about this great split of the population.

1. Ever since the Christian faith became dominant on the east coast of the Mediterranean until the rise of Islam, this region has been the scene of constant religious strife. The Nestorians, in order to escape from the Byzantine emperors, removed from Syria, after the schism at about 498 A.D., to the other side of the Euphrates and farther away. Most of the Syrian Orthodox were also squeezed out of Syria to the other side of the Euphrates, and only in the last century, especially after World War I, did thousands of them reach the Jazīra from Turkish Kurdistan. In the seventeenth century the Jesuits commenced to work in the Near East; and with other orders that followed them, they succeeded in winning over sections of the Eastern Churches to the Roman Catholic Church. The activity of the Protestants commenced in the first half of the last century.

2. The identity of three secretive communities—Ismāʿīlis, Druzes, and ʿAlawis—may have been preserved also by their isolation in the mountains. In some degree these three extreme offshoots of Shīʿism may be theologically related. Some scholars are inclined to see in Ismāʿīlism, the oldest of them, traces of a national and racial revolt of Persia against Semitic Islam. Others again lay more stress on its social elements, seeing in revolutionary Shīʿism "the natural expression, in a theocratic milieu, of the revolt of the depressed classes, Persian and Semite alike."[2]

3. The dualist tradition of the early Christian Gnostics and Manichaeans (opposition of Light and Darkness, divine abstractions beneath God, initiation and consequently division of the adepts into select and simple) may have left a residue in other sects, too (Yazīdis, Mandaeans). Manichaeism spread from Turkestan to North Africa and was still powerful in eastern Turkestan in 1000 A.D.[3]

4. Mass migrations.

a. Migration of Turkish peoples from the eleventh century onward, especially from the time of the Mongolian irruptions. During the Ottoman period, Turks were transferred to the territories of Iraq and Syria to protect communications.

b. The penetration of Kurds from Kurdistan southward. This movement had already taken place in the days of Saladin and has not ceased to this day. For security reasons, Kurdish settlements were established in Syria by the Ottoman government.

c. Transfer of segments of Caucasian peoples, and to a lesser degree groups from the Balkans, from the 1860's and 1870's.

d. After World War I, Syria and Lebanon became, through their mandatory government, an asylum for refugees from Christian and other communities fleeing from Turkey,[4] and to some extent from Iraq.

Kurds

Among the minorities the Kurds stand out most clearly as a national entity. In claiming self-determination, they point to the following:

1. A distinct ethnic group, one of the oldest within the human race. The question of their origin, as yet unresolved, has no relevance whatsoever to their claim.

2. Common fundamental characteristics of the dialects.[5] They have a vast folklore, a number of classical works and the beginnings of modern literature.[6]

3. Community of religion. Within Sunni Islam, mysticism embodied in orders, notably *naqshbandi* and *qādiri*, is the main characteristic. Outside it, a number of heterodox sects thrive among the Kurds.[7]

4. Almost unbroken territorial contiguity of the Kurdish settlements: from close to Marash in Turkey to the boundary of Iran, that is, on both sides of the Syrian-Turkish frontier, and then northward to Erzerum and Kars; in Iraq from the Iraqi-Turkish border southward to Mandalī; and in Iran from Maku on the border of Soviet Armenia to Kirmanshah. This contiguity is also confirmed by tribal ties across the frontiers. Large confederations of tribes live in or migrate between Iraq and Iran (Jāf, Bilbas, Kalhur, Harki) and between Iraq and Turkey (Mazuri).[8]

5. National self-consciousness combines with a centuries-old tradition of rule of Kurdish principalities, some of which still existed in the first half of the last century. The last century

witnessed social revolts there and risings of Kurdish feudals against centralization of government in Turkey and Iran. After 1908 the first shoots of a national movement emerged, in the form of a club and a literary society. After World War I, the Kurdish problem had been raised on an international plane for the first time. The Treaty of Sèvres provided for local autonomy in the Kurdish areas and acknowledged, under certain conditions, the possibility of independence "if the majority of the population desired it." A new and more advanced phase started in 1927 with the setting up of Hoybun (National Committee) in Syria which initiated cultural activities.[9] The outcome of World War II seemed to be favorable to the national cause, but the resulting cold war prevented the upsetting of the status quo in the Middle East.

6. All the national and social characteristics that entitle a people to statehood are found in them. It is the conflict of interests in this "seething cauldron" which facilitates, by means of negligence or support, a policy of oppression towards the Kurds. Power politics after the two world wars helped to establish states for peoples or tribal conglomerations far less fit for independence.

The main reasons against Kurdish statehood are given as follows: the isolation of the mountain districts and the consequent difficulties of communication among the three parts of Kurdistan; backwardness of the Kurds; particularism of the tribes; and multiplicity of dialects. But these and similar reasons can be applied, to a far greater degree, to all the states recently established in Asia.[10]

The problems concerning the position of the Kurds in Iraq and Syria are in many respects inseparable from those of the Kurds in Iran, Turkey, and the Soviet Union.

Turkey

In Turkey, where nearly half of the Kurdish people live, the policy adopted towards them since the end of World War I has been one of forcible assimilation, that is, "absorption in the Turkish nation." Officially, there is no Kurdish question and the

Kurds are regarded as "mountain Turks." Since 1923 the Turkish government has had to cope with rebellions, particularly in the years 1925, 1927, and 1937. Various methods of Turkification have been used: enrollment of the men in labor squads in distant camps, and, as during 1914–1918, deportation; transference from the mountains to the plains; ban on the Kurdish language in office and school; and denial of facilities for cultural and social activities. Steps calculated to destroy the tribal organization were also taken. After World War II, a more conciliatory attitude toward the Kurds was adopted, but the basic policy remained unchanged.[11]

Iran

In Iran, Riza Shah tried to settle the Kurdish question in his own way—by disarming the Kurds, by carrying off tribal leaders to Teheran as hostages, by forcing tribes to settle without providing the means, and by splitting up tribes and scattering some of them in remote districts. In the years between the two world wars, Kurdish revolts took place, and in 1932, during the uprising of Jalali in the region of Maku, many villages were laid waste. Conditions after World War II favored the emergence of a Kurdish republic in the Soviet-occupied part of their territory (end of 1945 to the end of 1946). Its government initiated social reforms, and it consequently became the center of Kurdish national aspirations. It was crushed by the Iranian government, and its leaders were put to death.[12] The republic of Mahabad was a combined attempt of representatives of different classes—tribal chiefs, religious leaders, and town dwellers. It was the first Kurdish movement preponderately urban.

The Kurds in Iran are regarded as Iranians and consequently are forbidden to carry on cultural work in their own language. It is open to question how far it is a means to an intended gradual absorption.[13] The authorities are not strong enough to destroy the tribal organization of the Kurds.

U.S.S.R.

The 120,000 Kurds in Armenia, Azerbaijan, and Turkmenistan enjoy, speaking in Soviet terms, cultural autonomy. Yerevan has become their intellectual center.[14] They have a network of elementary and secondary schools, and a pedagogical institute. A Latin alphabet, adopted in 1929, was replaced, in 1945, by the Russian alphabet supplemented by some Latin signs. Studies in the Kurdish language have been pursued with tangible results. Broadcasts in Kurdish are also designed to impress Kurds beyond the border.

Iraq

There are over a million Kurds in Iraq, forming at least 20 percent of the population.[15] Most of them live in the northeastern mountain range—the liwās of Sulaymāni, Arbil, Kirkuk and in the four northern districts of Mosul. Two of the four districts of Diyāla liwā—Khanāqīn and Mandalī—are to a large degree Kurdish. They are also found in Kūt and Baghdad liwās.

Kurdish society in Iraq is basically tribal. The continuous process of detribalization has been accelerated by closer control of the central authorities, by modern communications, and in a great degree by land settlement which, as in the whole of Iraq, tended to fix property rights in favor of tribal chiefs and other men of power. This could not but result in the transition from a tribal to a feudal pattern of society. The oil fields and the recently executed damming projects contribute their share to detribalization. The national movement, nowadays chiefly directed from the town, brings about a shift of loyalties from the tribal hierarchy and from the nontribal, merely residential associations, to the nation as a whole. If one may generalize, one might say that the mountain areas still are, in the main, tribally organized (Ruwandiz area in Arbil, areas of Pushdir and Halebja in Sulaymāni). In the lower parts, the nontribal groups of tenant farmers (Garmian area in Kirkuk liwā, the area around Qizil Rubat in Diyāla liwā, the valley around Sulaymāni) predominate. They owe much allegiance to landlords, mostly absentees, and their agents. In many cases they work as tenants on their old tribal land. Distinct social groups are subtenants and laborers, and in certain areas nontribal serf groups.

The once powerful seminomadic tribes (Harki, especially Jāf) are rapidly losing their nomadic character.

The town dwellers, also partly descended from tribes, are nontribal. In most towns the Kurdish element is predominant, but ethnically they show a great diversity (various Christian denominations, Turks, Arabs, and, until recently, Jews).[16]

The position of the Kurds in Iraq is in some respects far more tolerable than in Turkey and Iran, but there they have had the misfortune of being subjected, a second time in our own days, to the rule of a foreign people which like themselves has been subordinate to the Turks. The Kurdish question with all its implications was acute as early as 1918.[17] On account of the oil-bearing region, the British government threw all its weight onto the scale so that it was joined to Iraq in 1925. The R.A.F. played a decisive part in subduing Kurdish revolts against the government in 1922–23, 1927, 1930–31.[18] In 1930, on the eve of the abolition of the mandate, Kurdish leaders pressed their petitions on the League of Nations for the establishment of a "Kurdish government under the supervision of the League of Nations." In 1925 and in 1932 the Iraqi government pledged itself before the League of Nations to guarantee the use of Kurdish in school and office, and employment of Kurdish officials in Kurdish areas. At the same time it continued to foment dissension among Kurdish tribes.[19]

In the 1940's the main complaints of the Kurds were:

1. The Kurdish community in Iraq has no political existence because any political activity in a national framework is forbidden to it. By contrast, national feeling among the Arabs has reached its peak. There are two principal peoples in Iraq, but both domestic and foreign policy represent the Arab section alone. The ties between the Kurds of Iraq and those of Turkey and Iran are not different from the ties between the Arabs of Iraq and Syria. The policy of Turkey and Iran is to disintegrate the Kurds, and yet Iraq has entered with them into the Treaty of Saadabad, one of the purposes of which is to coordinate the suppression of the Kurdish aspirations by all of them.

2. The administration is inefficient throughout the country, but the districts of the Kurds have been deliberately neglected.

3. On paper, Kurdish is recognized as one of the official

languages in Kurdish districts, but in fact the law is not carried out even in the Sulaymāni liwā. Of the few schools in the area, only a small portion are Kurdish. The curricula and the history books do not deal with the Kurdish people, and printed matter in Kurdish is scarce.

4. The authorities dismiss or remove beyond the Kurdish boundaries those local officials who have any attachment to Kurdish nationalism.[20]

The answer to complaints about the economic plight was expulsion from the area or imprisonment. Power seekers, eager to pose before the public as heroes, exploited the situation by provoking racial and communal dissensions.[21]

After the revolt of the Barzani tribes in 1930, their leaders Mulla Mustafa and his brother Ahmad were removed to the south, and from there to Sulaymāni, where they were forcibly detained for about thirteen years. In June 1943, Mustafa escaped and joined his fellow tribesmen, and affrays involving bloodshed took place. In consequence of defeats at the hands of the rebels and desertion of Kurdish policemen and soldiers, the authorities decided, on the advice of the British, to open negotiations with the rebels. The Kurdish deputy Majid Mustafa associated some Kurdish officers with the negotiations. The Kurds assert that the following agreement was then arrived at:

1. All the Barzanis in detention should be released.
2. The Barzanis should retain their arms.
3. Foodstuffs should be equitably distributed in the Arab and Kurdish districts.
4. The Arab officials in the Kurdish districts should be replaced by Kurds.
5. Proper cultural autonomy should be guaranteed in Iraqi Kurdistan, and Kurdish schools and hospitals should be established.

Nūrī al-Saʿīd accepted these terms, but a majority in parliament rejected them. In consequence, Nūrī al-Saʿīd resigned in June 1944.[22]

The government of al-Pāchachī renewed the negotiations with Mulla Mustafa. In July 1945, the government troops suffered a severe defeat, and it was only after the air force hurriedly intervened that the rebels withdrew into the mountains. Finally thousands crossed the frontier of Iran. The Barzanis were joined by members of other tribes, officers, some of them of high rank, soldiers, civil servants, and teachers.[23] About 800 of them proceeded to Soviet Armenia.

The movement in Barzan had three aspects: local, national, and international. The district was one of the most neglected, and the inhabitants lived on chestnut bread and some fruit. The pick of the young men were imprisoned and removed on the pretext that they were busying themselves with the Kurdish question. The inhabitants complained of economic unfairness, particularly in the handling of the tobacco monopoly.

Government of the country appeared to rest on a constitutional basis, but in fact the constitution was a dead letter. Unscrupulous men sought to attain office by exaggerating differences of race and community.[23]

On the international side, the interests of the great powers prevented the Kurdish question from making itself heard in the world. The Kurds knew that as long as their aspirations for independence did not fit in with the prevailing trends of world politics, they had no hope of sovereignty.[24] Toward the end of World War II, the course of events seemed to be favorable to them. In the zone of Soviet occupation in Iran they were greatly encouraged. During the war, the British authorities evinced a certain sympathy towards them. American envoys also displayed interest in the Kurds in Iran, and after the war they counselled the authorities in Turkey to show patience. The Kurds thought that the time had come to call attention to the Kurdish question.

In the Iraqi parliament at that time, various attitudes on this question were voiced. Some denied its communal or national character. What people wanted was justice and fair treatment. The causes of the revolt were corruption, hardship, and official ineptitude. A state with many communities could not be united unless each community received its share of the benefits from reforms. Others again laid the blame on too great leniency in dealing with the rebels. One deputy pointed out that fifteen years earlier the government had brought forward a bill equivalent to an amnesty for the Barzanis, which was a proof that the causes which had produced the revolt were still operative.

There were two deputies who tried to get to the root of the matter. Sālim Namīq saw in the amnesty only a palliative. It was necessary to investigate the psychological and material causes of the revolt; moreover, it was necessary to examine the question in the light of the international situation. The latest events had reached a new stage, and it was only through the prompt action on the part of the government in sending a punitive expedition, and through the cooperation of a number of Kurdish leaders and their tribes, that a disaster had been averted. Comprehensive reforms were to be introduced in the zone. "The Kurds were a portion of the kingdom and in serving their interests we should serve the kingdom."

The deputy Uzrī called for a "philosophical and historical examination of the problem." Reforms were of secondary importance. "We must make clear to our Kurdish brethren, both by word and deed, that it is not our desire to subject them to exploitation." The Iraqi state was based on two large nations and some smaller ones, all of which had one fatherland. The Arabs would remain Arabs; they would work for the cultivation of their language and their nationality, and would link themselves with the Arabs of other countries; and they wished that the Kurds would also have success in cultivating their language and their nationality. Switzerland and Canada had shown how differences between peoples could be reconciled.[25]

The uprising of the Barzanis signaled a turning point in the Kurdish national movement. In some respects tribal organization offered many advantages. It helped to preserve a tradition of unity. Unlike the Arab tribes, Kurdish tribes are not, at least for the most part, based on traditions of consanguinity, but are nevertheless organic and territorial units headed by a nobility. Moreover, these units are associated with religious orders, so that the sheikhs sometimes combine hereditary temporal and spiritual power. On the other hand, dervish brotherhoods may encompass parts of various tribes. All this, however, is counterbalanced and even outweighed by the fact that the state possesses means for stirring up dissension among the tribes or taking advantage of existing feuds among them. In the last revolt of the Barzanis, the towns already took part so far as to provide it with political support. The Kurdish town resorted to the usual *modus operandi* of the Arab town—students' strikes, demonstrations, leaflets, side by side with negotiations.

The Kurdish society in Iraq has already reached a stage in which detribalization on account of economic development does not imply weakening of national bonds. On the contrary, the loss in cohesion is being offset by a broader outlook and closer attachment to the urban centers. We witness a shift of the center of gravity from landed aristocracy to socially more advanced associations.

Syria

The immigration of Kurds into Syria has been going on for centuries, and the increase in their numbers is already noted by Bazily.[26] Seminomadic, they used to go down with their flocks from Kurdistan to the pashalik of Aleppo. Since the eighteenth century, Kurds had been charged with the task of protecting the pilgrims on their way to Mecca, and immigrants followed in the wake of the protectors. Kurds settled in the towns as bodyguards for the Pashas, and as horsemen in the service of the government or some powerful faction. In Bazily's day there were about a thousand Kurdish families in Damascus.

In various parts of the country, especially in the west and in Hawrān, and also in Lebanon, upper Galilee, and across the Jordan, there are scattered Arabicized islands of Kurds. In some cases some remembrance of their origin is preserved in the name of a tribe or a place: Jabal Akrād in the northeastern slope of Jabal Ansāriyya; to the south of this mountain Krak des Chevaliers, which formerly was called Hisn al-Akrād; Akrād Ibrāhīm, Akrād 'Uthmāni, on the west of it; Hārat al-Akrād in Safed. Arabicized families took an active part in the civil and military life of the country (al-Barāzī, a family from the Euphrates region owning many villages in the districts of Hamā and Masyāf; Būzū, and others). There are tribes or large families in the east of the country, the origins of which are uncertain; some of them claim Arab origin although their Kurdish background is still remembered or they still speak Kurdish. A kind of symbiosis is represented by the Kurdish-Arab confederation of Millī, which is mostly Kurdish. At the beginning of the twentieth century they were in the service of the Turkish government (Hamidiyye cavalry, dissolved by the Young Turks).[27]

Alongside the Turkish frontier there are three Kurdish belts.

1. In the Upper Jazīra, Tigris region, sedentary Kurdish tribes are predominant. They are interspersed with Arab, Turkoman and Yazīdi elements. Since 1926 they have been joined by Kurdish groups from Turkey. In the Khabur area some thousands from the Millī confederation who crossed over from Turkey are settled. Here, too, they were joined by Yazīdis, Armenians, and Jacobites from Turkey. The new town of Qamishli is a kind of capital for the Kurds.

2. Kurdish tribes in the Euphrates belt make up a part of the population of the districts of Jarablus and Manbij, Bāb and A'zāz in the province of Aleppo.

3. A large Kurdish group is to be found in the district of Kurd Dag (Mountain of the Kurds). Its center is the townlet 'Afrīn. Although its tribal formation has been almost completely broken up, the influence of the sheikhs is still considerable.[28]

In the Sālhiyye quarter of Damascus, there are about 20,000 Kurds. They still retain their language and customs, partly because of the influx of fellow Kurds from the North.

After World War I, the Kurds of Syria enjoyed a spell of comparatively liberal treatment. The immigration from Turkey strengthened the Kurdish element in the Jazīra to such an extent that, with the Christians, the Kurds formed the majority of the population.

Although the voice of the Kurds is not heard in the peoples' assemblies, the Kurdish question is one of grave importance in the Middle East. Their claims for self-determination were not supported after World War II either. On the other hand, the Kurdish national movement has now reached a stage where partial concessions, such as language rights and a certain share in the administration, are likely to stimulate rather than curb it.[29]

Within a few months, in 1958, the Kurdish question became a factor in world politics. As far back as 1957, it could still be stated that Iraq "seems to have solved the Kurdish question," and that the Kurds "docilely accept the rule of Baghdad."[30] The reason was seen in the appeasement policy of Nūrī Saʿīd's government through an increased share of the Kurds in the development program and in government posts. The situation improved also in the field of education. As in the case of Iraq as a whole, it was a race with a mounting tide of discontent.

The Provisional Constitution of the new republic sees in Iraq "a part of the Arab nation" (art. 2), but considers Arabs and Kurds "partners in this homeland," and "provides for their national rights within Iraqi unity" (art. 3). Thus the policy of assimilation is explicitly abandoned. An abortive Council of Sovereignty was formed with one Shīʿi Arab, one Sunni Arab, and one Kurd. A member of the first government was Baba ʿAli, son of Sheikh Mahmud from Sulaymāni, since 1918 a rallying point of the Kurdish movement.

Mustafa Barzani, who led the Kurdish revolt in 1944-45, returned from his exile in Soviet Armenia and was acclaimed a national hero. Kurdish tribes helped to crush the rebellion in Mosul in March 1959. The Kurdish position became even stronger with the resignation of the pan-Arab Baʿth and Istiqlāl members from the government. In a greater Arab unity the Kurds would be reduced to a relatively small minority. Recently their impact on the government has lessened.

Repercussions of the changes in Iraq are felt in Iran. Prior to the upheaval in Iraq, Egypt espoused the Kurdish cause and inaugurated a broadcasting service in Kurdish. Its targets were the Baghdad Pact and Nūrī Saʿīd's regime. As in the case of the Negro south in the Sudan, it was a self-defeating undertaking. The Iranian government "retaliated" with broadcasting in Kurdish and allocations for the development of Kurdish areas. The Kurds are being assured that they are no match for Arabs. For the first time since 1946, a Kurdish weekly appeared in Iran, in June 1959.[31]

Lurs

Linguists differ in the classification of their language, some considering it a Kurdish dialect and others claiming that it is closer to the Persian dialects of the Fars province. They are thought to be Shīʻis; some of them are ʻAlī-Ilāhis. For the most part workers, they are to be found in villages of the eastern part of the country (ʻAmāra and Kūt) as well as in Baghdad and Basra. Some of them take part in the Kurdish national movement. The last word as to kinship and allegiance should be theirs.

Nusayris

They are an offshoot of extreme Shīʻism, secretive since the ninth century. One version traces the origin of Nusayri to Ibn Nusayr, the "gate" of the eleventh *imām* at the end of the ninth century. Being believers in the divinity of ʻAlī, they are also called ʻAlawis. Problems of their relation to Islam, particularly to Ismāʻīlism, and of the origin of syncretic elements in their faith, undoubtedly including ancient Semitic, Iranian, as well as Byzantine and perhaps crusaders' practices, remain to be cleared.

There are about 375,000 Nusayris in Syria, of whom 87 percent are in the Latakiya province, that is Jabal Ansāriyya, which in 1920 was extended by the French authorities towards the south and renamed the province of the ʻAlawis.

This is a tribal community. In their province they are linked, mainly, in five confederations (Haddād, Khayyāt, Metāwira, Kalbī, and Haydarī, the last seemingly representing a kind of *madhhab*, persuasion). Owing to migrations and feuds, the first three are not geographically compact, and since, in addition, they are sedentary, the stature of the tribes as social units is constantly diminishing.

Broadly speaking, the tribal bond, epitomized in allegiance to chiefs (*raʼīs* or *muqaddam*), is outweighed by the zonal bond, that is, the bond between tribes or parts of tribes living next to one another. Still more important is the personal bond which leads certain groups to form around a prominent and wealthy family which is able to afford them protection. These groups grow larger or smaller according to circumstances and to the leader's success.

The 'Alawis constitute the majority in the province—over 70 percent—and if the towns are excluded, over 80 percent. Of the towns, some are Sunni islands (Haffa, Ru'ād, Jabala); others Sunni with a considerable Christian minority (Latakiya, Tartūs), or inconsiderable (Bānyās); and one is Christian with a considerable 'Alawi minority (Sāfītā).

This community is preponderantly an agricultural proletariat—laborers, shepherds and foresters. There are comparatively few big landlords in it. Large estates are the rule in the east of the province, where towns are very few, and also eastward of the boundary toward Homs and Hamā, in the area overspread by 'Alawi tenants who are being brought over by Sunni and some Christian landlords. In the northern part of the mountain, medium and small ownership is predominant, but even here the peasant is oppressed by his dependence on the sheikhs and the middlemen who market the tobacco.[32]

Druzes

The eviction of Christian and Muslim elements by Druzes coming from Lebanon to Jabal al-Durūz began as early as the eighteenth century, but it assumed large proportions only in the last century, especially after the warlike feuds between the Druzes and the Maronites in 1860. By the middle of the last century, the Druze settlement in Jabal A'lā of the Aleppo province, at one time the strongest, still provided a refuge for war victims. From here, too, many emigrated to Hawrān.[33]

Other groups of Druzes are in Damascus (town and province), and in Homs and its environs.

The great majority of the 120-odd villages in Jabal al-Durūz are inhabitated by Druzes only, the rest of them by Druzes mixed with either Christians or Muslims or both.

Less than a third of the cultivated area belongs to large proprietors, and about 38 percent are medium-size holdings. As in most parts of Syria, the share-cropping system is prevalent. Seasonal workers are employed under contract.[34]

Although the 'Alawis have been settled in their province for probably seven to eight centuries, whereas most of the Druzes removed to Jabal al-Durūz only about a century ago, they have many features in common. Their numbers are large enough to inspire a certain self-respect. They have a recent tradition of struggle for autonomy, and they have followed similar lines of political evolution under the mandate.

Various attempts to confer autonomy on them were made by the French authorities, from the État du Jebel Druze and the État des Alaouites in 1920, to the *gouvernements* of these territories, in May 1930, which were a kind of tentative arrangement. In all these experiments they remained under direct control of the French. However, in view of the treaty of 1936, they were included as ordinary provinces in the state of Syria, at the same time being promised a special administrative and financial regime. The treaty was not ratified, but it was put into practice, on a trial basis, in regard to the two provinces. At the beginning of World War II, matters returned to the *status quo ante*. In January 1942 the union of the two provinces to Syria was proclaimed. In 1944 their administrative and financial autonomy was withdrawn.

The differences between the two areas are as follows:

1. In the degree of confessional homogeneity. Of the inhabitants of Jabal al-Durūz about 90 percent are Druzes, while of the seven minorities only three are represented among them considerably—Greek Orthodox, Greek Catholics, and Sunnis. In the region of the 'Alawis at least seven minorities stand out—Greek Orthodox, Sunni Arabs, Maronites, Ismā'īlis, Turks, Armenian Orthodox, and Greek Catholics.

2. Economically, and therefore politically, the town has almost no advantage over the village in Jabal al-Durūz. Its three district towns are Druze in character. By contrast, Sunnis and the Greek Orthodox are dominant in the towns and in the coastal

areas of the Latakiya province. And since the ruling class in the towns lives principally on the product of the villagers' labor—officeholders, landlords, and produce merchants—it is easy to see that from the political and social point of view the 'Alawis are nothing more than a minority to the dominant groups of the province.

3. The two communities differ in their geographical distribution. Adjoining the Jabal al-Durūz, there are 88,000 Druzes living in Lebanon. What is more, their position in Lebanon is that of a state-community, that is, of a partner in the government. They also have as neighbors the 18,000 Druzes in Israel, who form a compact group, politically and socially advanced.

By contrast, there are only some 46,000 'Alawis close to the Latakiya province, those in the provinces of Homs and Hamā, which are now their chief field of expansion. About 70,000 'Alawis lived in the region of Alexandretta before 1939, while about 80,000 live further north, in the neighborhood of Adana. Socially and economically these are better off than their brethren in the mountain, and some of them are town dwellers; but efforts of Turkification, especially by means of education and military service, are weakening their ties to the community. At any rate, the 'Alawis in the mountain cannot draw any communal sustenance from them.

A few thousand 'Alawis are to be found in the lowlands of 'Akkār (Lebanon).

4. Unlike the 'Alawis, the Druzes have not preserved tribal ties. They are usually grouped on a territorial basis, around a ruling family or a clan with a tradition of leadership and form a kind of party named for it (Atrash, 'Amir, Dervish, etc.).

5. The Druze community made a notable contribution to the revival of the Arabic language and literature and to the political movement among the Arabs. The younger generation also gave its share to the Arab interterritorial organizations (League of National Action, Syrian National Party). The more advanced state of the Druzes and their proximity to Damascus and Beirut helped them to a better political standing.

During the whole period of the mandate, the leaders of the

two communities argued with the leading Arab circles—the National Bloc on one side and, on the other, the *al-hay'a al-sha'biyya*, popularly called Shahbandariyya, after Shahbandar, their gifted leader who was murdered by his adversaries in 1940. To some extent, political affiliation or estrangement is founded on mistrust and considerations of personal gain. Political tergiversation, or sitting on the sidelines, is not considered reprehensible. Party affiliation may be decided by the relationships between the leading families in the community, by those between branches in the family, between houses in the branch, and sometimes between individuals in the household. These relationships spring from fear of the majority and yearnings for autonomy, from a desire for position in the government, and from land disputes. The confusion has naturally been increased by outside factors.

Any prominent Druze could not but adopt an attitude toward the mandatory authorities, toward the rival blocs in Syria, and toward the British and Transjordan. On the whole, Atrash, the leading family since 1850, inclined toward the British—following a long-standing tradition among the Druzes—and toward the Popular Bloc. The ambitions of King 'Abdullah also acted as a kind of stimulant on this family. Varying considerations also gave it a certain leaning toward the French, and, especially among the inferior branches of the family, toward the National Bloc. Of the other principal families, some supported Atrash while some—among others, al-Halabī and al-'Asalī—sought to undermine them. The common feature was that practically all of them were split internally, even the few Bedouin tribes in the Jabal who tended the flocks of the Druzes.

In 1947, the dissensions in Jabal al-Durūz almost assumed the proportions of a civil war, revolving around the representation of the community in the Chamber of Deputies. Sultān Atrash took offense at the abolition of representation of the Druzes in the government by a minister, at the neglect of the Jabal in fields of education and communications, and at the alleged barring of members of the community from government service. Other complaints concerned withholding of grants from the family, and, most of all, the support by Damascus of the opposition in the Jabal. There can be no doubt that at that time high hopes were pinned on a union with Transjordan, because in it the Jabal would have a recognized place of its own.[35]

The rivals of Atrash at that time formed a so-called Popular Party. They complained that the Atrash family fell in with the plan for a large Syria and the schemes of 'Abdullah, that they were opposed to family domination based on "divine inheritance" and not on popular choice, to "medieval tyranny and feudalism."[36] They demanded that the separate administration of the Jabal should be abolished and that the government offices in it should be redistributed.

In Jabal Ansāriyya the relations between the 'Alawis and Damascus were affected by those between its various communities. Most of the leading families in the Sunni community were attached to the National Bloc, though some of them threw in their lot with the Popular Bloc. The 'Alawi leaders also took sides in the quarrels between and within the ruling families in the minorities.

Feuds for influence went on at various levels among the 'Alawis: between or within leading families of the confederations (Raslān from Kalbī; al-'Abbās from Khayyāt; Hawwāsh from Metāwira and Kinj from Haddād); between them and the religious leaders, though in many cases temporal and spiritual powers were exercised by one person. The feuds sprang from claims to authority in the community or the tribe, or to positions in the government service, from attempts to lure portions of another tribe away from allegiance to their leaders, and from land disputes. Parts of some tribes even owed their allegiance to Sunni landowners. Even the attitude to Islam is sometimes colored by political considerations.

In this atmosphere of intrigue, a sort of internecine war on one side, with the ignorant masses of share-croppers completely under the heel of the landowners on the other, the way was open for land expropriation and misuse of government authority for private gain. This was stimulated by the fact that religion has been compensating the 'Alawi community for an actual condition of subservience as a minority by a sense of superiority and election, and that oppressed masses incline to attach themselves to adventurous leaders who claim to perform miracles.

The yearning for Messianic deliverance found satisfaction in Sulaymān Murshid. In the end, an enthusiastic mass movement sprang up around him.

This movement of Murshid contained a certain communal reaction against wiping out the traces of autonomy. 'Alawi leaders—among them Ibrāhīm al-Kinj and Munīr al-'Abbās—called upon the government to add an 'Alawi minister, to appoint an 'Alawi governor in the province, and to set free the group of Murshid. Otherwise, they said, the province would seek to attach itself to Lebanon.[37] 'Alawi leaders were also in contact with adherents of 'Abdullah.[38] The advocate of Murshid stated at that time that nearly all the leaders of the 'Alawis wanted to secede from Syria because they saw in independence the only means of extricating the province from its low status.[39]

The French policy in Syria was undoubtedly motivated by an urge to support the cause of minorities. On the other hand, there was the necessity of leaning on them so as to mitigate the pressure of the majority. No new stimuli were provided for the instinct of self-preservation such as might have raised it to the level of a communal consciousness as a positive force. Communal identity cannot be ensured for a long time by means of topographical isolation or of an obsolete social structure. It has not been provided with any new social basis and *eo ipso* a new élite, which might, by means of new values, compensate for communal confinement and counteract the temptations to join the majority.

The leaders of these self-centered communities themselves circumscribed the opportunities to make their political unity a reality. Nowadays the communities have to face a government which seeks to see their identity fade. How the relations of the majority and the communities would evolve when the country reaches a higher level of social advancement, and when the religious tradition fades, is uncertain.

Yazīdis

They form a self-contained community, Kurdish by origin and language. There are many versions of the origin of their name, one of them being the Persian Izād (God, angel). The current versions among the Yazīdis is that it is derived from the caliph Yazīd ibn Mu'āwiya, and it is therefore presumed that a political movement in favor of the house of Umayya gained a lasting foothold in Kurdistan.

According to some scholars, Yazīdism originated in Islam in the thirteenth century, but Persian beliefs and superstitions prevailed in it. Traces of Islam almost disappeared from it, and the Yazīdis do not consider themselves Muslims. To others, Yazīdism is to be traced in the religion practiced in Kurdish paganism. Similarly, there are questions as to how far other contacts are discernible in it: Semitic, especially its relations with Mandaeism, Christian, and others.

The Yazīdis are usually called Devil worshippers, and here again opinions differ on whether the much-revered Peacock Angel—Ta'ūs-é-Melek—embodies the Devil as a representative of God, or whether it is purely a defamatory name.[40] This Devil worship does not necessarily involve a denial of the principle of good in God. On the contrary, trust in the good may impel appeasement of evil in order to induce it to do good. They believe that the spirit of evil, originally good, is merely separated from God, and will ultimately arrive at a reconciliation with Him.

Yazīdism is distinguished by having a hierarchy of partly hereditary castes. The grand sheikh—*ikhtiyār*—is a kind of patriarch. Endowed with supernatural gifts, he exercises absolute power in religious matters, including excommunication. Some families of sheikhs are authorities on doctrine and ritual. The *pirs*—like the sheikhs hereditary descendants of Sheikh 'Adi, a twelfth-century Sūfi—perform similiar religious functions. The sheikhs and pirs are supported by a tax. There are also *qewwāls* (reciters), a kind of itinerant missionaries and collectors of offerings, who live in two villages in Shaykhān, and *faqiran,* ascetics of the sect, alongside with *küchaks,* visionaries and healers who live on gifts. Every Yazīdi is attached, as a *murīd* (disciple), to a definite sheikh and pir. Some of the clergy, especially the first two castes, are wealthy. Sometimes they compete with tribal chiefs for political influence.

There are about 70,000 Yazīdis scattered over five countries. Most of them (up to 40,000) live in the province of Mosul. The

Yazīdis in Turkey, in the region of Diarbekr and elsewhere, joined the revolt of the Kurds in 1927, and most of them escaped to Sinjār, to the Jazīra, and even to the Soviet Union. The rest of them are living in Syria (about 5,000), in Persian Azerbaijan (the mountains around Maku), and in the Soviet Union (Tiflis, Azerbaijan, and Soviet Armenia). Their centers in Iraq are as follows:

Jabal Sinjār, a lonely mountain range, is 100 miles west of Mosul. There are about fifty villages wholly inhabited by Yazīdis; and only in Balad, the capital of the district, are there some Christians and Muslims.

The Yazīdis in Jabal Sinjār are grouped in tribes, some of them almost sedentary and others seminomadic. In the early days of the last century they may have numbered about 150,000, but they suffered at the hands of Kurdish *begs* and Turkish *walis*, and were considerably reduced in numbers, especially in 1830–44 and 1892. During World War I they refused to hand over to the Turkish authorities Armenians who had escaped from Deyr el-Zor, and in 1932 they also gave refuge to Assyrians. After World War I they again gathered some strength, but factional strife over claims to the position of hereditary chief (*mir, amīr al-umarā'*) has weakened them considerably. The revolt of 1935 against compulsory military service failed because some tribes refused to take part in it and even supported the government. In this revolt the most important of the tribes—Mihirkan—was ruined and the back of the community was broken.

In the districts of Shaykhān and Mosul there are about fifty-eight Yazīdi villages. Eight of these have a mixed population—Christians or Muslims as well as Yazīdis, or all three.[41] Ba'adhrī, about forty miles north of Mosul, is the residence of the *mir*. Nominally he is the secular head of the community and as such levies a tax on it. North of Ba'adhrī lies the grave of Sheikh 'Adi, a sanctuary and a place of annual pilgrimage. 'Adi is said to have lived in seclusion in Hakkiari. If the assumption that he is the founder of Yazīdism is true, the religious structure of the Yazīdi society may have been patterned on a Sūfi order founded by him. But the tribal structure also may offer a clue to it.

In Syria about half of the Yazīdis live in villages around
'Amūda in the Jazīra. Since the eighteenth century, they have
been attached to the confederation Millī. In 1927 Yazīdis joined
the Kurds in their exodus to Syria. With the expansion of
mechanized farming they have been shifted by the landowners
from place to place and tend to submerge as an ethnic group.

The Yazīdis in Jabal Sim'ān and the valley of 'Afrīn have long
been sedentary. Practically all form an agricultural proletariat.
The stony soil provides a scanty sustenance for the flocks of the
mountain folk. The dwellers in the lowland grow corn and
cotton. Most of the land is the property of Muslims from Aleppo
and 'Afrīn.

The Yazīdis here seem doomed to disappear. They are not
recognized as a religious community but only as a Muslim
faction. They try to conceal their religious practices from outsiders, and they are also reluctant to defend their rights. Members of the community, especially landowners, are going over
to Islam in such numbers that in most of the villages they have
already been reduced to a minority.[42]

A characteristic feature of the Kurdish society is the dervish
brotherhoods within the Sunni faith. Secret ritual and fervent
allegiance seem to serve as a sublimated means by which the
underprivileged raise their moral and social status. Secret sects
related to extreme Shī'ism—*ghulāt*—or Yazīdism represent a
higher degree of cohesion. Al-'Azzāwī stresses the affinity of
their beliefs.[43]

Kakā'iyya, the largest brotherhood which became a kind of
sect, comprises town dwellers (Baghdad, Mosul, Sulaymāni)
and tribes, or tribal segments. Groups of their villages are to be
found in Kirkuk and Diyāla liwās.[44]

The *Shabak*, a community of 10-15,000 souls, live in about
twenty villages of their own or in mixed ones (Bajorān, Kurds,
Turkomans, Arabs). Like the Bajorān they speak a language
that is a mixture of Persian, Kurdish, Arabic, and Turkish. In one
breath they mention Allāh, Muhammad and 'Alī. Shī'i elements
are easily discernible in their creed. Their head (*pir, baba*)

exercises immense power over them. He is the forgiver of sins.[45] They are close to the Yazīdis and have their shrines in common.

Persians

They number about 140,000. For centuries Persians have made a yearly pilgrimage to the Shī'i shrines in Iraq. They are numerous in Kerbelā. Najaf, on the other hand, is more Arabic in character, but there are also various elements—Persian, Indian, Pakistani, and Turkish. Students from the Shī'i countries attend the numerous colleges in these towns. Here and in Kāzimayn the great theologians, *mijtahids*, reside, some of whom are of Persian origin, and whose influence extends beyond the borders of Iraq. In Baghdad and Basra the Persians are dealers in carpets, textiles, and tea.

Bahā'is

Their religion developed away from Bābism, which emerged in Persia in the first half of the last century as a kind of protest against the Shī'i clergy and the social conditions. Its founder escaped to Baghdad in 1852. Bahā'ism represents a universal religion holding to humanism and pacifism. It has neither clergy nor ceremony. As in Persia, the small Bahā'i community in Baghdad is to a great extent underground. It gained some foothold in the United States. Its center is in Haifa, Israel.

Armenians

Armenians have been settled in Syria and Lebanon from ancient times, notably in some villages in the north of the 'Alawi mountains. Owing to massacres in 1894, Armenians moved there from Turkey, and before 1914 they numbered about 5,000. Because of massacres and deportations during 1915-1918, a large part of the Armenian nation perished (estimates range up to over a million).

Three waves of Armenian immigration into Syria and Lebanon are to be noted:

1. The survivors of 1914-1918, who had returned and settled in Cilicia, left this region with the departure of the French in 1921.

2. Armenian refugees who settled in Iran, Iraq, and Greece gradually moved to Lebanon.

3. During 1938-39, when the region of Alexandretta was ceded to Turkey.

Of the 100,000 Armenians in Syria, 73,000 are Gregorians, 20,000 Catholics, and 6,000 Protestants. Their main centers are Aleppo (70,000), Damascus (6,500), Qamishli (9,300), Latakia (950). Armenian settlements are scattered over the three northern provinces, notably in the Jazīra.

The sixty-eight primary and secondary schools are attended by 16,850 pupils.

The Armenians in Lebanon and Syria are divided into two major political groups. The Armenian Revolutionary Federation (Tashnag) advocates complete independence of Armenia and, in consequence, pursues an anti-Soviet policy. The other faction, mindful of past experience and present world conflicts, sees the nation's survival in the protection given to the small republic by the U.S.S.R.; but ideologically they are not Communists. This faction is composed of the Armenian Democratic League (Ramgavar), the Huntchag Party, the Progressive Party and non-partisans. It represents the majority of the Armenians in the Diaspora.

Armenians had been living in Iraq before 1914. Most of them, however, came there during World War I and after it. Of the 15,000 Armenians in the great refugee camp in Baʿqūba, a part returned at the time to Iran or were transported by boat to Batum. They are estimated to number about 24,000, including 2000 Catholics and an Evangelical congregation. Their main centers are: Baghdad (8,000), Basra (3,000), Kirkuk (2,200), Mosul (2,000), Sulaymāni (1,200), Zakho (950). As elsewhere, church and school are the mainstay of the community.

After World War II a movement to return to the Armenian republic in the Soviet Union started among the 300,000 Armenians in the Middle East. About 20-25,000 migrated from Syria and Lebanon alone.

*Circassians**

In the 1860's and 1870's Muslim refugees from the Caucasus reached Northern Mesopotamia. Chachans settled alongside Rās al-'Ayn in the Jazīra, but their numbers were greatly reduced by malaria and pressure of the Bedouin. At present a small Chachan tribe is encamped there.[48]

After the Russo-Turkish war of 1877–78 Circassians settled in Jawlān (Damascus) and in the district of Manbij (Aleppo);[49] also some in the Latakiya province.[50] Qunaytra in Jawlān, then a deserted village near the ruins of a Roman town, was rebuilt by them. The Circassian community was enlarged as a result of the Franco-Turkish agreement of 1921, by which the Turkish frontier with Syria was moved southward. Circassian groups were at that time enrolled in the French army. Before 1939 Circassians still lived in tents in the area of Upper Khabur.[51] On the whole, there are some forty villages scattered over the country, with about 35,000 inhabitants.

The future of this community, which is a national minority in every respect, is problematical. Apart from close settlements in Jawlān and to a certain extent in Jordan (about 12,000 souls),[52] there are only a few isolated islands left in this region, two of them in Israel; and of these some have become Arabicized.

Settled for political reasons, the Circassians were assigned the task of maintaining order as gendarmes and officials of the Sultan. In the revolt of 1925 they fought vigorously for the French. Throughout the period of the mandate, they took a prominent part in local security units. The freedom they enjoyed stimulated in them the sense of national separateness, and in the 1930's they went so far as to demand autonomy for the district of Jawlān and representation in the parliament as a national minority. They also became conscious of the bonds they had with other fragments of their community in the Middle East. On the other hand, some of them inclined to assimilation. The Daghestanis and the Chachans became absorbed politically, and mixed marriages occur between them and the Arabs.

---

* Caucasian peoples of different origin are generally called Circassians (Chachans, Daghestanis, etc.).

Most of them are small landowners; there are very few traders among them. The tribal bond is still strongly in evidence in the way in which they herd in villages and in the assemblies of the elders. Unlike the Arab tribes, the elders practice no economic or social exploitation. Nevertheless, the influence of the leading families is considerable.

Various factors help to preserve their particularism in Syria—common language, customs, an urge for independence, connections with their brethren in Jordan, Turkey, and Egypt, where they have attained to wealth and influence. Some factors work in the opposite direction—a weakening of attachment to their language, which in spite of all efforts remains a spoken tongue only, education in Arab schools, lack of opportunities for the young people in a small community.[53] With the abolition of the mandate, their hopes for national self-assertion waned. Statistically, they are regarded as a part of the Sunni majority.

Turks and Turkomans

Their settlements are scattered over a line stretching from northwest (the predominantly Turkish Tall 'Afar, 47 miles west of Mosul, and a dozen villages adjoining it in the Mosul liwā, where traces of tribal structure are still to be found) to southeast (Altun Köprü and Tuz Khurmatu in the Kirkuk liwā and the Khanāqīn district, where there are some Turkoman tribes). Qizil Rubat and Khanāqīn, Kirkuk, and Arbil are predominantly Kurdish-Turkoman towns.

Turkoman settlements were established by the Turks at strategic points as a defense against Persians and Kurds. In a way this is a kind of enclave separating the Arab from the Kurdish zone. In 1947 they numbered 108,000. They are mostly Sunnis and partly adherents of secretive Shī'i sects.[54]

In Syria Turkomans are concentrated in villages in the districts of Latakiya, Tall Kalakh, and Sāfītā, 13,350 in all. They have preserved their language and to some extent their tribal grouping.

Remnants of Turkoman tribes are also found in the Jazīra, where they had been nearly decimated by the Kurdish and Shammar tribes at the beginning of the last century, and in the Euphrates province (Jarablus). Turks are found in the towns of Syria, and some of them have extensive estates in the northern area.

As in Iraq, Turkoman settlements were established here to protect the traffic routes. In the interior they have become more or less Arabicized. There are three large villages of Turkoman origin south of the 'Alawi mountain, around Krak des Chevaliers, and five in the south of the Hamā district; also some in the subdistrict of Qunaytra. They are estimated to number 75,000.

Jews

Before the great exodus to Israel in the years 1950–51, about 130,000 Jews were living in Iraq: 90,000 in Baghdad, 10,000 in Basra, and 16,000 in the northern districts. They were divided roughly into three classes. A small wealthy class was almost dominant in some branches of commerce, especially in export and import trade, and in banking. Then there was a professional class—lawyers, physicians, teachers, government officials, and business managers. Lastly, there was the great majority of very poor people engaged in petty trading and handicrafts. A special class was formed by some thousand Kurdish Jews in the north, mostly manual workers (woodchoppers, tanners, dyers, weavers, porters, also silversmiths and peddlers). In the highlands they were scattered in agricultural groups under the protection of Kurdish aghas. Their vernacular is *targum* interspersed with Kurdish, Arabic, or Turkish elements.

The Jews in Iraq have passed through many vicissitudes. In 1921–30, they were comparatively well off politically. Owing to the personal influence of Faysal, the British control and the policy of appeasing the minorities in order to prove fitness for independence, as well as lack of training among the Arabs, opportunities were thrown open to Jews in the government service and in commerce. A feeling of confidence strengthened the attachment of the Jewish intelligentsia to Arabic culture, and this attachment even found expression in literary activity. This is the first and only attempt that has been made in our day at conscious assimilation.

In the 1930's, a decisive change took place in the position of the Jews, due to the attainment of political independence by Iraq, the impact of fascism on Arab nationalism, and the Palestine problem. The Jews were driven out of government posts, educational establishments, and business situations, although no legal sanction was given to this discrimination. On the other side, the authorities sought to sever the ties which bound the Jews to Palestine and the Hebrew language. Even teaching of Jewish history was forbidden. This period reached its climax with the massacres of May 1941.

Between 1941 and 1945, when the British army was encamped in Iraq, the confidence of the Jews revived, but they did not recover their former social position. In spite of an official ban, migration to Palestine continued.

After the war, tension because of the Palestine issue increased and spread fear among the Jews. From November 29, 1947, and still more from May 15, 1948, a policy of persecution against the Jews, which also had legal sanction, began. It took the form of mass imprisonment, maltreatment, and economic exactions.

At the beginning of 1950 permission was given to the Jews to emigrate to Israel. Whereas between 1919 and June 1950 about 19,000 Jews had gone to Palestine, by the end of 1951 the number had risen to about a hundred thousand. Several thousand Jews went to Europe, the United States, and India. Only a few thousand remained.[55]

In the early 1940's there were about 30,000 Jews in Syria, for the most part town dwellers (Aleppo, Damascus, Homs, Latakiya). Of these some 18,000 were Sephardis, mostly engaged in petty commerce and trade, some 4,000 indigenous and extremely poor, the rest Kurdish Jews, fellahin and some peddlers in the Jazīra, and Ashkenazis, mostly professionals. Large-scale immigration into Palestine, to a lesser degree to Lebanon and Europe, started in the 1930's, and increased in the war years and after 1948. Of the remaining Jews some 2,000, mostly refugees, are confined to two narrow streets in the Jewish quarter; some 2,000 are less restricted in Aleppo; and some hundreds of families are in Qamishli. Stripped of their property, they are denied elementary rights. It is a slow death of starvation and degradation.[56]

Ismāʿīlis

Their name is taken from the shīʿi imām Ismāʿīl (d. about 760), seventh in the line of the imāms descending from ʿAlī by Fātima. By the end of the ninth century, they represented a strong politico-religious movement involved in a fierce struggle with the Baghdad Caliphate, and its successors. By means of highly refined propaganda they built up strong centers in Persia, Yemen, North Africa, and Salamiya, southeast of Hamā. The great Ismāʿīli dynasty in Egypt—the Fātimis—reigned over a large part of Islamic territories for more than 150 years. At the end of the eleventh century, a related movement of Nizāris—named after Nizār, who was murdered by his brother after the death of his father, the Fātimi caliph Mustansir (d. 1094)—issued from Alamut in Northern Persia, through the medium of the order of assassins (hashshāshin) and in fight with the Sunni Saldjuqs and the crusaders, and spread terror for more than 150 years.[57] By the middle of the twelfth century the Ismāʿīlis were still scattered over all Syria, but their mainstays were a few centers in the ʿAlawi mountains (region of Qadmūs and Masyāf). According to their own tradition, they dispersed from Salamiya in the wake of the invasion of Tamerlane. In 1843, they started to move from the mountains to the then derelict area of Salamiya, and the process of colonization still goes on.

Under the French mandate, the Ismāʿīlis were recognized as a community with a personal status, but they took little advantage of this, so as not to expose their tenets. Similarly they refrained from taking part in politics. Most of their leaders were emirs owning large estates, and some of them have held religious offices, too. These represented the community with the authorities, and they were also entrusted with government posts.

The Ismāʿīlis have two centers in Syria. In Salamiya and in about thirty villages east of it, they number over 30,000. In the ʿAlawi mountains, there are about thirty small villages on both sides of the river Ismāʿīliyya and a few encampments with about 10,000 souls. Urban settlements are found in Qadmūs and especially in Masyāf (about 2,000). The Ismāʿīlis in the mountain region are very backward, and because of the pressure of the neighboring 'Alawis some of them cross over to the zone of Salamiya either permanently or for seasonal labor. Some of their settlements are becoming depopulated or mixed with an influx of 'Alawis. On the other hand, in the towns, through the very fact of their being a minority requiring coherence, they have managed to set themselves up in trade and moneylending, and in consequence, they have become landowners also.

The Ismā'ilis in the zone of Salamiya differ from the others in several respects. They are Nizāris, pay allegiance to the offspring of Agha Khan as descendant of the Nizāri imāms, and turn to him for assistance in religious and educational matters. This connection with a kind of world movement helps to keep alive in them a spirit of independence. Their position is distinctly better, another reason being the fertility of the irrigable land.

And yet, World War II threatened the existence of the Ismā'ilis in this region. The opportunities for trade and employment opened up by the presence of Allied forces brought abundance of money and a spirit of enterprise into the community, and this accelerated the transition from dry farming to irrigated crops. The authority of the emirs weakened more and more, and with it the dependence of the share-croppers on them. With the introduction of motor-pumps, some of the large estates are being broken up. A new middle class of officials and traders is gradually displacing the feudal families from their positions in the community and in government offices. Some have even left the community. With the independence of Syria a shift in the political loyalties of the leading men took place. The economic and social intercourse with the majority brings with it a danger of extinction.[58]

Mandaeans

The original home of this ancient community is still a matter of controversy (the Hawrān plateau in the west or the highlands in Media), and it remains to be answered how they moved to Khuzistan in Persia and to lower Iraq. European travellers since the first half of the seventeenth century called them, erroneously, "Christians of John the Baptist." They themselves referred to him as their prophet, probably in order to keep in touch with the Christians. Their faith seems to have been subject, directly or indirectly, to Babylonian, Hebrew, Nestorian, and Islamic influences. Recently, more and more attention is drawn to Persian elements in their beliefs, ritual, and language. No answer has yet been found to the question of how far the common element in Manichaeism, Mandaeism, and Christian Gnosis are coincidences or could be traced to common sources.[59]

The core of their faith is worship of the principles of life and fertility, with rushing water as its symbol. An elaborate system of baptisms and ritual meals serves to ensure purity. To the Mandaeans, the celestial and infernal realms of the world are peopled with male and female beings of different ranks—spirits of light dispensing health, virtue, and justice as against spirits of darkness and evil. Health of the body is to be combined with health of mind and with upright conduct.

They practice certain crafts with artistic distinction. They are well-known as goldsmiths and silversmiths, especially providing tribal jewelry, armorers, carpenters, ironworkers, boat-builders. The priests supply charms.

This community, persecuted down through the ages, is threatened with extinction. Their ceremonial language is Mandaean, an ancient Aramaic dialect, but the spoken Mandaean (ratna) is falling into disuse, and Arabic is spoken by all members of the community. Under the British mandate, they were inclined to emphasize their identity, but in face of rising nationalism, they have to be very guarded. The younger generation is adjusting itself to the environment; they attend general schools, in defiance of their precepts, and serve in the army. Even the priestly caste is dwindling because their sons who should inherit the office are deviating from the tradition. Mixed marriages are also diminishing the community.

They are scattered in towns and villages of southern Iraq (Muntafiq, Basra, and ʻAmāra, especially in Qalʻat Sālih, Sūq al-Shuyūkh). They are also found in Baghdad and Mosul. In 1949 they numbered 6,597. There are a few groups in Muhammera and Ahwaz in Khuzistan, and some individuals live in Damascus, Beirut, and Alexandria.[60]

Communities of the Eastern Churches

These communities are the Assyrian Nestorians (Church of the Orient), the Chaldean Catholics (Uniate Eastern Church), the Jacobites (Syrian Orthodox Church) and the Syrian Catholics. In many respects they constitute small nations. Each has its spoken Aramaic dialect, or memories of it (with a liturgical Aramaic), its own church, a tradition of self-governing entities (millet), and a measure of historical conscience. For centuries they have been oppressed by neighbors and invaders. Before World War I, they were mainly concentrated in the Turkish vilayets of Mardin and Mosul up to Lake Van, and in Persia, in the lowlands of Urmiya. Eastern Aramaic dialects were then spoken by the Nestorians and the Chaldeans, and Western by the Jacobites in Tūr 'Abdīn (vilayet Mardin), in the Jazīra and in Aleppo, and also in three villages in central Syria (two Muslim and one mixed). Cognate dialects were spoken by the Jews (*targum* in Kurdistan, and the dialect of the Jews in Salmas, northwest of Lake Urmiya). Through the pressure of the environment the dialects received an infusion of foreign elements, Turkish or Kurdish, Persian or Arabic, and in many places they were entirely driven out.[61] At present, members of these communities, insofar as they still cling to their own dialect, are often bilingual, all according to their contact with neighbors and the route of their wanderings.

Assyrians

At the turn of the tenth century, Nestorian congregations were scattered over a large territory, from Basra to Nisibis in the Jazīra. In the following centuries the community shrank more and more, and its center shifted to Mosul. By the middle of the fifteenth century the leadership of the community, secular and religious alike, passed to a militant family—Shim'ōn. The Church, hitherto interterritorial, became more and more a millet, a kind of church-bound coalition of tribes.[62]

Owing to its closely knit character, the Assyrian community comes nearest of all these communities to the concept of a nation. It stands out by memories of religious expansion, by its social structure, and by a stronger political consciousness. Most Assyrians speak their dialect (*soureth*) and understand Arabic, or Kurdish, or Persian. Before World War I, most of them, about a dozen tribes, were grouped together in the midst of Kurds and Armenians, on the heights of Hakkiari, northeastward of Iraq, in an area assigned in 1925 by the frontier commission of the League of Nations to Turkey. About a quarter of them lived in valleys on the west of Urmiya. Their numbers were then variously estimated at between 100,000 and 200,000.

In 1916, after they joined the Allies, they were forced to leave Hakkiari, and those who had not starved to death or been killed by Turkish or Kurdish bullets reached Urmiya. In 1917, when the Russians retreated, they had to seek refuge once more. About 70,000 set out from Urmiya and less than two thirds reached Hamadan. In 1918 about 35,000 were transferred by the British to the camp of Ba'qūba, northeast of Baghdad. Thousands moved to the Caucasus.

Great Britain recognized them as allies in this war. In 1919, and later on, they were employed in the pacification of the Kurdish districts in Iraq. In 1922, when an invasion of the north of Iraq by the forces of Kemal Pasha was imminent, two thousand of them enrolled within three weeks and helped to foil the Turkish plans. Later, Assyrian levies served at the British bases in Iraq. A number of factors combined to frustrate the aspirations of the Assyrians. They had no leadership worthy of the name to which the fate of the community could be entrusted, and what leaders they had were at variance with one another. The refugees from Urmiya wanted to return, and some of them actually did return to their former homes. In 1920, a plan was hatched among them to occupy an area on the borders of Turkey, Persia, and Iraq and to set up a state in it. The British authorities, it would seem, desired to consolidate the community in one area, but they were not determined enough to take risks. An attempt was made to settle them in scattered groups, chiefly in Mosul liwā, thus causing friction between them and the Kurds. Several thousands moved to Baghdad, Mosul, and Basra. Their cause was already killed in the years 1925-1928, in the course of a futile argument between the League of Nations, Turkey, and Great Britain.

The problem of settling the Assyrians occupied the attention of the British up to the cessation of the mandate. The Iraqis saw them as tools of a foreign power. But even without this it was clear from the first that an Arab government would do everything in its power to suppress any idea of a close settlement, and still more, that it would have no intention to further administrative autonomy. In the autumn of 1931 the Assyrians appealed to the League of Nations with a request to be transferred to Syria or to some European country. The Assyrian units gave up their service and asked that the Assyrians should be recognized as a millet and their Patriarch as its temporal and spiritual leader. If there was no possibility of annexing Hakkiari to Iraq, a national home for all the Assyrians in the world should be established in Iraq, for which an area was proposed in the province of Mosul. The authorities of Iraq succeeded in inducing a section of the Assyrian leaders, mostly from among the old established villages, to demonstrate their loyalty by a counter petition. Attempts were made also to divert the antipathy of the Kurds to the Assyrians. The tension reached its climax in July 1933, when eight hundred Assyrians crossed the border to Syria. They were induced by the French authorities to return. Part of them returned. Those who were not caught and shot by Iraqi guards dispersed to their villages. These events culminated in massacres perpetrated by the Iraqi army in the village Sumayl. Assyrian villages were devastated and hundreds of persons were murdered.[63]

After these events, up to nine thousand Assyrians were settled in 30-35 villages, under the auspices of the League of Nations, on both sides of the upper Khabur in the Jazīra. A few scattered over Syria and Lebanon. In these villages they preserved their own modes of life; every village contains one subtribe and has its own *malik*, whose influence varies, and clergymen.

As in Iraq, they did not cease to dream of returning to their native country and at the same time looked for a country to which they might emigrate—even casting eyes on Brazil.

In Iraq there are still 23,000 Assyrians. Some of them are in the towns (Mosul, Kirkuk), others are employed in the Iraq Petroleum Company works or until recently at the British air bases, and the rest live in villages in the Mosul area. Of these, some are in ancient settlements (Barwar) while others have settled on their own land or as serfs.

Assyrians are found in the Soviet Union, and some 15-20,000 of them in the United States. In all, they may number 80,000. The community is diminishing owing to a sizeable conversion to the Catholic Chaldean faith in the Jazīra and in Iran.

This ancient community is still striving, under an exiled patriarch who resides in Chicago, to preserve its identity. The Iraqi authorities are on the watch to prevent any contacts between the Assyrians in Iraq and other branches of their church. Their excellent service in both world wars has availed them nothing. The Western Powers have not been able to secure a home for them.[64]

Chaldeans

This community has about 170,000 members in the Middle East (145,000 in Iraq, 11,500 in Iran, 5,500 in Syria (diocese of Aleppo-Jazīra), and the rest in Lebanon, Egypt, Turkey. The Chaldean church in the region of Mosul was definitely established under Dominican guidance in 1750, but organized attempts to secede from the Nestorian Church go as far back as 1553. In 1845 the Chaldeans were recognized by the Ottoman government as a millet. The Patriarch of Babylon resides in Mosul.

Their chief center is the Mosul plain. There they have some dozens of villages, among them Tell Keif with a population of several thousands, Batnai, Alqōsh and Tell Uskūf. During World War I, thousands of them escaped from the south of Turkey to these places and also to the Jazīra. The rest of their centers are Baghdad with 15,000 souls, Basra with 10,000 and Kirkuk with 8,000. They are of enterprising spirit and are also represented in the government service. A few thousands of them have migrated to North and South America. Their centers in Syria are the Jazīra, Homs and Aleppo.[65]

Jacobites

The Syrian Orthodox (Jacobite) Church takes its name from Jacob Baradai (d. 577) who helped to reorganize and consolidate it. It originated from a fifth-century schism. During the period of its renaissance (1150-1300), Jacobites were scattered in compact groups comprising a large area; suffice it to mention Tabriz, Mardin, Urmiya, Mosul, Damascus, Jerusalem and Cyprus.[66] Despite persecutions at the hands of Turks and Kurds, they may have numbered 200,000 by the middle of the last century. Their center was Tūr ʿAbdīn with 150-200 villages. Nowadays there are about 23,000 in Iraq, most of them in Mosul and, together with Syrian Catholics, in some villages within this province (Baʿshiqa, Bartelli, Karaqōsh); also in Baghdad and Basra.

Most of the 50,000 Jacobites in Syria live in the Jazīra, Homs, and Aleppo. After World War I the seat of the Syrian Patriarch of Antioch was transferred from Zaʿfaran near Mardin to Homs. They have congregations in Lebanon (5,000), Jerusalem and Cairo (3,000), Turkey (Tūr ʿAbdīn 20,00, other regions 10,000), North and South America (25,000).

Syrian Catholics

These are the Jacobites who have joined the Roman Catholic Church since the seventeenth century, especially at the end of the eighteenth century. Within the jurisdiction of the Patriarch of Antioch of the Syrians, who resides in Beirut (the former Ottoman Empire and Egypt), they number about 70,000: 35,000 in Iraq (Mosul and villages within the province, Baghdad, Basra), about 20,000 in Syria, chiefly in Damascus, Aleppo, Homs, and the Jazīra. Many of them fled after World War I from Turkish Kurdistan. There are some 18,000 Syrian Catholics in the United States, South America, France and other countries.

The disintegration of these communities, especially since World War I, is closely bound up with the gradual displacement and disuse of the Aramaic dialects. As far back as the 1830's, missionaries who found their way to Urmiya (Presbyterians in 1835, Lazarists in 1840) fixed a script for a basic Aramaic and began to collect and publish educational and religious literature in it. Scholarly interest in these dialects arose in Europe, too. This literary work was not carried on regularly, so that traces of changes in these dialects have been lost. It came to an end with the outbreak of World War I.[67]

In the 1880's Aramaic dialects were still spoken in a large area bounded roughly by Lake Urmiya to the east, the lower Great Zāb to the point of its confluence with the Tigris to the south, the Jazīra, the north area of Van, and pashalik Diarbekr as far as Mardin. One may assume that despite conversion and massacres there were then some 300,000 Aramaic-speaking Christians in this area.

At the end of the last century, Aramaic was little spoken in Mosul, having been supplanted by Arabic. In the plain of Solduz south of Urmiya, Azerbaijan-Turkish elements found their way into Aramaic, and in many villages it had almost been displaced by Turkish. In the mountains Aramaic had been affected by Kurdish and in the plains westward by Arabic. The same applies to *fellihi* (dialect of fellahin) which had been spoken to the west of the Tigris and in Mosul.[68] The dialects were preserved, mainly, in village centers.

These peoples defended themselves for centuries, and it was just in the period which raised the standard of self-determination that they were condemned to dispersal and decay. What was left by famine and massacres during World War I was liable to fall a victim to the policies of the one-nation state. They are far from identifying themselves nationally with the majority; but against this the desire for self-preservation works toward assimilation.[69]

Arabic-speaking Christian Communities

These communities—the Greek Orthodox, and the Greek Catholic (Melkites)—are a tiny minority in Iraq. In Syria, the Greek Orthodox are the largest of the Christian communities, numbering about 174,000 of whom about 72,000 are in the province of Latakiya, while the rest are in Damascus, in the districts of Homs and Hamā, and in Aleppo. The Greek Catholics are fewer in numbers—about 58,000—in the province of Damascus, in Aleppo, in Hawrān, and elsewhere. A considerable part of these communities live in villages, or even groups of villages, and in small towns. The groups are found in the 'Alawi province, especially in the southern part of it, around Hamā, and in the south of the Ghāb valley on both sides of the Orontes.[70]

With the exception of a few Russians and Greeks, all the members of the Greek Orthodox community in these two countries speak Arabic. At the end of the last century, the Greek Orthodox Church secured autonomy with the assistance of the Pravoslav Church, which before World War I had succeeded in gaining the hegemony of the Orthodox Church.[71] The Greek Catholics, who at the beginning of the eighteenth century acknowledged the supremacy of Rome, retain, too, a certain measure of independence. Their Patriarch ordinarily resides in Damascus.

Various factors molded the characteristics of these communities. Their superior education, derived from the activity of missionaries, has opened up to them more opportunities in the fields of commerce and civil service. Both the regime of the capitulations and that of the mandate benefited them in many respects. The community controls a large part of the individual's life from birth to death, and of his attachment to the society (education, mutual assistance, representation). Each community has maintained relations with outside bodies, and this has given it a sense of ease, in the main imaginary, and inculcated a dangerous feeling of lasting security.

On the other side, the Christian minorities are affected by the social conditions in the country as a whole. The affairs of the community have largely been in the hands of families of distinction. The interfamilial—sometimes intrafamilial—dissensions, frequently on questions of office in the church itself, decided political affiliations or links with external elements. The deeply ingrained habit of camouflage, which is a powerful force in the life of the country, assumes a communal coloring and maintains itself toward the majority. The members of the community oscillate between an urge to throw in their lot with the rest of the inhabitants, and fear for their autonomous framework which in any case may be a shield against encroachment from the majority.

Two further factors:

1. Emigration. It assumed large dimensions about 1890, with the migration to America, and grew even more after World War I.[72] This, on the one hand, weakened the communities by markedly depleting the Christian villages and urban groups, while on the other hand it helped to improve their cultural and moral status.

2. The future of the community is bound up with its demographic trends. The improvement of education and living standards tends to upset the equilibrium in natural increase which is conditioned by the birth and death rates, and especially by the infant mortality, by the age and frequency of marriage, and the frequency of divorce. Experience shows that in a period of transition from a backward to a higher stage of social development, the decline of the death rate is greater than that of the birth rate. The proportion of the Christian communities in the population (at present about 14 percent in Syria) tends to decline.[73]

The differences in the social and cultural status of the two communities spring in part from the fact that the Greek Catholic Church kept uninterrupted contact with the West, whereas the Greek Orthodox Church renewed its contact with the Pravoslav Church after a break of about thirty years.

The Orthodox Church sees itself threatened by an expansionist activity on the part of the Catholic Church with its greater resources, world-wide connections, especially in North America, its schools and philanthropic establishments, and, moreover, with its acute sense of vocation and devotion to work in villages. At the beginning of this century, the Greek Catholics in Syria and Lebanon numbered 60-70,000 members and nowadays about 140,000. Being given to one authority, there is a wider scope for interconfessional activity in it, especially through its lay organizations (Action Catholique). In contrast, the Greek Orthodox Church, the largest Christian minority in the Middle East, is rent by rivalries within the hierarchy. It even knew local and regional splits with a double hierarchy. The connections with the Hellenic church are weak and are affected by those with the Russian Church.

Nowadays a new *modus vivendi* seems indispensable. Despite the sad experience of the past and the present-day hardships due to discrimination in government service, educational policy, etc., Christians are called upon to discard the "minority psychosis," the perpetual search for protection, and to assert themselves in the life of the country. Not that they have to give up their ties with the West or their function as link between East and West. Being culturally more advanced, they have a mission to fulfill within the majority, especially within the weaker layers in it. After World War I, they seemed sheltered under the mandate and therefore withdrew into themselves. They have to revive their interest, once keen and creative, in the social renascence of the majority.[74]

It is a grave decision to make. The prerogatives of the Greek and Armenian Patriarchs are traced to 1453. Eastern Christian communities were recognized as millets in the first half of the last century. Their institutions became, to a varying degree, focal points of loyalty to the members, and with the deterioration of the state, the political standing of their leaders became stronger and stronger. The Patriarch is still the representative and shield of the community. Oddly, European nationalism, itself born of speech-bound entities, made these mostly creed-bound groups equate millet with nation.[75] It is open to question whether the current authoritarian trends within the majority can encourage a development toward integration.

Other Christian Minorities

Maronites. There are about 18,000 of them in Syria, roughly a half in the Latakiya province, some of them in villages close to the borders of Lebanon, and about a quarter in Aleppo. In Iraq there are only a few.

Protestants. Some of them have come from the Orthodox communities in Syria. They have a good social position on account of their education and cultural advantages derived from links with missionary institutions. They number about 13,0000 in Syria, and about 3,500 in Iraq.

Latins. These are the western branch of the Roman Catholic Church in the Middle East. Most of them, or the ancestors of most of them, came from Europe. They are about 7,000 in Syria. They, too, enjoy a good social and economic position. In Iraq they may number 1,300.

In regard to the proportion of the Muslim Arabs to the total population, Syria does not differ much from Iraq; it is estimated at 66 to 70 percent. The Muslim Arabs of Syria, however, with the exception of the 15,000 Shī'is, most of whom live in the province of Aleppo, are Sunnis. Of the Arabs in Iraq, on the other hand, a large majority are Shī'is. In the 1930's the Shī'is in Iraq still felt discrimination in the government service. The royal house was Sunni, and around it had been gathered Sunnis from the entourage of Faysal. Since the power of the state was mainly in the hands of this tiny group, members of their families had the first claim to high positions in the state. In spite of this, the share of the Shī'is in the administration has been growing.

Evidently the problem of the minorities is also different in the two countries. In Iraq it is mainly centered on the North, where an autonomous basis is being claimed by a national community, while in Syria it has other aspects. Most of the provinces of Syria are a kind of ethnic and religious mosaic. Only Jabal al-Durūz and Hawrān are near-homogeneous.

Throughout the period of the mandate, the French and the British policies vied with regard to the minorities. Previously the Christian communities had been accustomed to view foreign protection as a kind of favor. Now they enjoyed protection of a Western power as a right, and all the minorities, including the non-Christian, gained self-confidence. But when the era of promises was over and the workday period of the mandate arrived, dimmed as it was through the 1920 and 1925 insurrections, Great Britain adopted a well-designed policy not to encourage autonomous leanings of the minorities. Through Great

Britain's influence, the Sunni kingdom in Iraq was established, and the Shī'i South was attached to it. The interests of the British Empire were declared to lie in the stability of Iraq, and this was regarded as being bound up with the unification of the country. No due regard was paid to the consideration that factors making for national self-assertion cannot be forcibly and permanently subdued, and that the stability of the state depended on its social and economic soundness.

The French policy was at first one of federation and of preserving the identity of the minorities. But the autonomist impetus shrank more and more, no doubt also on account of pressure by the majority. All the same, during the whole period of the mandate the administrative autonomy of Jabal al-Durūz and Jabal Ansāriyya continued. French policy also resulted in the opening of the mandated territories to waves of refugees, Christians and Muslims, from Turkey and from Iraq. Of course, this may partly be ascribed to motives of expediency, to the necessity of mitigating the pressure of the majority. But at the same time the mother country behaved in the same way to refugees from all parts of the world. Another point, too, is that political motives do not lessen the value of humanitarian action. On its administrative side the French policy was harsher than the British, especially in times of crisis. The British and the French left a lasting imprint in the civil administration; the former in the judicial system, too. The French left behind a valuable legacy in the shape of the brilliant research of such observers as Weulersse, Lescot, Savaget, Charles, Thoumin, Rondot, and others in the field of "géographie humaine."

The march of events frustrated both policies. For whatever reasons, the British view had to acquiesce in the authoritarian approach of the ruling circles, and in the deficiencies of a regime which could not assure elementary rights even to the majority. The French system was not calculated to give a proper social and cultural basis to the cohesion of the communities and so to enable them to hold their ground against the majority. Thus the opportunity of securing autonomy for the communities was missed.

With the cessation of the mandate these communities entered

into a new phase. Arab nationalism in these countries had been centralist and legalistic, and practically identified with a social system based on large landownership. The first and foremost object of the governing class was to increase its social and political power. Just as it was not capable of a constructive approach in the social field, so it was incapable of dealing constructively with minorities. This kind of nationalism possesses no such social and economic dynamism as would enable it to absorb the minority politically and culturally.

The Arab state does not see itself under any obligation to change its attitude. Present-day circumstances seem to leave no room for international discussion of the problem. Still, if one is not prepared to accept disappearance or decay tamely, it is imperative to examine some possibilities. There is no question that the existing social order is also anchored in the structure of the communities. Let us assume that an enlightened regime should enable the communities to do away with the domination of leading families, whose leanings toward isolation or assimilation are also determined by considerations of personal advantage. The sources for political exploitation of confessional particularism would be cut off. The remnants of tribal structure, which help preserve the separateness of the community, would pass away. Further, some of the asocial elements in the secretive religions for which there is no more room, would cease to exert any influence. What shape would the aspirations of the communities then take?

No doubt, the identity of the communities would be sapped by modes of life that cut across old loyalties. Hence there are possibilities in both directions—either for absorption or for a kind of regeneration. Formerly the desire of self-preservation drew strength from the very oppression by the majority and from distrust of its intentions. In the new conditions it would not have to feed mainly on assessment of the merits or demerits of the majority.

In any case it is out of the question that an enlightened policy would seek to uproot the language of any people or to hamper its progress. It is humanly possible that the lot of a minority should be determined not by the interests, genuine or fancied, of a ruling oligarchy, but by social and cultural needs of human groups. A community which has been formed by historical causes should be treated with respect for its traditions and its identity. Various fruitful plans to deal with the needs of minorities have been tried by Switzerland, by Sweden, and by Canada.

Chapter Two

Problems of Lebanon

The problems affecting the integrity of Lebanon are so many and various that in comparison those which it shares with the neighboring states at times seem to pale into insignificance. There is a conflict between forces making for disintegration and for unity which makes its very existence problematical. Weak and not homogeneous, it is exposed to political, religious, and cultural influences from the West, alongside of the pressure of geographical proximity, kinship of origin, and community of language from the East. The hold which these factors have on each separate community in Lebanon greatly varies in strength. The country is tossed violently from one extreme of reaction to the other, and it is no wonder that it is left in a state of suspense and indecision.

In August 1920 the autonomous region of Lebanon was augmented by the addition of Beirut, Tripoli, 'Akkār, the Biqā', and the stretch between the former frontier of Lebanon and the new frontier which was given to Palestine. In these new areas the Christians formed only about a third of the population. The rest of it were Shī'is, especially in the south (Jabal 'Amil), and Sunnis and Druzes in the Biqā'. Thus in the enlarged territory the proportions between the communities were altered. While the Syrians maintain that these changes were made arbitrarily and forcibly, the Lebanese assert that these areas—parts of "historic Lebanon" in the sixteenth and eighteenth centuries— were torn from Lebanon in 1861, when the autonomous region was established, and that the frontiers of the Arab states themselves were not drawn according to the wishes of the inhabitants, let alone of the territorial minorities.

The distribution of the communities in the country as a whole and in its regions is variegated. The current estimate, according to which the Christians form 53 percent of the population, has become a sort of myth, calculated to preserve a tenuous equilibrium. Besides the fourteen communities which are mentioned in the official statistics, there are about 5,000 native 'Alawis in the northern 'Akkār district, about 3,000 Kurdish immigrants, chiefly in Beirut, and Assyrians. The various communities at the end of 1951 were as follows: Maronites, 378,000; Sunnis, 272,000; Shī'is, 237,000; Greek Orthodox, 130,000; Druzes, 82,000; Greek Catholics, 82,000; Armenian Orthodox, 67,000; Armenian Catholics, 14,000; Protestants, 13,000; Jews, 6,000; Syrian Catholics, 6,000; Syrian Orthodox, 5,000; Latins, 4,000; Chaldeans, 1,400; others, 7,000.[1]

The Maronites have a clear majority in Mount Lebanon and the Shī'is in Southern Lebanon. The Shī'is have a relative majority in the Biqā' (about a third), and the Sunnis in Beirut (about a third) and in Northern Lebanon (about 40 percent). On the other hand the Christians taken all together have a large majority in Beirut, chiefly on account of some 40,000 Armenians, a majority in Northern Lebanon, a large minority in Southern Lebanon and about 40 percent in the Biqā'. The Druzes are concentrated to a preponderating extent in four districts in Mount Lebanon ('Alayh, Shūf, Matn, and Ba'bda) and in the district of Rashayya in the Biqā' (settlements of Hermon). The districts and the large towns have a mixed population, and so have small towns and villages.

The numerical proportions between the communities are not stable. The large birth rate of the non-Christian communities is bound not only to upset the present delicate balance between the communities, but even to threaten seriously the position of the Maronites in Mount Lebanon itself. The natural increase in the country as a whole is about 2 percent.

This demographic trend has been strengthened by emigration. In consequence of the massacres of 1860, Maronites, Greek Catholics, and Syrian Catholics emigrated to Cairo and Alexandria. A great exodus to the United States and Canada commenced about 1890. In the years 1889–1914 there was an average annual emigration of 6,000 persons, from 1919 to 1924 of 9,000 to 10,000, and from 1925 to 1938 of 3,217. The centers of immigration were America (North, Central, and South), Africa, especially French West Africa, and Australia.[2] The annual average in 1951–1957 was about 3,300. It may be presumed that the number of emigrants and their descendants amounts to at least a million. There is scarcely a village in Lebanon, and not a Christian family in the whole country, without representatives abroad. Against the adverse effect of the exodus on the position of some communities in the country—the Christian emigration being overwhelmingly larger—has to be set the economic and cultural benefit derived from it both by the families of the emigrants and by the communities themselves. Having ties with various countries produces a feeling of confidence. To a certain extent, returning emigrants acquire neglected lots and work them through terracing and planting. Enterprising and less inhibited, they contribute to breaking the hold of the traditional leadership in the communities.

In its political structure, the country is unique in the Arab East. There is no state religion. The Constitution secures the personal status of every community and the management of its own religious affairs. This is not a majority country which at best extends benevolent protection to minorities. The six large "majority" communities are the "state-nations," and the principal offices of state are shared among them. Thus the president of the state is a Maronite, the head of the government a Sunni, the speaker of the Chamber of Deputies is a Shīʻi and his deputy Greek Orthodox. Each of the six communities is represented, not always in proportion to their numbers, in the eight- or ten-man government. Article 95 of the Constitution provides, temporarily, for a proper representation of the communities in the public service, and in the cabinet, insofar as the general welfare of the state is not affected. In theory the state is meant to be a model of communal cooperation, especially as nearly all the communities are bound together by a common language. The very fact that no one community has a decisive majority helps to keep in check ambitions for domination and to maintain equilibrium, although by no means a sense of equality. Of no small weight, too, is the tradition, if at times marred, of cooperation in the past between the Maronites and Muslims in "historical Lebanon" and between Maronites and Druzes in Mount Lebanon, and of about thirty years of joint rule, however shaky, in our own time.

To indicate the uniqueness of Lebanon, an ideology has been coined with two aspects, of its historical continuity on one side and on the other of its mission extending from the distant past to the future. The Maronites reckon the days of their independence from the end of the seventh century A.D., when from the fear of the Jacobites and the Arab invaders they left the northern plains of Syria and settled in the mountains of Lebanon. Their exodus came to an end only in 939.[3]

Throughout history freedom-loving peoples gravitated to Lebanon. The land, too, is singled out by its topographical features and its beauty and by its central position on the earth's surface. Here "Western thought with its philosophy and logic, and Eastern thought with its imagination and feeling met and mingled together. And this synthesis was spread through the world by Christians."[4]

According to this concept, the cultural mission of Lebanon has been continued since the period of Sidonians. The first mathematician in the world was Hiram, King of Tyre; and a Lebanese was also the first colonizer in the world. Perhaps it was its geographical smallness which stimulated its ambition. The land has been extended by ships and towns and gods, as if it sought to take revenge for its small compass. Both nature and history have constituted it a link between East and West. In our day, too, the emigrants carry their cultural mission to the ends of the earth. They are also fostering Arabism in the world.[5]

The cultural mission is also being discerned in the fact that this land was the cradle of a cultural awakening from the middle of the nineteenth century; or, following an Egyptian version, it was the first that answered the call for a new life that went forth from Egypt. The first Arabic printing press was established in Lebanon by the Melkites in 1734. It was in Lebanon that in the

1830's the Catholic and Protestant missions commenced their educational work. It was here that polymaths arose who worked for the revival of Arabic and the dissemination of knowledge in it. *Émigrés* from this land contributed much to the development of the press and of literature in Egypt.

Actually this kind of full-fledged nationalism had a chance of establishing itself first and foremost in the midst of the Maronite community.[6] Its nursery was mainly in the circles close to the Maronite Patriarch of Antioch and the Orient. In the Ottoman sanjak of Lebanon with its majority of Maronites the Patriarch represented, alongside of the governor, the secular authority also. Under the mandate, when his authority was curtailed, he strugggled for influence, by various political methods, in secular matters also.[*] This concept, however, which gained currency after World War I reflects the conditions in the community as a whole. The Maronites are the largest single group, and they are mostly concentrated in a single territory. This community has an historical self-consciousness and a keen sense of a common destiny. Unlike the other communities, the Maronites see in Lebanon their one and only fatherland, and their brethren in other countries are, apart from a few thousand villagers and town dwellers in Syria, practically all people who have gone forth or descended from it. The Maronite Patriarchate,[**] with its numerous clergy, religious and secular congregations, had exercised greater influence than the highest authorities of the other communities. Unlike them, the Maronites are, or had been until recently, for the most part independent tillers, and through them the village in Lebanon exercised a marked influence on the town. The protection which they have enjoyed for many generations at the hands of France and Rome has inspired them with a kind of double-edged feeling of both self-confidence and dependence. Attachment to Mount Lebanon and anxiety for

---

[*] It was to assume that with the election of a new Patriarch, in 1955, at which the influence of the Vatican has prevailed, the attitude of the highest dignitary, especially as to Lebanon's position in the Arab world, is to be somewhat modified. The new trend of "indigenization" is not confined to the Catholic church.

[**] Under its jurisdiction are twelve archbishoprics in Lebanon, Syria, and Cyprus.

maintaining its individuality have even prompted some Maronite circles to demand a narrowing of the country's frontiers in order the better to preserve it.

An offshoot of this has been the Mediterranean idea. Although its population is mainly of Semitic descent, Lebanon has been in direct human contact with other parts of the Mediterranean world (Greeks, Romans, crusaders). Lebanon is likely to turn toward the Mediterranean; another version, toward the Latin culture. The culture of Lebanon will represent a fusion of Arabic culture with the modern culture of the West, especially that of France.[7]

Charles Malik, who looks on the Mediterranean basin as a unity, assigns to Lebanon a "positive vocation" in the international field: "to be true to the best and finest in the East and West alike," and to carry "the burden of mediation and understanding." Lebanon is the one country in our day in which "East and West meet and mingle on a footing of equality." The Islamic-Christian combination contains the possibility of a "creative confrontation of East and West."[8]

This concept gives scope to legend for improving on reality. It is nurtured by anxiety and concern for maintaining the historical distinctness of the country. Contrary to general assumption, social conditions, apart from Mount Lebanon, do not differ greatly from those in the neighboring countries; only here, apart from dividing each community in itself, they contribute in a marked degree to distinguish from one another communities of legally equal status. World War II sharpened the consciousness of these differences in the social structure of the communities. The hundred million pounds brought into the country by the Allied armies benefited chiefly a thin stratum of merchants, industrialists, and contractors and helped to widen the gap between rich and poor. True, a number of factors have contributed to improve conditions in the country, such as continuous contact with the West and its help in raising the standard of education, emigration, and an agreeable climate with a heavy rainfall. The death rate is lower than in any Arab country; the position of woman is higher; the rate of literacy is 60-65 percent, and in Mount Lebanon much higher. There is in

Lebanon a larger proportion of small landowners (158,185 own less than five hectares). All this, however, is due mainly to Mount Lebanon. Here, especially in the districts of Zagharta, Kisrawān, Batrūn, Jazzīn, and Matn, where the largest groups of Maronites are concentrated, small ownership is dominant. Security of life and produce has rendered possible great density of population (186 per sq. km. in Mount Lebanon against 38 in the Biqā') and a higher standard of living. These regions do not send men to the hovels in the suburbs. On the contrary they supply educators, professionals, even public servants and leaders.[9]

For all this, the traditional picture of Mount Lebanon is to be corrected. It is in a state of transformation, in some respects bordering on disintegration. True, in consequence of the agrarian upheaval during 1850–1860, small landholdings prevail, but there are larger estates of families with a tradition of authority and large estates owned by convents. Land tenure appears, as elsewhere, in many forms and combinations. There are small owners who supplement their earnings by work as share tenants or as wage laborers, especially during the harvest season. There are owners who farm only a part of their land and let the rest to tenants, partly from outside. There are landowners—residents or absentees—who are not farmers. In many villages the land base is poor or inadequate.

Broadly speaking, there are in Mount Lebanon two classes of villages. The summer resorts area, mainly above Beirut, is rapidly being commercialized. A part of the land here has been acquired by city merchants. The great increase in fruit production is partly due to their efforts. The rest of the Mountain maintains its agricultural character.

The chief disturbing trend is steady depopulation due to migration to the towns. In many villages, up to half the population moves daily or weekly between the village and the city. The surplus population is growing, owing to the decreasing death rate and the relatively high birth rate, and is drifting from the village in search of better earnings. In consequence, there is a rapid reduction of the productive population in the village, the decline in the number of agricultural workers being offset only to a negligible extent by the development of nonagricultural occupations. Apart from the new fruit orchards, archaic methods of cultivation are still prevalent.[10]

In the towns the Maronites are represented in the manifold social classes ranging from shopkeepers to big businessmen.

In the rest of the country the land tenure problems are not much different from those in the neighboring countries. Half of the surveyed area in Lebanon is owned by 171 persons, that is, 0.2 percent of the landowners.[11] As in Syria the large estates are let on a share-tenancy basis (*murāba'a*); its effects are visible in the degraded position of the fellah, and also in the desolate aspect of the landscape. The characteristics of this system are absentee landownership, heavy indebtedness of the tenant due to exceedingly high interest on loans, and extreme fragmentation of holdings.

In the plantation areas, especially around the coastal towns, a system of share-cropping known as *musākā* is still in use. In the case of new plantations the system of *mughārasa* is sometimes applied, a form of association between the owner of the soil and the planter entitling the latter to a share of the trees and sometimes both of the trees and the land.

The forms of partnership are varied and allow of many devices for squeezing the *métayer*. This is also expressed in the fact that nearly half the seats in the parliament have been occupied by large landowners.[12]

Large ownership is prevalent in the districts inhabited mostly by Shī'is (Matāwila, Mitwālis)—Jabal 'Amil in the south and the northern Biqā'. Socially and politically theirs is the most backward of the communities, and before World War II the rate of illiteracy in it was 83 percent. The great majority of them are share-croppers, nearly half-slaves of the rich Mitwāli landowners who enjoyed, until recently, especially in Jabal 'Amil, unquestioned authority. Within their community some of the chieftains preferred illiteracy to education and even sought to prevent the government from promoting it.[13] The Mitwāli village supplies unskilled labor to the towns and to Christian villages. In the northeast of the country Shī'i tribes are to be found, the most restless among them being Danādisha. Their economy is, to a degree, a closed one; some of them combine agriculture, including hashīsh, with sheep-rearing, and in consequence are on perpetual move between their summer and winter residence.[14] The leading feudal families (al-As'ad, its chief Ahmad being the most powerful, al-Zayn and al-Fadl in the south, Haydar and Himāda in the Biqā') had been dominant in the community, and it is they who represent it, through perpetual strife, within each region and on a regional basis, sometimes even within each family, in public service. Associated or competing with them are families of merchants and professionals in the towns ('Usayrān, Baydūn). At the same time a group of middle-class spokesmen has grown up in the town which began to take part in the affairs of the community, recently with considerable success.

Large Shī'i groups exist also in North Lebanon and in Beirut.

The Sunnis form more than a half of the town dwellers (the largest single community in Beirut, a majority in Tripoli and Sidon). In these towns there is a class of Sunni merchants, owners of estates and of plantations, alongside artisans, shopkeepers, and workers. In the predominantly Sunni district of 'Akkār—together with the Biqā' and Southern Lebanon one of the wheat granaries in the country—large ownership of the land is the rule. Rich Sunni landowners are also found in the Biqā'.

Next to the Christians, the Druzes are the most advanced community. Commonly none of the Druze groups forms the majority of the population in any district; in almost all regions where they are grouped together (mainly in Mount Lebanon and the southern Biqā') they live close to the Christians in villages of their own or in mixed villages. The majority of them are engaged in agriculture, to which they cling more tenaciously than their neighbors; the town dwellers are engaged in trade, manual labor and liberal professions. The chief spokesmen of this community are representatives and associates of two feudal families, Janbalāt and Arslān, whose influence has spread beyond their own boundaries.

The Greek Orthodox are grouped mainly in the towns and urbanized areas adjoining them. There is a large group of them in Northern Lebanon, especially in the agricultural district of Kūra. A comparatively large section comprises powerful merchants, bankers, landowners, and professionals. The common people, including the lower clergy, stand out in their primitive and retarded existence.

The Greek Catholics are scattered almost all over the country. An agricultural element is to be found in the northern Biqā' (regions of Hermel and Zahla) and in Southern Lebanon. In Beirut they have a considerable number of men of affairs and professionals. The educational level of the community is among the highest.

The Armenians came to Lebanon and Syria extremely impoverished. In Beirut they congregated in quarters named after their home towns, such as Nor-Hajin, Nor-Marash, Nor-Sis, Nor-Adana (nor=new). Through their enterprise and diligence they gained a respectable position in the country's industry. There has gradually grown up the nucleus of a well-to-do class engaged in industry, commerce and banking.

The majority of the Armenians are artisans and skilled workers (mechanics, masons, carpenters, tailors, shoemakers, goldsmiths, weavers). They are markedly represented in the liberal professions (educators, notably in the universities, architects, physicians, pharmacists), and arts (musicians and composers, art photographers, painters, writers).

The 115,000 Armenians (87,000 Gregorians, 22,000 Catholics, and 6,000 Protestants) own seventy primary and high schools, attended by 73,502 pupils, and some colleges. The schools are maintained by the Armenian community and supported by Armenian benevolent societies abroad, notably in the U. S. A.

The churches of the Armenian Apostolic faith (Beirut, Zahle and nearby 'Aynjar, where the remnants of Musa Dag are settled, and Tripoli) are under the jurisdiction of the Catholicos of Antelias, Lebanon. The Armenian Catholic community is headed by the Patriarch-Catholicos, Cardinal G. Aghajanian.

Five Armenians are members of parliament.

The differences between the communities are also marked in education. The rate of illiteracy among the Christians and the Druzes is comparatively low. The educational level among the Shī'is is on the whole lower than among the Sunnis. The percentage of Christian and Druze students attending school is higher than that of other communities.

In 1944–45 the 308 government schools had 20.9 percent of the pupils (30,113), the 963 private (denominational) schools 49.4 percent (71,524), and the 326 foreign schools 29.7 percent (43,065). About seven-eighths of the pupils in the foreign schools were Christians, mostly Catholics. In 1947-48 there were 48,795 pupils in 275 foreign schools: 232 (40,500) French, 22 American, 14 English and others.[15] In 1955–56 there were 102,738 pupils and 3,472 teachers in 1,107 government schools, 110,966 pupils and 3,912 teachers in 907 private schools, 39,148 pupils and 1,633 teachers in 111 foreign schools.

The choice of a school is largely motivated by communal considerations. Each community strives to get its children into its own schools or into those akin to them, so that the schools help preserve the confessional spirit. Though government schools, the underlying aim of which is a unified system of instruction, are increasing markedly, they can hardly cope with the contradictory trends in public life.

Although there are, relatively speaking, more highly educated people in Lebanon than in any other Arab country, the character of its public life does not differ much. Foreign education and knowledge of languages, often amounting to bilingualism in certain strata of the Christian communities, has certainly heightened the feeling of self-confidence among the Christians. The universities have already trained generations of professionals. The Université Saint-Joseph has carried out much research work in Arabic culture and ethnology, while the American University of Beirut is trying its best to train young men and women for public work and social research. Nevertheless, foreign establishments alone could not succeed in training a disinterested élite qualified to make a bold attempt to take the destiny of the country into its hands. The very connection of education with manifold missions and institutions entails a distinct relativism in approach to values which may also spring from competitiveness, especially as the secular attitude becomes stronger. Against this background, attachment to façade and virtual worship of material things is conspicuous.[16] And insofar as there is a cultural élite, it submerges or is forcibly kept away from public affairs.

An ambivalent strain also marks the attitude of the communities toward the Arab countries. It takes on a different color within each community, since cultural or ethical motivations are intertwined with political considerations, whether of principle or of tactics. Extreme opportunism, fed on self-interest, has long become nearly second nature to the *homo politicus* in Lebanon, a kind of artistic game. It finds a fruitful field in the political structure of the country, since in spite of everything the communities cannot dispense with a certain amount of reciprocity at the national or regional level. It is accompanied by a kind of denominational neurosis—permanent fear of a setback now, foreboding about survival in the future. Even among the Maronites, to whom Lebanon is the historical and only fatherland, there are differences of outlook and purpose. Integral Lebanese nationalism has been the watchword of the clergy. To them independence is a kind of national faith, and they do not regard the attachment to the Arab world in its existing image as axiomatic and unquestionable. For them the neighboring countries are in fact Islamic countries, and Arab culture is mainly Islamic culture. They desire therefore to maintain the Christian character of the country. Those circles that in their time gathered around the National Bloc of the late president, Emil Eddé, or nowadays around Pierre Eddé, or the preponderantly Christian Phalanges Libanaises, were anxious not to attach the country, without reservations, to a pan-Arab organization, and they also sought to establish some connection with France. For them Lebanon has an "ethical individuality" and a historical right to existence, based on "spiritual and political traditions and friendships of past generations." The adherents of the recently revived Dustūri Bloc of Bishāra al-Khūri have, chiefly from political motives, tended toward closer cooperation with the general body of the Arabs and, consequently, to eliminating or weakening French influence. It may be presumed that their basic outlook was not greatly different from that of their rivals in the National Bloc. Opposition between them has in fact

been fed by quarrels between families with a tradition of authority (as the al-Khūri family from Shūf had for two centuries),
and there is no doubt that the orientation towards foreign
powers has been partly determined by them. For them the bell
tolled with the rise of British influence in Lebanon in 1942. It
was al-Khūri who in 1943 negotiated, presumably with British
blessing, a "National Pact" with the Sunni leader Riyād al-Sulh,
providing for the preservation of Lebanon's independence with
its "Arab face" and maintenance of the Christian-Muslim equilibrium with a "slight pre-eminence" of the former.[17] Nowadays
all factions among the Maronites acquiesce in the "National
Pact," although they differ widely as to its implications.

Naturally, the pan-Arab feeling is stronger among the Sunnis.
Syria is a Sunni state, whereas in Lebanon they are merely one
of the ruling communities. The four districts in which most of
the Sunnis live were attached to Lebanon only in 1920. Although
the leading circles in the Sunni community have consolidated
their political influence and economic activity within the borders
of Lebanon, the community's natural solidarity with Syria is a
motive force, especially in regard to the foreign policy of
Lebanon; and there is no doubt that it is influenced through
channels of advice or pressure from Damascus. The spokesmen
of the community hold that with the attainment of independence
Lebanon is apt to find greater scope for action in cooperation
with its "brethren in language, origin and national sentiment"
in the other Arab countries. To them Lebanon is a land which
"in character is Arabic but absorbs what is best in western culture." Its geographical position and economic conditions impel
it to make its relations with the Arab countries its chief concern.
The Sunni organizations point time and again to cooperation
with the Arab countries to the furthest limit. In the 1930's a
pan-Arab union, 'Usbat al-'Amal al-Qawmī, was formed, principally from Sunnis, and in our days the al-Nidā' al-Qawmī party
has been in touch with the Istiqlāl party in Iraq. The youth
association Najjāda, at present an ardent protagonist of the
United Arab Republic, professed a closer, if at times equivocal
attachment to Lebanon. Generally speaking, in Beirut, where
there is a somewhat more enlightened and content class of

Sunni merchants and professionals, the attitude of the Sunnis to the state seems more favorable. For all this, the lower middle class was easily swayed to favor alignment with the U.A.R. In Tripoli, with its strong Sunni majority, more centrifugal forces have been at work. Here there was a strong leaning, partly nurtured by the interest of citrus planters in the Syrian market, toward absorption into Syria, or at any rate to economic union with it; Tripoli is jealous of Beirut. The internal tension in Tripoli revolved to a large extent around a long-standing quarrel, often leading to blood-feuds, between and even within Sunni families of high standing. Local organizations are grouped around them. Owing to the turmoil, nearly chaos, following the attainment of independence in Syria, the leanings toward closer attachment to it had been weakening. With the merger of Egypt and Syria, the current in favor of unity again prevails.

The Mitwālis gained confessional autonomy under the French mandate. In 1926 they were allowed to set up religious courts and thus put on a basis of equality with the Sunnis. They are one of the three large "twelfers" communities in the Middle East, that is, believers in the resurrection of the twelfth *imām* (Iran, Iraq, Lebanon).* Tactical moves or motives of prestige aside, the community as a whole appreciates its standing in an independent Lebanon. Their attitude is partly determined by their links to the Shī'is in Iraq.

The Druzes have traditions of political existence even in a wider sphere than the sanjak of Lebanon. Up to the middle of the last century the Mount Lebanon was known as Jabal al-Durūz. They have memories of numerical superiority there. With the great waves of Christian refugees in the seventeenth and eighteenth centuries, as this superiority passed to the Maronites, the solidarity with the Christian communities was preserved, and at times even a kind of political symbiosis with the Maronites was established. Some leading families trace their descent back for centuries. In our days, the faction which had gathered around the family of Janbalāt has been emphatic in

---

* They are referred to as Ja'faris, because Ja'far ibn Sādiq, the sixth imām, is considered the founder of their legal system.

its eagerness to see the independence of Lebanon preserved. It is noteworthy that, prior to World War I, this family maintained close links with Great Britain. Its members were among the supporters of the mandate regime and adherents of the National Bloc. In 1949, its leader, Kamal Janbalāt, founded the nondenominational Socialist Progressive party, but its followers are more and more reduced to Druzes from his native Mountain. Their rivals, the family of hereditary emīrs Arslān in Shūf, where they have been established since the eleventh century, seemingly represented the pan-Arab leanings and allied itself with Bishāra al-Khūri. This family produced Shaqīb Arslān, a distinguished writer and versatile champion of the Arab cause. Janbalāt and Arslān enjoyed the allegiance, not always continuous, of other families and strains. Some branches of these two families departed from their adopted attitude. Unusual policies were also to be observed within other families, such as Talhūq and Taqī al-Dīn. Many of the Druze intellectuals, who had entered the American University of Beirut, were captured by the pan-Arab idea; they left their impression on the Syrian Popular Party. Of late years they have formed a kind of moral support for their brethren in Jabal al-Durūz in Syria, where they practically lost their autonomy and have almost been ousted from share in public affairs.[18]

The Greek Orthodox Church in Lebanon is under the jurisdiction of the Patriarch who resides in Damascus. The conflict between East and West cuts through this community, too. Three candidates contended for the vacant post of Patriarch: one, Bishop from Zahle, rather Soviet-oriented, another, Western-minded, from New York, and a neutralist, supported from Damascus.

It would seem that nowadays the concept of political independence is common to all the communities. All the same, it is put to a severe test at times of crisis. An equivocal attitude also prevails with regard to the Arab League Covenant, which, although it binds Lebanon to a supposedly joint policy, at the same time may assure some protection for its independence.[19] Lebanon's membership in the United Nations also may help to strengthen its political position. Meanwhile, it sometimes found enthusiastic supporters, such as Egypt and Sa'udi Arabia, which sought to frustrate the Hāshimite plans for union, in regard to which Syria itself has been divided. The *coups d'état* in Syria could certainly not have much attraction. Through the discord between and within the neighboring states, Lebanon obtained a breathing space and was sometimes able, despite pressure from both sides, to derive moral advantages from trying to mediate between them. But the attempt, in the controversy over the Mutual Co-operation Pact between Turkey and Iraq, to take up a somewhat equivocal stand, seemingly more favorable to one side, incurred a move to economic sanctions from Sa'udi Arabia. Previously it had been pressed to agree to a bilateral military agreement with Syria, an issue on which the government of Lebanon cannot but be divided. Professing integral Arab nationalism is necessarily among the fundamentals of Lebanon's politics, but in any dissension between Arab States it cannot afford to take sides, although the means of gross interference, current in inter-Arab power politics, may leave her no alternative.

Politics being mixed with an irrational strain, this tenuous equilibrium may one day be utterly upset. The controversy raging, avowedly, over the Baghdad Pact and the Eisenhower Doctrine, in reality over the 'Abd al-Nāsir issue, stirred up a hornet's nest of political emotions with the usual surprising changes of sides. Leading personalities among Muslims, even Christians, were carried by motives of power and position, or concern for the future.

All the same, merely negative factors are not calculated to preserve independence for any length of time. The communal spirit galvanizes public life and at the same time frustrates it. In relation to the state it is essentially a centrifugal factor; it powerfully fosters an aggressive spirit, often fed on alleged unfair representation of the community in public service. From time to time the share of each community in the Parliament is being fixed after keen struggle. Sometimes a fierce battle is fought on an issue as, for example, jurisdiction in matters of personal status or education. In consequence a sharp turn to communalism is the rule. There usually emerges an ephemeral Muhammadan Bloc comprising groups of Sunnis and some heterodox Muslims. Islamic associations, under Sunni guidance, give vent to grievances (The National Committee, The Congress of Parties and National Committees, etc.). The Catholics turn for guidance to their religious heads, usually to conferences at the seat of the Maronite Patriarch. The Greek Orthodox turn to their lay councils and religious hierarchy. At times of intense discord, the confessional youth organizations or parties (Phalanges, instituted in 1936 as a counterweight to the Syrian Popular Party of Sa'āda by Maronites and Greek Catholics, Najjāda of the Sunnis, and the less conspicuous Ghassāsina of the Orthodox and Talā'i of the Shī'is) come to the fore. More considerate elements of the communities intervene and try to bridge the rift at conferences outside the Parliament.

Thus clashes were caused by a Muslim pamphlet *Moslem Lebanon Today* (in 1953) and by a Christian one allegedly offending Islam and the Prophet (in 1954). Muslim circles demanded revision of the Constitution with a view of curtailing the prerogatives of the president and transferring some of them to a Muslim vice-president. A long overdue population census should be conducted honestly and include only the emigrants who had retained their Lebanese nationality. Other demands: actual participation in the administration on a basis of equality, economic unity with Syria.

The attitude of the heads of the Christian communities, as far as they are unified, implied preservation of Lebanon with its "traditional physiognomy." To them, the country belongs to all its descendants, residents and emigrants alike, and a census should cover all of them. The existing Constitution already ensures equal rights of all citizens. More outspoken circles, such as the Phalanges, maintained that a just redistribution of public offices should take into account moral and intellectual ability and that equality of rights implies equality of duties. They argue that Christians pay 80 percent of the taxes. To them economic unity with Syria is bound to put an end to Lebanon's sovereignty, and place it at its mercy. Abolition of confessionalism should begin with general laicization of the state, elimination of the sharī'a courts, and introduction of a unified civil code.

The confessional representation, which postulates a certain cohesion of each community, is bound to strengthen the spirit of cooperation in it, and on the other hand to accentuate the differences between the strong clan leaders over the representation itself. At the same time, being regional, partly list-bound and therefore intercommunal, it has a certain centripetal force. Rigid confessionalism may be mitigated by the interdependence of the candidates. The electoral list, usually headed by a leader of the dominant community in the administrative or electoral unit, comprises members of the minority or minorities in it. Even small minorities not represented in an electoral list may decide the outcome of the elections in a given unit. The struggle for representation in the same community is therefore partly decided by connections with members of other communities, and through this, common power interests grow up. The political groups in the parliament are usually intercommunal in appearance, but they are kept together not so much by identity of outlook as by temporary considerations, personal rivalries, etc. This state of affairs explains such political curiosa as temporary alliances between extreme political foes.

The political ferment is reflected in the ever-changing electoral laws and in the oscillation between grand lists with powerful leaders and smaller constituencies. From 1943 to 1951 the Parliament numbered 55, elected from five constituencies, and from 1951 to 1953, 77 deputies (nine constituencies). The electoral law of 1952 abolished the multi-seat constituencies and introduced 22 one-seat and 11 two-seat constituencies (1953-1957). It soon proved disadvantageous, providing no scope for the incessant political game within the communities, between them and between parliament and government. The electoral law of 1957 altered anew the subdivision of the constituencies and raised the number of the deputies to 66. The law of 1960 raised it again to 99 (54 Christians, 45 Muslims), to be elected in 26 constituencies.

Against this tangle of divergencies certain possibilities can be set which, given favorable conditions, may diffuse an influence transcending the boundaries of Lebanon. There is a good deal of myth in the concept of Lebanon's mission toward East and West. But there is no exaggeration in the current view that this land has served, and is likely to go on serving, as a place of refuge for religious minorities, a kind of national home for Christians in particular, and to ever-changing political exiles from Arab countries. Much of this is due to France. For all internal and external pressures, there is far more personal freedom in Lebanon than in any other Arab country. In theory, there is an amount of religious freedom; actually, formal adherence to a community is indispensable. In Lebanon no community is able to dominate another without endangering the existence of the state. Through the very fact of its existence Lebanon is bound to heighten the self-confidence of the Christians in the whole region, while the Sunnis, who form the majority in many countries, learn to be a partner and not sole judge. As for the Shi'is, it is not difficult to assess the change in their status in case of absorption into Syria. The communities are in a state at once of mutual fear and mutual dependence. If we exclude the possibility of the country being absorbed by some other state, it is imperative for them to live together, for no attempt to draw new frontiers for the state and reduce its size will succeed in isolating regions with a single community.

Up to World War II, the economic future of the country was open to question. Syria was then, in large measure, its hinterland. It supplied Lebanon with cereals and in return relied to a great extent on its service, mainly as middleman, in commerce and transit trade. Today the Syrian market, although still of some importance, is falling from her grasp, and, with the development of the port of Latakiya, Syria has become largely independent from Beirut. At the same time Lebanon is capable of supporting herself. Owing to some climates (15 subclimates)—the lowland with its coastal Mediterranean climate, the mountain range of Lebanon rising from 400 to 1,600 metres, the northern plateau of the Biqāʿ with an average height of 1,000 metres and a semiarid climate—the country is able to develop a variegated agriculture. It produced, in 1956, 62,000 tons of wheat and 25,000 tons of barley. With the possible extension of the cultivated area (up to some 390,000 ha.) and with increased yield, it could produce a great part of the 120,000 tons of wheat imported yearly. Since 1945 the area under irrigation is being enlarged (up to 44,000 ha. in 1957). In the last few years unirrigated fruit production on the slopes of the mountains (vines, figs, olives, almonds) and irrigated in the coastal strip (citrus fruits, apples, bananas) have considerably increased. There is also wide scope to develop light industries, especially food processing.

An important item of the national income, amounting to 55 percent of the export value, are remittances sent by relatives abroad. Lebanese foreign colonies, some of which are very wealthy, could be called upon to share in the financing of enterprises. Through its schools, the country has become an educational center for the whole region. Although the requisites for a highly developed tourist trade are still lacking, it is already an important income source.

All the same, the economic and social trends do not accord with the potentialities of the country. Nearly half the population is concentrated in five towns, and the capital alone holds more than a quarter of it. As against this trend of urbanization, only 140,000 persons depend for their livelihood on industry. Nearly half the population derives its livelihood from trade and its auxiliaries (100,000 clerks and shop assistants, 30,000 merchants). The steady drift of workers to towns increases unemployment and lowers the purchasing power of the population. The bulk of investments is being absorbed in the building industry and real estate. Only about 300,000 persons derive their livelihood from agriculture. A great part of the income of the village consists of remittances, earning in the town, renting summer resorts. Mulberry groves, which until 1928 occupied 17,000 ha., and provided the chief cash crop, decreased in the 1930's to small areas. Of the 70 spinning mills, which in the past could absorb the whole produce of cocoons, only a few are working. Wheat culture in Mount Lebanon has also decreased, especially in low-grade terraces on the hillsides, as the yield is not worth the cost of hired labor and taxes. Only in the last three years has there been some increase in wheat production.

Unlike Syria, Lebanon produces services mainly. Agriculture and industry account for about a third of the national income. The wide trade gap, which decreased to the 1:5 ratio in 1954, but increased to 1:6.5 in 1955 and 1:6 in 1956, is chiefly covered by transit trade (including gold) and benefits of a free currency market, by remittances, expenses of foreign representatives, foreign cultural and social establishments, foreign companies (trade, shipping, air lines), Point Four allocations, aid under the Eisenhower doctrine, and proceeds from the pipelines of I.P.C., which terminates at Tripoli and of the Tapline Co., which terminates at Saida. Hidden sources of income are trade in hashīsh, Lebanon being the planter, and contraband trade (gold, narcotics, arms). But a balanced budget, the bulk of which is being assigned to salaries, and a favorable balance of payments do not make for social reconstruction.

The chief problem for Lebanon lies therefore in a peculiar sociological phenomenon, namely, a community the main distinguishing feature of which is not ethnic origin but religion, and, on the other hand, its separateness as a human entity, by way of "community of blood." More precisely, the problem is whether, and how, a sense of joint citizenship, of Lebanese nationhood, based on common values, can be created, strong enough to counterbalance the centrifugal forces in the communities. The state, which is here the destined instrument for forming a single nation, maintains the basis for preserving confessionalism, which at best can insure a kind of intercommunal equilibrium. A modern state can hardly function properly as long as the basic loyalty to the national community is far weaker than the traditional set of loyalties (confessional community, tribe or kinship group, a regional family rule by virtue of property or tradition, quarter or clan in a village grouped around a headman, quarter in town, even local churches and saints). The demographic trends of the communities intensify the fear of domination, so that political solutions that are not anchored to the sentiment of attachment to a national community are liable to come to grief on the apprehensions of the minorities.

Unlike Switzerland, in Lebanon almost all the communities speak the same language. The forces that preserve the confessional unity are, therefore, tradition of independence or separate identity, and a sense of superiority or inferiority with the resulting isolationist reactions. Numerous questions arise from this. What are the prospects for a community when the religious sentiment commences to weaken as a unifying force, and *ipso facto* as a political factor? Or when the vested interests of the ruling circles in the communities—omnipotent landlords, rich entepreneurs, versatile lawyers—are curbed, and with them, at least to some extent, the fears of being overruled and the need, real or imagined, for self-defence, which promotes aggressiveness? What will be the result of the continuous social differentiation in the backward Muslim villages and of the weakening of the upper stratum's grip? Is the weakening of communal consciousness going to strengthen the pan-Arab feeling in several of the communities, or will a secular Lebanese nationalism arise from it?

Thirty years of Lebanese parliamentarism could not but contribute somewhat to mutual tolerance. Yet it was marked by lack of an enlightened policy towards the weaker communities and social strata.[20] The rudimentary social legislation does not serve the barest needs of the weakest in the society, especially the agricultural tenant and worker. Rigid control and interference by security organs hindered the growth of supracommunal voluntary associations, based on common economic interest or social concept, that could gradually replace confessional associations or short-lived coalitions of self-interested landed and urban plutocrats. Nonetheless, this kind of association, for what it is worth, has emerged: the Syrian Popular Party, the Communist Party, the nearly defunct Progressive Socialist Party, and some of the trade-unions.[21]

Meanwhile, there is a good deal of confusion. Everyone recognizes the evils of communalism and the advantages of Lebanese nationalism, or at least pays lip service to it, and yet all cling to it, for it seems to safeguard rights and equality to all. This barren struggle is apt to crush every constructive effort in the society; moreover, religious sentiments, easily inflammable, may cause an explosion on the smallest pretext.

An intercommunal nationalism cannot be established on sharp distinctions in the social life of the communities; a supracommunal one even less. It is conceivable only if it has roots in the whole people, not in a small class possessing political and economic power with a frightened middle class following in its wake. Formal abolition of communalism, without supplanting it by a higher social order, would lay the state open to abuses by communities bound to be strengthened from outside in undermining the foundations of the state. Social levelling would undoubtedly increase the attachment to the whole. A social vocation may have the power to sublimate the consciousness of national unity.[22] But economic and social renovation of the country is hardly conceivable without fundamental land reform coupled with bold social legislation.

A showdown took place earlier than could have been anticipated. In September 1952, an innocent popular uprising, born of indignation at a corrupt government, united heterogeneous elements in an eloquent protest, and swept away the nine-year-old regime of Bishāra al-Khūri. A frightened Chamber of Deputies, mostly partisans of al-Khūri, elected Sham'ūn to succeed his rival, by 74 to 3 votes. Four years passed, and the forces of division became stronger than ever. Of course, the main causes can be traced to influences from the neighboring countries. The *coups d'état* in Syria and the growing impact of Egypt reverberated strongly in this tiny country whose policy seemed to be a kind of pro-Western neutralism. As usual in the Near East, agitation in Lebanon meant activities of foreign agents, promises and intimidation, bribing of newspapers, attempts on lives. The outcome of the British-French campaign in Egypt in 1956 precipitated the crisis. In April, 1957, the government of Sāmī al-Sulh accepted, and the Chamber approved, a policy to work with the United States for mutual defense against Communism. At once various elements of opposition combined to settle accounts, in which personal dislikes, tactical moves or matters of conviction are hardly to be disentangled. The elections of June, 1947, manipulated as always, resulted in a majority (47 to 17) in favor of Sham'ūn. Defeated traditional leaders launched a violent anti-Western campaign. In September, 1957, the government indicted 400 persons, including three former premiers, on charges involving an attempt at an armed coup. The crisis came to a head with the merger of Egypt and Syria. Open interference by the U.A.R. took shape in infiltration of armed bands, inflammatory broadcasts, press attacks. Kamāl Janbalāt, the leader of the once promising and now defunct Progressive Socialist Party, reverted to family leadership, and bands of his followers indulged in terrorizing the government. He was helped with men and arms from Jabal al-Durūz. The tiny faction of Sāmī al-Sulh within the Sunni community was swamped by the factions of Sā'ib Salām and 'Abdallah Yāfī, both former pro-Western premiers, who became, each in his own way, violent opponents, with slogans ranging from alignment to fusion with the U.A.R. 'Adnān al-Hakīm, leader of the Najjāda, openly discarded the pretense of independence and called for fusion. A large segment of the Shī'i community, headed by Ahmad As'ad, and Sabri Himāda, his son-in-law, plunged into the battle. Both the Sunni and Shī'i *muftis* took sides with the rebels. Dissatisfied Christian leaders, among them Greek Catholics and even some Maronites, raised a "third force." For personal and ecclesiastical reasons, the Maronite Patriarch, too, joined the opposition against Sham'ūn, and stirred up strife within the clergy.* He pleaded for Christian-Muslim

---

*A reconciliation came about in 1960.

co-existence, even if it meant neutralism in the East-West conflict. The opposition demanded closer cooperation with the U.A.R. and fought a possible amendment of the Constitution to allow the President to succeed himself for another six-year term. Lebanon was to adopt a policy of neutralism or of alignment with pan-Arabism, which later on proved to receive differing interpretations in Baghdad and in Cairo. Fortunately, the civil war which raged during May-October 1958 in Beirut, Tripoli, and on the mountain, was not conducted along strictly religious lines, at least not in religious terms. But it is safe to say that the overwhelming majority of the Christians desired ardently to see the independence of Lebanon preserved. The burden of resistance to the rebellious factions was borne by the Phalanges and, curiously, by the Syrian Popular Party, protagonists of a Greater Syria that turned to defenders of independent Lebanon. An independent Lebanon seemed a lesser evil than Egypt's dominion.

On September 24 Fu'ād Shihāb, former commander-in-chief, assumed the office of President. An eight-man cabinet was formed under Rashīd Karāmeh, who led the rebellion in Tripoli. It was a compromise in favor of the rebels, with a prospect of a Muslim victory. In the judgment of Jumayil, leader of the Phalanges, the government was made up of rebels and neutrals. After four months of a Muslim strike an effective Christian strike was staged. Both sides shrank from the imminent danger of open Christian-Muslim warfare. On October 14 a Sunni-Maronite four-man government was formed, with the Premier Karāmeh in charge of defense, and Jumayil in charge of interior. The two moderate members were Raymond Eddé, leader of the National Bloc, and Husayn 'Uwaynī. Thus an uneasy "balance of fear," as *The Times* of London put it, was established, a kind of neutralized regime, from which the other communities were excluded. Its watchword in foreign policy was conciliation, between Arab factions and between East and West, while the United States healed the economic wounds of a rebellion which cost over 2,000 lives.

On October 24, 1958, the evacuation of the United States

forces that had landed in July was completed. The landing itself was a bold undertaking: it put to the test apprehensions and conveyed some lessons to those concerned.

The Chamber elected in June-July 1960 produced an 18-member cabinet, evidently to appease various factions. It comprises leaders of the rebellion (Sā'ib Salām, the new premier, Janbalāt) and of the counter-rebellion (Pierre Jumayil, leader of the Phalanges), also Arslān, the leader of the second Druze faction. As against this, Sham'ūn's National Liberal Party, the National Bloc and some Sunni factions are not represented in it.

Thus a tenuous equilibrium has become an uneasy truce.

Part Two

PARTY POLITICS

Chapter Three

Egypt

On January 17, 1953, political parties in Egypt were dissolved by order of Muhammad Naguib, and on the tenth of February of the same year, "principles and rules" of government, effective during a transition period of three years, were declared. This was the termination of nearly thirty years of party strife, carried on under the shelter, for the most part fictitious, of the Constitution. In its wider aspects, this strife had been three-cornered, the contestants being the king and his entourage, the Wafd, and Great Britain.

Political life in Egypt suffered from a great many drawbacks: on the one hand, centuries of Ottoman misrule, an obsolete land system, maldistribution of the national income; and on the other, lack of any movement for reform with a revolutionary urge, also of a disinterested élite willing to speak up for the needs of millions of voiceless people. After the rebellion of 'Urabī Pasha in 1882, contact with the West increased. The nationalist movement adopted the watchwords of the French Revolution; it sought the aid of France against England. Religious modernism was fostered by ideas that were prevalent in France and England. With the first stage of independence, after World War I, the external signs of democracy, such as parliamentary trappings and party struggle, came to the fore. But the balance of social forces was such as to secure almost unlimited power for a strife-torn propertied class; and this class dominated every sphere of national life.

The struggle between the ruling groups was bitter and stormy, but it hardly affected questions which were a matter of life or death to the nation. It was a struggle within a class whose whole existence and prestige depended on the very fact of its domination. Having no social or economic program of its own, every party, on being ousted from office, accused its rival of having obtained power by various malpractices, principally, of falsifying the elections, of corruption, or of leniency towards the British. The highly charged appeal to the masses, who were ready at any time to rise in revolt, was not meant to cut off the sources of their rebellion. For the most part, it ran into two channels: one was nationalist, which meant, mainly, conflict with the British, and the other religious; at times these channels merged. In this way, its inherent social character was perverted.

In the very act, however, of fomenting and exploiting rebelliousness, the ruling class, as it were, fell captive to the street. The government was afraid of the mob, since it could easily be made an instrument for dislodging it or hastening its fall. In many cases, it fell a victim to methods of conduct which it had adopted for its own convenience. It had to take the wind out of the sails of an opposition which resorted to trickery and deliberately whipped up the fury of the mob against "indolence and complacency." It had to put itself at the head of a "national campaign," as it were, to represent all the "national aspirations" of the people. An attempt of this kind was made by the Wafd in 1951, but, unlike in 1919, this body was then far from being identified with the people. The current of events proved too strong for those who had set it in motion, and when the rebellion was unleashed, it was followed by Black Saturday, on January 26, 1952, when the center of Cairo went up in flames, and by the downfall for the Wafd which brought with it a decisive turn in the affairs of the state.

Dr. Ahmad Husayn saw in Egypt only a "single ruling class in control of the land, industry and commerce, holding all the high offices of state and sitting in parliament by virtue of the votes of economically enslaved and starving workers."[1] As a final estimate this came very near to the truth. Urban Egypt has had intercourse with the West for about 150 years. Thousands of educated Egyptians have been in contact with its culture, and the country has always enjoyed a greater degree of independence than its neighbors. Nonetheless, the landowning class was dominant in it. Politically, the fellahin and the workers were nonexistent, and the direct influence of the middle class was also negligible.

The two world wars gave a powerful stimulus to the development of industry in Egypt, due to the requirements of the Allied armies. Nevertheless, the landowner remained the "ideal type." Land was the most desirable form of investment since it brought in an assured income without great effort. Large numbers of lawyers and other professionals, businessmen, and high officials had come from this class, or had sought to join it by investing their savings in land, sometimes running into heavy debts. True, intellectuals who were steeped in Western culture did not accept this state of society without protest. Since, however, public argument was bound to undermine their social position, it was inevitable that an ambivalent mentality should prevail, leading to a kind of forced hypocrisy.

Many of the rich landowners, including former ministers and high officials, joined governing boards of companies, local and foreign.[2] The profits made from commerce and from contracts and supplies to the Allied armies were invested in buildings, industrial, insurance and transport companies, hotels, etc. A characteristic feature of Egyptian economy had been the capitalization of agriculture in the form of limited liability companies. This partnership between capitalists and landowners could not but slow down the pace of social advance. While it may have been in the interest of industry to increase purchasing power by raising the standard of living, it was in the interest of the landowners to prevent a minimum wage being granted to the agricultural worker, and also to hinder the spread of education.[3] In the last resort, it was the landowners' interest which gained the day. The best guarantee for speedy profits for industry without effort lay in a plentiful supply of cheap labor from the villages, and in a strict political supervision of trade unions.

Almost all agreed that unfair division of the land was the

root of evil in the country. As far back as 1939 'Alī al-Shamsī warned the House of Deputies that if the government did not encourage small landownership, it would eventually have to confiscate the big estates and divide them up.[4] The moderates proposed a graduated tax on land so that it would not be worthwhile holding more than 100 feddan, a tax on legacies with the right to pay them in kind from the land, and only in the areas of big estates to expropriate a part for compensation.[5] In addition, proposals were made for a nonrecurrent levy on profits, a graduated income tax, and the abolition of the waqf. The more outspoken saw no remedy except in dividing the big estates.

All the while certain interests were at work to silence the well informed. "There is a kind of double policy pursued in the sittings of the parliamentary committees and of parliament itself of making promises for deceiving people," said Khattāb, a member of the Senate.[6] In February 1944, he brought forward a bill forbidding owners of more than 50 feddans to acquire further land. By this proposal, which did not apply to inheritances, he sought to put a stop to the extension of large estates and so do away with a position in which a third of the national income found its way into the purses of one-half percent of the population.[7] His intention was to divert the surpluses invested in land to industry, or to government bonds for public works.[8] The proposal was referred to a committee and thus pigeonholed. In 1946, the social affairs committee of the Senate approved a bill for distributing government land to fellahin, in lots of 5-15 or 16-50 feddan, but, on the request of the finance ministry, the consideration of it in the Senate was indefinitely deferred.[9]

Black Saturday in Cairo was directed against foreigners, but underlying it was also a protest against an urban center which typified the situation: a display of splendor and comfort in most glaring contrast with the surrounding misery. The whole of the ruling class was alarmed by it. In the period 1919-1950, the standard of living of the masses had fallen while that of the wealthy class had risen. True, one of the causes of this was the rate of natural increase. In spite of solemn warnings, no enlightened demographic policy had been planned for the country.

Before World War II, the main assault on the bickering parliamentary parties came from the aggressive nationalism of Young Egypt which derived inspiration from fascism. Later the chief attack came from the Muslim Brethren. In the late 1940's, almost all the groups vied with one another in making social demands, and nearly all of them espoused socialism. But no immediate spokesmen for the needs of the working population came to the fore. Trade-unions were run by or placed under the control of parties and individuals of the ruling circles. Independent associations, motivated by the real needs of the members, repeatedly sprang up, but they soon disappeared. The Federation of Industries, which was founded in 1922, also sought to narrow the field of their activity.

The Trade Unions Act of the Wafd government in 1942 withheld the right to form unions from millions of agricultural workers and from civil employees; and it also forbade trade-unions to discuss "political or religious questions" or to establish a countrywide organization. The Wafd then took over the trade-unions. When the Wafd government was overthrown, Makram 'Ubayd, a dissident Wafdist, managed to give them his blessing. Prince 'Abbās Halīm also, after having been detained during the war, espoused the cause of unionism. Later on, the Wafd again entrenched itself in the trade-unions, and relied on them in its political warfare. At the end of 1945, an attempt was made at a countrywide organization—the near-Communist Workers' Congress, which got in touch with the Trade Unions International. In its activities, it associated itself with the National Committee of Workers and Students, which was under the sponsorship of the left wing in the Wafd. They had to vie for influence with the Muslim Brethren.[10]

The small Nationalist Party (*al-hizb al-watanī*) was founded in 1907 by Mustafā Kāmil, and although after 1918 the Wafd assumed the lead, it continued to bask in the glory of its past and its founder. Prior to World War I it had gathered round it the pick of the younger intellectuals, many of whom afterwards became leaders of various parties. At first it was Islamic in its leanings, and it did not shrink from relying on Constantinople. It is generally assumed that it was supported by the khedive ʿAbbās Hilmī whom the British deposed in 1914. It opposed a compromise agreement with Great Britain, or even discussions with it before the evacuation of its army. It did not join hands with the National Front, which endorsed the Anglo-Egyptian Treaty of 1936. It eyed foreigners with suspicion and protested against every real or fancied injustice. It had only a few members in the House of Deputies, but its voice was much in evidence there.

This party was not particular about its political connections. In the 1920's, it sought the support of the Left, and Hāfiz Ramadān, its president, took part in the anti-imperialist congress in Brussels in 1927. With all its extremism, it showed no consistency of attitude. After the dissolution of the predominantly Wafdist House of Deputies, it did not hesitate, on December 30, 1937, to join the *coup d'état* government of Mahmūd Pasha. In the elections of March 1938, which were boycotted by the Wafd, it joined the Constitutional Liberals (*al-ahrār al-dustūriyyūn*), the remnants of the People's Party (*hizb al-shaʿb*), and the Unionist Party (*hizb al-ittihād*), to form a National Bloc. During World War II, it adopted an attitude which was, at best, one of cold neutrality, and it sought to derive political advantage from any favorable circumstance. For all that, its representative, Hāfiz Ramadān, joined the government of Hasan Sabrī in 1940. It was chiefly on account of its joining the government of Ahmad Māhir (1944-1945), who used every effort to bring the country into the war on the side of the Allies, that ʿAbd al-Rahmān al-Rāfiʿī's group left the party. The two divisions were reunited at the end of 1946. In the years 1950-51, when relations with Great Britain grew more strained, the party argued in favor of a nonaggression pact with the Soviet Union.

Fathī Ridwān, the spokesman of the youth element in this

party, did much to foment the tension which preceded Black
Saturday in Cairo. In August 1952, he seceded from it along
with his adherents, and they founded a New National Party.
He joined the government of Muhammad Naguib.

After World War I the national movement became a mass
movement—that is, the movement of the Wafd. It commenced
with a delegation of three, headed by Sa'd Zaghlūl, which presented itself before the British High Commissioner in November
1918. In April 1924, the Wafd assumed organizational shape
with the establishment of its parliamentary bloc.

In the periodicals of fascist countries, the totalitarian features
of the Wafd were deliberately emphasized. Particular stress
was laid on the habit of the Wafd of identifying itself with the
nation, as the mouthpiece of its will. In line with this was the
designation of the head of the Wafd as leader of the people
(*za'īm al-umma*). The Wafd saw in the Egyptian people a
"national society" in which the divisions between classes do not
necessitate class conflicts. In this view, however, it did not
differ from the other ruling parties.

This twofold identification of the Wafd—with the nation
and with its own leader—was to be the cause of divisions within
it. The pashas 'Adlī Yeghen, Muhammad Mahmūd, Ismā'īl
Sidqī and Hāfiz 'Afīfī left the Wafd and in October 1922 founded
the Liberal Constitutional Party. After its partnership in the
coalition government of 'Adlī Yeghen, in 1926-1928, the Wafd
made it a binding rule not to enter any coalition. And, in fact,
from that time it took part—for the purpose of preparing for
the elections—only in the third government of Husayn Sirrī,
in July-November 1949. From time to time, the wisdom of
this rule was questioned by leading members. In 1930, Hamīd
al-Bāsil left the party and founded the Sa'dist Party (*al-hizb
al-sa'dī*), which did not take root in the country. From similar
causes, one of them being that the head of the Wafd was under
the influence of Makram 'Ubayd, al-Nuqrāshī and Ahmad Māhir
left the party in 1937 and founded the Sa'dī Bloc (*al-hay'a
al-sa'diyya*). Only five years passed and 'Ubayd himself left it.
In November 1950, al-Hilālī was expelled from the Wafd; he

had come to the conclusion that the central problem of Egypt was corruption. In March 1952, he became prime minister, and he undertook to clear away what he regarded as a plague spot of the country.

No doubt, the insistence of the Wafd on governing alone helped to prolong its existence as the dominant power as well as the system of single-member constituencies. In the elections which took place during the period 1924-1950, under the electoral law of 1923, the Wafd obtained a majority eight times, and twice it boycotted the elections. It never succeeded in remaining in power for the full term of the election, and in this way it retained some moral authority till the next election.

Through thus identifying itself with the nation, the Wafd became a rival to the king, alongside of whom stood the "leader of the nation." On account of quarrels with the British, the tension resulted more than once in fatal affrays; it was calculated to raise apprehensions for the whole regime in the royal palace. Hence, almost from the beginning, the Wafd was openly or covertly at variance with the king, and, naturally, republican aspirations began to stir in it. A complete rupture between them took place in February 1942 when the British, pleading military necessity, compelled the king to appoint a Wafd government. This was dismissed by him in October 1944. The Wafd then remained out of office for about five years. The last attempt to compose the differences between the king and the Wafd, at the elections of 1950, also came to nothing.

After World War I, the Wafd represented the nation's aspirations for independence. "In the vague political conscience of the fellah, the Wafd held the first place in the scale of esteem. It had its representatives even in the smallest villages."[11] Sa'd Zaghlūl, its founder, and Mustafā al-Nahhās, his heir, were themselves of fellah stock. All classes of the people rallied round the Wafd. Before very long, however, it lost the affection of a portion of the rich landowners, and also of the banking and industrialist class which had grown numerous and powerful during the war. Their interests necessitated more moderation in dealing with the British. They shrank in some alarm from the restlessness of this seething conglomeration, and they therefore saw in the royal court and in the parties which had seceded from the Wafd a better guarantcc for their position in the state. During the 1930's, in the wake of the ideological polarization sweeping through the world, groups arose which after the example of fascism employed religious, national, and social demagogy to offer solutions for all problems and all difficulties (Muslim Brethren, Young Egypt). Within the Wafd itself, a group of intellectuals sought to call attention to the needs of the masses. The socially conscious elements exercised more influence toward the end of World War II and later, when the Wafd fell from power. A number of newspapers and magazines—*al-Wafd al-Misrī, al-Ba'th* and others—adopted a markedly socialistic tone. Capitalist companies and their heads were subjected to sharp criticism, and in the sphere of international politics a strident antifascist note was sounded. The position of the town workers became their principal concern. In 1949, on the eve of the elections, not only the head of the Wafd, but his secretary,[12] a rich landowning "boss," declared for a Socialist program. It must not be supposed, however, that at any time the Wafd would have embarked upon bold reforms. Under the Wafd government of 1950-1951, ministers with a lively social feeling, like Dr. Taha Husayn and Dr. Ahmad Husayn, were prevented from carrying out their designs in the field of education and welfare, and the latter left the government.

What became of aspirations for a cultural awakening in the framework of social relations can be seen from the vicissitudes of the Liberal Constitutional Party. On the cultural side, it continued, at the start, the efforts made by a group of enlightened men (among whom was Husayn Haykal), which in the year 1907 gathered round Lutfī al-Sayyid, an editor of the reform-minded journal *al-Jarīda*. In the 1920's the daily *al-Siyāsa* became, under the editorship of Haykal, a forum for the ideas propounded by these men. Without rejecting the Islamic outlook, this group sought to extend the scope of cultural concept beyond the contact with the Arabs, in such a way as to link it with the legacy of the Egyptian and classical past, and with Western enlightenment.[13] This party counted among its members the remarkable brothers 'Alī and Mustafā 'Abd-al-Rāziq. A handful of individuals could give no guarantee for the intellectual trend of a party, but in their day they did impose some of their authority on it. In the 1920's, this party displayed a critical attitude to some of the institutional features of Islam. In consequence of the removal of 'Alī 'Abd al-Rāziq, author of *Islām and the Bases of Government,* from al-Azhar and the dismissal of 'Azīz Fahmī, the minister of justice, the other two members of the party resigned from the government of Ziwar Pasha. In the "Principles" of its early days, it paid tribute to the liberal concept, and sought to defend the rights of the individual "in so far as they did not detract from the welfare of the whole," and was anxious to place the relations between workers and employers on a "basis of justice" so as to "avoid social maladies and the domination of one side."[14]

All the same, on the social side this party was perhaps the most conservative of the larger parties. It represented staunchly the interests of the large landowners. Its founders and active workers, including some who seceded from it, were men like Dasūqī Abāza, a descendant of a long line of property owners. For tactical reasons, it did not exercise much moderation in its declarations, especially when it was out of office, but in practice it was more favorable to the royal court and to the discussions with the British. On account of the balance of power between the king, the British, and the Wafd, on most occasions it served as a partial alternative. The party boasted that it always had been a kind of engine used whenever the country needed to be brought back on the right track. In 1921, Adli Yeghen had discussions with the British, which resulted in the declaration of independence of February 28, 1922. In 1927, Tharwat Pasha negotiated with them, and Mahmūd Pasha in 1929. The members of the Committee of Thirty which drew up the Constitution of 1923 were almost all drawn from this party.[15] Its members participated in most of the coalition governments. For some six months they supported the *coup d'état* government of Ziwar

Pasha (1925) which dissolved the parliament with a Wafdist majority as soon as it had been elected and ruled by decrees. The government of Mahmūd Pasha dissolved the parliament, rescinded a number of paragraphs in the Constitution, and in this way held office for about fifteen months (1928-1929). On the other hand, they assisted the Wafd to overthrow the *coup d'état* government of Sidqī Pasha (1930).

The Unionist Party was founded at the beginning of 1925 for the purpose of supporting the government of Ziwar Pasha, that is, for strengthening the position of the royal court. The People's Party emerged in 1930 in order to support the *coup d'état* government of Sidqī Pasha which abolished the Constitution and drew up another in its place. In virtue of the elements which supported it, and of its aims, it was close to the Unionist Party. In 1938, under the leadership of Hilmī 'Isā, these parties were fused into the Popular Unionist Party (*hizb al-ittihād al-sha'bī*). It was never anything more than a group of individuals, seceders from Wafd, Liberals, and others, and in later years it faded away almost entirely.

In August 1937, four members of the government of al-Nahhās resigned, one of them being al-Nuqrāshī. In an open letter the latter strongly criticized the leanings of al-Nahhās to dictatorship, his anticonstitutional actions and the violent conduct of the Blue Shirts, the Wafd's youth organization.[16] In another manifesto Ahmad Māhir and al-Nuqrāshī accused al-Nahhās of being too much under the influence of Makram 'Ubayd and, in consequence, of driving from the Wafd the adherents of Sa'd Zaghlūl, stifling the freedom of the press and the individual, and causing the interference of Great Britain in the Egyptian crisis.[17] Al-Nahhās tried to disprove the claim of the seceders that they were acting out of loyalty to the king.[18] This split provided further opportunity for an alternative to the Wafd's rule. In the elections of March 1938, which were all but boycotted by the Wafd, the seceders became a considerable bloc in parliament. From that time the Sa'dists had a share in most coalition governments, mainly in partnership with the Liberals, and in some of them they were at the head. Among the governmental parties, they became second to the Wafd in political importance. Like the Liberals, they also opposed the limitation of land ownership, although with less rigidity.

In May 1942, Makram 'Ubayd left the Nahhās' government, and at the beginning of July, he and his colleagues were expelled from the Wafd for violating the constitution of the Wafd and for accusing the head of the Wafd and his colleagues of contempt for the rights of the country.[19] The crisis commenced with the refusal of 'Ubayd to confirm the promotion of three of the chief officials, two of whom were related to the premier.[20] The quarrel was also fanned by the granting or withholding of export permits.[21] From the discussions in parliament it may be inferred that al-Nahhās was no longer able to endure the superiority of 'Ubayd, whose strong and dynamic character made him the life and soul of the Wafd. The incident of promotion was the last straw.

About twenty members of the House of Deputies and the Senate then formed an Independent Wafdist group (*al-kutla al-wafdiyya al-mustaqilla*). 'Ubayd was able to give full rein to his political passions; by bold questions he sought to show his zeal for the independence of Egypt.[22]

In the Black Book presented in March 1944 to the royal court and to foreign representatives, charges were brought against al-Nahhās which would have taken the law courts years to judge. In the words of the book: "The premier has used his office as a source of private profit for himself, his family and his ministers. He obtains for them houses to live in or to let; he makes them presents of lands and posts in banks; he releases commodities for export, and merchandise for import." The debate on the Black Book took place in the House of Deputies and the Senate from April 12 to May 23. In the House of Deputies alone, 37 questions were posed on this matter. In the course of their answers, the premier and some of his ministers brought charges against the Opposition.[23] In June 1944, the House of Deputies expelled 'Ubayd for "disgraceful conduct" and for "setting a bad example to the members of parliament."[24]

In May 1944, he was jailed for agitating against the government, and in October of the same year he became a member of the coalition government of Ahmad Māhir, and later on a member of that of al-Nuqrāshī (1946-1948).

In the election of 1950, this group failed to obtain any representation in the House of Deputies. 'Ubayd formed a National Front with the Nationalist Party in order to combat the project of Middle East Command of the Four Powers.

The Young Egypt group (*misr al-fatāh*) was founded in 1933 by Ahmad Husayn and in 1938 it became a party. In some of its views and in its externals it was greatly influenced by fascism; nationalist extremism (a great empire of Egypt and the Sudan), pan-Arabism, and pan-Islamism were all combined in it. In 1936, when its leader visited Rome, he adopted the language of his surroundings, reviling "parliamentary plutocracy," and extolling the "true democracy" of Rome and Berlin.[25] At the end of 1937, its Green Shirts, comprising mainly students of Azhar and the universities, were banned.

During World War II, Ahmad Husayn was detained, but on being released in the winter of 1944, he resumed his activities. As before, these activities were closely linked with his aim of fanning hostility against the British and foreigners, only now was socialistic demagogy added to them. The weekly *Young Egypt* dealt widely with the affairs of the Soviet Union, and it sought to use the fact of that country's military superiority to bring pressure to bear on Britain.[26] Members of the organization took part in acts of terrorism.

In August 1949, Young Egypt was turned into a Socialist Democratic Party, the aims of which were to spread socialistic ideas by "legal, constitutional and democratic methods within the framework of the heavenly religions"; to avoid all dependence on socialism in foreign countries; to work for the individual's freedom, and to oppose violence.[27] In 1951, it joined the extreme section of the Nationalist Party and the left wing of the Wafd in an agitation against the Middle East Command project. It played a prominent part in the incidents which led up to Black Saturday; Ahmad Husayn was then jailed. Strange to say, at the end of 1952, he attended a conference of Socialist parties in Rangoon.

The Muslim Brotherhood was founded in 1928-29 in Ismāʿīliyya by a teacher named Hasan Bannāʾ. In 1934 its headquarters were transferred to Cairo and from there it spread throughout the country. In the 1940's, it already numbered tens of thousands and had many sympathizers as well. Corresponding organizations arose in Syria and Lebanon, in Palestine and Iraq and in other countries.

In its structure it was highly centralized and authoritarian, consisting of a hierarchy in which the officials of each grade were appointed by the grade above it. At its head was the Supreme Guide (*al-murshid al-ʿāmm*). It had at its disposal a well-disciplined and carefully-picked military organization, built up in cells. A suicide squad (*al-fidawiyyūn*) was available for special purposes.

Its first activities consisted in holding evening classes for instruction in religious principles and in reading and writing. It also established clinics and sports clubs. In the course of time, it took up economic activities.

The Muslim Brethren stood for a theocratic state administered according to the Qurʾān and the *sharīʿa* (canon law). Islam was considered capable of coping with all modern problems, and it was only right that it should be the oracle of young Egypt. The young king, in their view, had to choose between Islam and the West, which was in the throes of decay and which was waiting for "a strong eastern hand resting in the shadow of Allah and the Qurʾān, and possessing a strong army of the faithful so that the whole world could be secure and all mankind could sing praises to Allah who had shown the right path."[28]

They were prepared to support any government that would pledge itself to work for the following aims: regulation of political and social life according to Islam and the customs of the early caliphs; abolition of parties and bringing the Constitution into line with the sharīʿa; strengthening of the bonds with the Islamic states as a first step to the revival of the caliphate; elimination of the western spirit.

Their world outlook[29] is so comprehensive and eclectic that there is something in it for everybody. Its dominant feature is fanatical devotion to an ideal, thus enabling its devotees "to blow up mountains, to sacrifice life and property, to struggle against difficulties until victory or death."[30] Islam is a universal religion which acknowledges the equality of peoples. The patriotism of a Muslim is not bounded by a single country, for "wherever he can say: There is no God but Allah, etc., there is his country."[31] Their nationalism is not racial, but is founded on faith, nor does this conflict with the fact that the Arabs are "the most advanced among the peoples of the world."

One aspect of nationalism is the desire for conquest and domination in the world; Islam shows the best method of attaining this end. Along with this an ethical interpretation is given to Islam, namely, the desire for truth, humility, and a generous attitude within Islam to a rival, even if he is not easy to convince.

Egypt had been plagued by imperialism from without and party strife within, usury and foreign companies, nihilism, weakening of morality and traditional values, selfishness and assimilation.

The Muslim Brethren offered an Islamic answer to the evils of society, and there was no demand for reform for which warrant could not be found in the words of the ancients. It could be proved from the Qur'ān that an Islamic government was bound to be democratic and socialistic.[32] In the sayings of the caliphs, precedents could be found for demands to seize the property of the rich and give it to the poor or to divide up large estates. In the zakāt tax on behalf of the poor, and in the law of inheritance, it was possible to discern an anti-capitalist tendency. Under this façade of piety, powerful ambitions were lurking which involved those who cherished them in a net of opportunism from which there was no escape. Historical precedents for this can be found in such brotherhoods as the Assassins and the Wahhābis. The enemies of Western innovations did not disdain the vilest weapons used in the West. Though being enemies of party strife, they negotiated with every party, including the Free Officers and the Communists. They also attempted to embark on political ventures in other countries.[33]

At the beginning of 1945, after the Wafd left the government, the Muslim Brethren negotiated with it. In May 1946, the Wafd declared war on them for "abandoning the principle of religious propaganda," so that they became merely a "Nuqrāshī-Sidqī party group." In opposition to the National Committee of Workers and Students, which had been founded by the Wafd, they established a Supreme National Committee for Workers and Students and used force against workers who went on strike.[34] As a result of the storm caused by the Sidqī-Bevin negotiations, relations with the Wafd improved. In October 1946, a national covenant was concluded between them for "joint efforts on behalf of the fatherland."[35] On the "day of burning," November 25, they vented their wrath on English books and periodicals.[36] In 1947 relations with the Wafd were again shaken.[37]

Their influence revived with the war between the Arab states and Israel, and several groups of them volunteered for military service. At home they rioted against the Jews, throwing explosives into their quarters. The humiliating outcome of the war seemed to give them their chance to seize the government by force. In December 1948, al-Nuqrāshī dissolved the Brotherhood; a few days later he was assassinated. The murderer confessed that he belonged to one of their terror gangs. In March 1949, al-Bannā' was shot and killed, and his followers saw in this an attempt to remove them from the public stage. Bannā's death set off a feud over leadership. The activities of the Muslim Brethren did not cease in 1949; when the Wafd came into power in January 1950, it began to negotiate with them. Many of the detained Brethren were released.[38] In May 1951, they were allowed to resume their activities, and it was observed that they adopted a more restrained tone. In October, al-Hudaybī, a former judge, was officially placed at their head. The king, who, but for a short spell in 1946, was relentless in his enmity to them, favored this appointment. They renewed their connections with other countries, and their envoy got as far as to Kashani in Persia.[39]

In the years 1951-1952 they threw themselves into the struggle with the British, especially in the guerilla war in the Suez Canal Zone. The horrors of Black Saturday, to which they lent a hand, cooled their ardor for a while. They welcomed the government of 'Alī Māhir and adopted the watchword of purification proclaimed by the government of al-Hilālī. In July 1952, their hour seemed to have arrived. Jailed Brethren were released and the three men who had escaped to Libya on account of the murder of al-Nuqrāshī were allowed to return. The authorities started an inquiry into Bannā's assassination. No doubt calculation lay behind this association on either side. The order for the dissolution of political parties did not apply to them, as they pretended to be a nonpolitical organization. They were asked to appoint one representative in the government of Naguib but preferred abstention to minor representation. One of their leaders, al-Baqūrī, joined the government and was expelled.

At best, there was a kind of truce between the new regime and the Brethren. They sought to gain foothold in the armed forces, the police, the labor unions, and later in the National Guard. The truce was broken on account of the successful negotiations with the British for a new treaty. The Brethren attacked the policy of the government but did not refrain from seeking contacts with the British. A strife of factions, with their commandos plotting terror, lessened their striking power. On January 11, 1954, they staged riots on the grounds of the University of Cairo, and on the next day 'Abd al-Nāsir, without consulting Naguib, banned them. The least one may say with assurance is that both maintained contacts with the Brethren, but one is inclined to say, for different purposes.

During the frantic days of February-March 1954, they took sides with Naguib in demanding democratic liberties. On October 19, 1954, the agreement with the British was signed, and seven days later an unsuccessful attempt was made by a member of the Brotherhood on the life of 'Abd al-Nāsir. Six men were condemned to death. The Brotherhood was again dissolved.[40]

The Young Muslim Association (*jam'iyyat al-shubbān al-muslimīn*), which was formed in 1927, was overshadowed by the Muslim Brethren on the eve of World War II. In the years when fascism was on the ascendant, it showed authoritarian leanings. Its leader, Sālih Harb, who had been minister of defense in 'Alī Māhir's government in 1939, was detained during the war. In 1947, Sālih Harb was made vice-president of the Workers' Party of 'Abbās Halīm.

This Workers' Party adopted as its motto "Allah, Fatherland and King."[41] It did not regard the strike as a legitimate weapon for recovering lost rights. It was anxious to establish relations between employer and employee on a "basis of justice and equality."[42] In its view only its own brand of socialism was suitable for Egypt. The root of this socialism was the religion of Islam, which "has outlined the best Socialist regime in the world." The various schools of socialism had not succeeded in realizing social justice, unlike Islamic socialism which had already lasted 1,300 years.[43]

A Wafd newspaper saw in the formation of this party an attempt of the government to divert the attention of the workers from its acts of oppression and from their class warfare.[44] After the war, it changed its name to Workers' Socialist Party.

The Communist Party, which had been banned from the very beginning, had always worked secretly and in disguise. At the end of World War II and immediately after it, when the political temperature warmed up slightly, it succeeded in getting control of some trade-unions, especially in the large textile centers, and in making converts among the students. Its intellectual element produced some popular literature. At the end of the 1940's, when relations with the British grew worse, it was granted a certain degree of toleration, especially under the guise of the Peace Movement. The object of the government was to increase the pressure on the British.

From what has been said, it is clear that between the five or six parliamentary parties there were no differences of social outlook. They were all alike in having no plan for economic or social reform, though the desire for reform (islāh) was voiced by all of them. In the words of 'Allūba Pasha: "Their aspirations and their inclinations are confused and ambiguous, they work for today and not for tomorrow, for themselves and not for the future of their people."[45]

With all the sharpness in disputation, there were no differences in principle between them in regard to "national demands" either, the principal of which were *jalā'* (evacuation of the British army) and the incorporation of the Sudan. On the other hand, there were differences in regard to the tactics to be adopted in dealing with the British. The arguments of all the parties in the opposition were practically the same: the banning of elections, and if not that, complaints that constituencies were not properly drawn and that village heads were prompted to serve the government in the elections; party favoritism in the control of the press and in the appointment or promotion of officials; and persecution of political rivals. The motto of every opposition was *nazāha* (purity)—removal of corruption.

When the government of Ahmad Māhir was set up in October 1944, the country rang with charges against members of the Wafd and their associates. The newspapers of the coalition were filled with revelations of serious offences. According to them, the state treasury was any man's property, and laws and decrees were utterly without power. The purpose of these charges was to crush the Wafd. Denials were published in the organs of the Wafd, and these were followed by denials of denials. Enough material was collected to occupy the courts of justice for many years.

There was a testing period of some months for the new government, whose chief motto was "purity and stainlessness, clothing and food for the poor." When the war came to an end and the rigors of the emergency regime had been somewhat mitigated, the battle between the parties became intensified beyond measure. The roles were reversed. The Wafd newspapers brought charges, while the government papers continued to pillory the offences of the previous government. The press was like a battlefield strewn with victims of bitter accusations. The Arabic language has no equal as a vehicle both for flattery and pin-pricks (*tajāmil* and *hijā'*). The leading writers of the country were also drawn into this conflict—Taha Husayn on behalf of the Wafd, al-ʿAqqād in *al-Kutla*, al-Māzinī in government papers. The charges did not cancel out one another, and between them they gave a lurid picture of Egyptian society.

Corruption was not a monopoly of any one party or parties, not even in conjunction with the institution of the monarchy. The whole fabric of society was permeated with it. Ability to circumvent the law and to get on politically and financially by any and every means was greatly admired in all quarters, and the successful competitor in this game was highly applauded.

To the fear of the mob was added the fear of terror. The period of political terrorism was opened in 1910 with the murder of Butros Ghālī, a Coptic premier, by a member of the Nationalist Party. The list of assassinations and attempts on the lives of Egyptians and Englishmen included General Lee Stack, the chief commander of the Egyptian Army.[46] After World War II, terrorism became a frightening factor in Egyptian politics. Among the assassinated were Ahmad Māhir in February 1945; Amīn ʿUthmān, one of the Wafd leaders, in January 1946; the judge who sentenced those who were charged with the murder of Amīn ʿUthmān in March 1948; and al-Nuqrāshī in December 1948. In December 1945, an attempt was made on the life of al-Nahhās, and two more attempts were made later.[47]

In many respects, too, the Egyptian constitution had a share in influencing the course of events. At the outset, it was formulated to pay tribute to the liberal period which followed World War I, but it helped, also, to erect a façade that hid the real state of affairs. Article 3 put all Egyptians on an equal basis; all equally enjoyed political and civil rights and were equally subject to civil obligations. Article 4 assured "personal liberty." Article 19 promised compulsory free education to both sexes.

The judges were independent (art. 124). These provisions were hardly translated into practice. But even if they had been, they were nullified by other articles which qualified and restricted the liberal provisions of the constitution. Freedom of speech was assured, and as far as the law went, a man was allowed to express his thoughts in speech or writing (art. 14). The press was free within limits laid down by the law. A paper might not be suspended or suppressed unless this was necessary for the "protection of the social order" (art. 15). Egyptians had the right of free assembly, but this right should not infringe on any regulation made for the protection of the social order (art. 20). The king had the power to dissolve the house of deputies (art. 38) and to dismiss the government (art. 49). Two-fifths of the members of the senate were appointed by the king. Thus the last three articles left decisive powers in the hands of the king. It was around these powers that the struggle between the king and the Wafd revolved, and in the last resort it was his clinging to article 49 that drove Fārūq from his kingdom.

In the period 1924-1936, the Constitution was suspended or arbitrarily amended for a number of years.[48] Of the thirteen framers of the Constitution who were still alive in 1943, no less than nine had helped, as members of the government, to suspend or annul it.[49] No constitution, however enlightened, can serve its purpose without a proper economic and social background. Its stipulations, and what is more, their execution mirrored the inherent tensions in the society.

Chapter Four

Syria

Broadly speaking, a distinction should be made between the old-line parties, composed of followers grouped around leaders, and the recently formed parties, nearly all labeled Socialist. For all the accentuated differences, there may be detected in the latter, more so in the former, a great degree of similarity.

The National Bloc (*al-kutla al-wataniyya*), since 1935 the main force behind the national struggle, had disintegrated within two or three years of Syria's independence. Its main issue had been the National Party (*al-hizb al-watanī*). It had been in power during 1947-1948 under al-Jābirī and later under al-Quwwatlī, and again, as a part of a coalition, since the downfall of al-Shīshaklī, in 1954, until the merger of Egypt and Syria. The People's Party (*hizb al-sha‘b*) emerged in 1948 from a parliamentary Constitutional Bloc; it was headed by a group from the north with the aim of breaking down the monopoly of Damascus in the high offices. They hardly differed from each other in their social background and outlook. Both represented, mainly, big landowners and the propertied class in the towns. With all the stress on reforms (al-Sha‘b even ventured to advocate "moderate socialism"[1]), both had been determined to preserve the status quo of the last three decades. In its program, al-Sha‘b dwelt on fixing an upper limit to landownership with no retroactive validity. Both parties called for distribution of newly reclaimed land to farmers. The National Party laid stress on the republican regime and demanded that no kind of Arab union should impair it. Al-Sha‘b emphasized Arab federation, and the dominant monarchical faction in it was inclined, as was a faction within the National Party, to bringing about a union with Iraq.[2] Of course, in their wildest dreams neither had envisaged a merger with Egypt under an Egyptian dictator.

The Popular or National Front (*al-jabha al-sha'biyya* or *al-wataniyya*) was formed in 1932. Once a powerful rival of the National Bloc, it declined after the assassination in 1940 of Dr. Shahbandar, its enlightened leader.[3] Efforts to regain strength under various names, such as Liberal Association, came to nothing. It had strong leanings toward the Hashimite countries and, unlike other groupings, sided unequivocally with the Allied Powers. Before the war it had evinced strong pro-British sympathies, but during 1941-1945, dominant British influence in Syria helped to further the cause of the National Bloc.

The League of National Action (*'usbat al-'amal al-qawmī*), was founded in 1933 by young men, among whom were Sabrī al-'Asalī and Ahmad al-Sharābatī. In a sense, it was a fore-runner of al-Ba'th. It took an extreme view in matters Arabic: the Palestine issue, negotiations with the French, and admittedly sent men to Iraq during the revolt in 1941.[4] It was an advocate of Greater Syria with its center in Damascus. After the fashion of the time, it adopted a socialistic tone and spoke of division of estates. Before the war it took an active part in street fighting against the French and the National Bloc government. It had branches in other Arab countries. In 1944, and later in 1954, it tried to resume its activities but could not recover its vigor. It stood for an all-embracing Arab unity, pointed to Arab virtues like: "generosity, manliness, vigor, courage, audacity in justice,"[5] and condemned corruption of social life, lack of social discipline, and so on. It denied the existence of minorities, be they sectarian, racial, or linguistic.[6]

The remnants of the Arab Liberation Movement (*harakat al-tahrīr al-'arabī*), launched by al-Shīshaklī, renewed their activities in 1956. They employed extremist phraseology, such as all-pervasive *inqilāb* (revolution). To them, too, the Arab lands extend from "Taurus . . . to the Ethiopian mountains, the great Sahara and the Atlantic ocean,"[7] and they are a "complete unit." The movement is republican and condemns confessional, tribal, and class strife; it respects private property "within the limits of social justice," and stands for distribution of uncultivated state land or land that was "acquired by illegal means."[8]

The Syrian Popular Party (*al-hizb al-sūrī al-qawmī*) was founded clandestinely in 1932 by Antūn Saʿāda. It soon became a breeding ground for fascism in the Near East. In 1934 it commenced to work in public and within a year had a mass following, especially among the students of the American University of Beirut. Because of its inimical attitude to Lebanon as a state and its paramilitary structure, it was proscribed in 1937 and went underground. Later on, Saʿāda fled to Germany and from there proceeded to Argentina. In 1944, after having professed, through equivocal phrasing, a change of attitude to Lebanon, the party resumed its activities as a Popular Social Party. Saʿāda returned to Lebanon in 1947. In the 1940's the party endorsed the Great Syria project sponsored by the ruler of Jordan.

In the 1930's it came nearest to the then powerful Fascist and Nazi parties. Its members swore allegiance to the lifelong leader. The structure of the party was hierarchical. Its concept showed traces of national-socialist dialectics; however, on account of Syria's ethnically mixed population it had to be based on a "natural cultural unity," not on unity of race. To them, Syrians are a "complete nation," a Mediterranean and not an Oriental one, with a Mediterranean mentality—a "mentality of modern civilization whose foundations had been laid in Syria."[9] It is one of the Arab nations and yet is "absolutely sovereign." Syria's soul "contains all the knowledge, all philosophy and all art of the world."[10] The origin of the Syrian nation goes back to prehistoric times. Syria is capable of leading the Arab world; it is "its heart, its sword and its honor."[11] But Syria's problem is a national one in itself: Syria is a "geographical-agricultural-economic-strategic unit."[12] It stretches "from the Taurus mountains in the northwest and the Bakhtiyari mountains in the northeast, to the Suez canal and the Red Sea in the south, and from the Persian Gulf to the Mediterranean."[13] After the Syrian nation has gained strength, it will be in a position to bring about a revival of the entire Arab world.

The party stands for separation of religion and state and "removal of the sectarian barriers between the communities"[14] through restriction of communalism to religious matters only. Traces of Nazi and corporate ideology are to be discerned in the aim of establishing the nation as a "social-national unity" on the basis of production or "equilibrium between distribution of work and distribution of capital."[15] The "unity of interests" of the nation, from which flows its "unity of life," does not admit rivalry between classes, hence the necessity of cooperation between capital and labor. Nowadays it rejects Marxist philosophy, which, alongside its counterpart, "capitalistic materialism," strives to "banish spirit from the world," as well as Fascist and Nazi philosophy, which seeks to "dominate the world."[16] The party professes to provide a "philosophy of cooperation of all forces in humanity."[17]

In Lebanon, the party was disbanded after an armed uprising in June 1949. Its leader fled to Syria and received protection, only to be extradited, tried by a court-martial and executed. A year later, Riyād al-Sulh, premier of Lebanon, was assassinated in Jordan in July 1951 by members of this party.

In Syria, the party was disbanded in 1955 after a successful attempt on the life of al-Mālikī, the deputy chief of staff, a spokesman for al-Ba'th in the army. Syrian authorities accused the party of serving the aims of the Baghdad Pact. During the uprising of May 1958 in Lebanon, the party, seeing its concept of Syrian nationhood fall to pieces, took sides with the Lebanese government. It apparently chose the lesser evil.

The Cooperative Socialist Party (*al-hizb al-ta'āwunī al-ishtirākī*), founded in 1940, represents a curious blend of articles of belief drawn from various sources:

1. Belief in the "almighty divine providence."
2. Myth of cooperativism. Cooperative socialism is a "faith that believes in Allah."[18] A union of "Arabs and Muslims" is to be established under a federal government and a federal assembly.[19]

3. "Moderate socialism" aims at "narrowing the class differences and bringing nearer the viewpoints of owners, employers and rich, on one side, and the fellahin and the poor, on the other, in accordance with the sharī'a."[20]

4. Sanctity of physical and intellectual work. The party seeks to eliminate "feudalism and exploitation," to nationalize public utilities and means of large-scale production, to protect ownership rights except those "illegally acquired," and to ensure common utilization of land by "the owner, the toiler, and the state."[21]

This concept of cooperativism, easily interpreted as corporativism, may stem from the trends prevalent in Europe in 1940—hence, "blind obedience" to the leader.[22]

It opposes any kind of Arab Union which would curtail the sovereignty of Syria. Its members were recruited, mainly, from among intellectuals and salaried workers.

After 1935, some Muslim groups emerged under various names and in 1945 united as the Muslim Brotherhood or Islamic Socialist Front. To them, Islam "contains all the elements of renaissance and of all-embracing reform."[23] Islam provides the answer to all "moral, economic, social, philosophical, scientific, legal" problems.[24] "Islam is religion and state, book and sword, mosque and school, law and literature, justice and brotherhood, matter and spirit, this world and the world to come."[25] The Muslim Brotherhood stands for Islamic socialism, and for the unity of Arabs and "more than five hundred million Muslims"; they form a formidable power capable of being the center of gravity in the struggle between East and West.[26] It supports the republican regime and condemns the Greater Syria project as an imperialist plot. In its vehemently anti-Western zeal, it endorses neutralism and even pro-Soviet policies, and some of its leaders have sponsored the Syrian Peace Movement.

The Arab Socialist Renaissance Party (*hizb al-ba'th al-'arabī al-ishtirākī*) came into being in September 1953. Its two constituent parts were:

1. The Arab Resurrection Party (*hizb al-ba'th al-'arabī*), founded in 1940 by a group of students. Its first practical activity was to form an Association of Partisans to further the

cause of Rashīd 'Alī in 1941. The first conference of the party was held in 1947. It supported Husnī al-Za'īm at the start, and for some time one of its leaders served in the government of al-Hinnāwī. It laid stress on the "eternal message" of the Arabs and on "Arab socialism springing from the spirit of the Arab nation and its deep needs."[27] It cherished a kind of revolutionary mystique, an "all-embracing revolution in modern Arab life, in spirit, thought, morals, and social conditions."[28] It condemned projects of Arab unity as sponsored by "foreigners" (Jordan, Iraq). It called the Arab League "dead" and maintained that it had to be replaced by an Arab peoples' league. It stood for nonalignment with either of the two world blocs.

2. The Arab Socialist Party (*al-hizb al-'arabī al-ishtirākī*) was founded in 1949-1950 by Akram al-Hawrānī, a versatile politician with a stormy record in parliament and in the "movement" that led to the *coups d'état*. Al-Ba'th confined itself, primarily, to educational work among students, while the party of al-Hawrānī preferred mass actions.

To the amalgamated party, too, Arab renaissance will be an outcome of an all-pervasive revolution: "Socialism is a necessity stemming from the essence of Arab nationalism"; it will allow the Arab people to "develop its genius in the best way."[29] The party is striving to "renew the human values, to stimulate human progress and strengthen co-operation and harmony between the nations."[30] Violence is not part of the party's program; it does not believe that "our nationalism will become aggressive." The "motive force in the Arab world is suffering," and this is the guarantee against aggressive or narrow nationalism.[31] The party is rationalist in that "it believes in the need for emancipation of thought"; "it does not condemn religion— only religious fanaticism."[32]

As against this, the boundaries of the Arab lands are the same as delimited by the Arab Liberation Movement.* The Arab countries "must have the same political structure before they

---

*They stretch to "Taurus mountain, mountains of Gulf of Basra, the Arab Sea, Ethiopian mountains, Great Sahara, Atlantic Ocean, Mediterranean."

can unite," or their structure, with all the differences, "is to be based on popular government representing the will of the people and emanating from it."[33] The party supports the republican and parliamentary regime and the freedoms "within the limits of supreme national Arab interest,"[34] or using a recent version: "in the countries where the popular movement has grown to the extent of participating in government, as in Syria and now in Egypt, we believe that we can admit some enlargement of the power of the executive and restriction of personal liberty to speed up the process towards our objectives."[35] The "recognized language" of writing and instruction is Arabic.[36] Every one who "calls for or joins racial associations against the Arabs or attacks the Arab fatherland for an imperialist purpose will be expelled from the Arab fatherland."[37] The party combats denominational, communal, tribal, and regional ties.[38] It is not clear how all these aims can be attained without violence.

At the elections of September 1954, the party succeeded in sending sixteen of its members into the parliament. Having been the political arm of a dominant faction in the army, it became a decisive factor in the government and no doubt the driving force in the merger between Egypt and Syria. Thus, in the process of ideological integration, many an article of its faith was watered down. In spite of the dissolution of parties after the merger, al-Ba'th has continued to be active.

Finally, al-Ba'th, once believed to be indispensible as the chief provider of ideology, was silenced.

In December 1959, the four members of al-Ba'th resigned from the U.A.R. government. After the Mosul affair they may have become a liability. The dispatch of marshal 'Āmir as a kind of proconsul to Damascus, the watering down of the land reform law and the toying with "hierarchical democracy," instead of a genuine attempt at democratic processes, may have prompted their ouster. According to 'Abd al-Nāsir, they became "opportunists" and "individualists," to be blamed for the growing pains of this democracy. Nowadays they are to be found among the Syrian exiles in Lebanon.

The Communist Party began its public activities under Khālid Bakdāsh in 1937-1938. At the outbreak of the war it was suppressed and came into the open again only in 1942. It gained utmost importance after the last *coup d'état* in 1954, especially since the officers' group linked to al-Ba'th won the day, and the economic agreement concluded with the Soviet Union enhanced its prestige out of all proportion. Bakdāsh was the first Communist to be elected, in 1954, to an Arab parliament. Having a minimum and maximum program, the party enjoys a wide scope for flexibility in its activities.

With the merger of Egypt and Syria, its leader left the country.

For all the differences in phraseology between the parties of the younger generation, they have many characteristics in common. All, even al-Ba'th, which appeared to grope for original ways in matters of ideology, are addicted to verbosity, and employ inflated slogans (fantastic frontiers, fanciful concepts of Arab unity). They stand out through authoritarian and formal approach to human issues of a subtler nature (language, ethnic distinctness, relations between majority and minority) and are extremely flexible in their loyalties. In defining frontiers, they do not consider worth mentioning some five million Berbers in North Africa, three million Negroes in the Sudan, one and a quarter million Kurds in Iraq, and distinct Christian communities. The Syrian National Social party has entered into curious internal or external alliances. The Ba'th party, though loaded with principles, saw no blemish in surrendering to an unprincipled (in terms of social concepts) ruler from Egypt, and it consented to stage a 99.9 percent plebiscite to confirm the merger. All the parties cherish a kind of revolutionary populism and profess democratic concepts until the appropriate moment for employing other means. Through their nationalism, they maintain, in varying degrees, an ambivalent attitude to things western. A driving force towards nationalism is *isti'mār* (a curious blend of imperialism and colonialism), so much so that it is even believed that the long struggle against it "will be transformed into a positive quality in our thinking."[39]

Chapter Five

Iraq

From the inception of the state, in October 1922, until 1945, almost no political party in the proper sense came into being. Parties emerged or merged or vanished, but they represented small circles, within or without the parliament, of tribal sheikhs or propertied townsmen, grouped around leaders, sometimes around the incoming prime minister. The real power in the state was vested in forty or fifty families.[1] The main divisive issue between these groups was not their social outlook. The strife centered on internal positions of power and relations with the British, that is, on the means to attain independence, or on denominational grievances (Shi'is versus Sunnis).[2] But even these groups were dissolved as far back as 1935.

Between 1936 and 1941 the state passed through a period of military coups. In 1941, when the pro-Axis revolt of the army under Rashīd 'Alī had been crushed and the tide had turned in favor of the Allied powers, pressure was brought on the government, both by the press and the public, to permit the forming of parties. Public opinion began to assert itself. The social ferment in the country caused apprehension.[3] Periodicals in Baghdad and other towns began to appear.[4] There was a spread of trade-unionism in various branches. Opposition bodies began to form in the parliament.

A new spirit seemed to prevail in the country under the government of Tawfīq al-Suwaydī (February-May 1946). It seems that Iraq had never enjoyed such a period of comparative freedom. The government contained some new men, younger members of the opposition, who were eager for reforms. The emergency regulations were annulled, and the formation of five new parties was permitted. In three of these parties some advanced middle-class elements, intellectuals, and skilled workers were represented in various degrees.

The Liberal Party (*hizb al-ahrār*), the leaders of which were the moving spirits in Suwaydī's government, laid stress on modest reforms, on safeguarding the constitution, and on attachment to the throne. It did not reject the Anglo-Iraqi treaty, but it sought to establish it on a basis of equality. In December 1948, it broke off its activities on account of persecutions, and since then it has practically ceased to exist.

The National Democratic Party (*al-hizb al-watanī al-demo-krātī*), the core of which was formed by members of the *ahālī* group, was socialistic from its inception. Only at the end of 1950 did it openly adopt the principles of democratic socialism.[5] At the same time it had reservations against the foreign policy of social-democratic parties, especially that of the Labor Party. One of its lines of action, in which all classes were to be united, was to abolish the British bases and to put an end to the British influence in Iraq. It took as its guide the foreign policy of Nehru, and it regarded neutrality as the right policy for the Arabs in general. It saw in the state a framework for the co-operation of Arabs, Kurds, and other communities. Among the reforms it proposed were the division of large estates and an increase in the proportion of direct taxes—especially a graduated income tax and an inheritance duty.

Owing to persecutions, the party suspended its activities in 1948 and did not resume them until 1950. Since its forced dissolution in September 1954, members of the party were active in the peace movement launched by the Communists and violently opposed the Baghdad Pact. Starting with participation in the *coup d'état* government in 1936, there were many inconsistencies, even grave disgressions, in the activity of its leader, Kāmil Jādirjī,[6] one of them the way he handled internal dissension within the party. Its daily, *Sawt al-Ahālī* (Voice of the Citizens), may be considered one of the best publications—in intellectual level and lucidity of exposition—in the Arabic press.

On July 14, 1958, one of its leaders, Muhammad Hadīd,

emerged as finance minister of the revolutionary government, and many of the economic decrees bear the imprint of this party's program.

The People's Party (*hizb al-sha'b*) was more outspoken in its leftist trend and decided in its leanings toward the Soviet Union.

The National Union Party (*hizb al-ittihād al-watanī*) differed very little in its program from the People's Party. Its weekly—later daily—*al-Ra'y al-'Amm* was edited by the poet Mahdī al-Jawāhirī. In September 1948 the two parties merged into the Popular Unity Party. Shortly afterwards the party was suppressed.

The Independence Party (*hizb al-istiqlāl*) contained extreme nationalist elements. Among its leaders, mostly lawyers, were members of the pro-Axis al-Muthannā club of the 1930's[7] and some of them were detained after the Rashīd 'Alī revolt. It is a vehement pan-Arab and xenophobic group, devoid of understanding for the needs of non-Arab minorities. It advocates abolition of the foreign concessions and neutralism. It stresses the need for social, especially agrarian, reforms.[8]

The Communist Party was founded in 1924 but emerged as an influential group only during World War II. In 1945 it was not allowed to establish itself as the National Liberation Party (*hizb al-taharrur al-watanī*). On the other hand its Jewish branch, the League against Zionism, was allowed for a time to exist. Its organ, *al-'Usba,* sought to rouse the Jews against Zionism.

In the 1940's the Communist Party was tossed between conflicting trends and experienced various splits. Even before World War II the Kurds in the northern districts formed a national branch of it with a paper of its own (*Azadi,* freedom). After the war, it expanded into a kind of popular front, and apparently the Communist Party took fright. The nascent Kurdish Communist Party then decided to form a National Front (*Ruzgari Kurd*) which took in left-wing fragments of the *Hewa* (hope) group, and members of *Komali i Ziani Kurd.* The latter was an association of Kurdish youth which had originated in 1943 in Mahabad and from there had spread to the towns of Iraqi

Kurdistan. The National Front drew up a National Covenant with a view to promoting the Kurdish cause in general. The Kurds were to attain self-determination, and administrative autonomy for Iraqi Kurdistan was to be one of the first steps toward this goal.

The Kurdish Communist Party continued its separate existence, its organ being *Shursh* (revolution). Its members complained that the Arabs were not able to understand their difficulties. The mere realization of Arab aims would not benefit the Kurdish people. As against this, the Communist Party of Iraq called for cooperation between the Arabs and the Kurds in the "struggle against exploitation and feudalism." The Kurdish question was a part of the Arab question, and with the liberation of Iraq all the national groups would automatically be freed. It was childish to dream of a union of the Kurdish areas after they had separated themselves from the revolutionary movements in the three countries.[9]

The breach with the Communist Party of Iraq was closed in 1947.[10] The remainder of Ruzgari Kurd was turned into a *Parti Democrat Kurd*.

In September 1954 the existing four parties were finally dissolved:

1. The Constitutional Union Party (*hizb al-ittihād al-dustūrī*) grouped around Nūrī al-Sa'īd.

2. The Socialist Nation Party (*hizb al-umma al-ishtirākī*), whose leader was Sālih Jabr. In its social outlook it hardly differed from that of Nūrī al-Sa'īd. Its backing came mainly from the Shī'i south.

3. Istiqlāl.

4. The small United Popular Front Party (*hizb al-jabha al-sha'biyya al-muttahida*) which, being an opposition, represented a strange agglomeration of reform-minded men within the ruling group and held to neutralism.

Before the uprising of 1958, the following parties were known to be active underground: the Communists, the Kurdish Democrats, al-Ba'th, and the Liberation Party, which insisted on "renewal of Muslim life and uncovering the intrigues of imperialist infidels."

There are some distinct features in the political landscape of Iraq. It was the first state in the Arab Near East to achieve independence in 1930, and to be admitted to the League of Nations in 1932. It was also the first to inaugurate the era of military coups in 1936. The issues of division between the Sunni Arabs (about a third) and the Shī'is, though diminishing, left an imprint on the course of events. The tribal structure of the population, though disintegrating, has been the strongest. The social basis of the government, at least until the mid-1940's, has been the narrowest, and the dimensions of landownership, nearly all over the country, are the largest. It has a large ethnic and territorial minority—the Kurds—which under any circumstances could never be made voiceless. On the borders of Iran, especially towards the Persian Gulf, territorial claims and counter-claims are dormant. And last, but not least, it is the nearest to the Russian borders, a fact that has manifold implications.

Iraq enjoyed the stabilizing influence of Faysal, although even during his reign (1921-1933) it had no less than fifteen governments. Faysal sought to maintain a kind of equilibrium between the nationalist factions and the mandate administration, but in his last years his authority was diminishing. The discontent of the Kurds culminated in revolts, and the extremist groups gained in strength. With his death the tenuous equilibrium vanished.

From September 1933 until the revolt of Rashīd 'Alī in 1941, Iraq had another thirteen governments. Tribal revolts became an effective means to combat a government. Tribal support would be enlisted by granting larger representation to the House of Deputies, or by giving preference to minor sheikhs and agents over major sheikhs. As this means, employed by government and opposition alike, lost its efficacy, the army became a decisive factor in politics.[11] Victories over Kurds and Assyrians, real or imaginary, served to heighten the prestige of the government or the army. From 1936 until May 1941 various factions of officers took part in removing and setting up governments. The grave lesson of May 1941 seemed to have been effective, and no open revolt in the army was recorded afterwards. Since 'Abd al-Nāsir's star had begun to rise, however, signs of ferment in the army could not be brushed aside.

Nūrī al-Sa'īd, premier of Iraq fourteen times, had been the main stabilizing factor. Iraq seemed sheltered under his shadow, which meant arbitrary application of the constitution and law, semilegal, or illegal activity of parties, electoral processes that nearly always made the party in power victorious. Meanwhile, the urban population had grown, the number of vociferous students was increasing, and the class of share-cropping tenants became more and more restive. Added to this, a new factor emerged: prosperity amidst abject poverty.

The oil industry is among the largest employers of industrial workers (12,800 in 1956) and benefits local industries and services. The oil revenue is nearing the ID 100,000,000 mark. Immense tasks have been undertaken or still lie ahead: water control, which is already nearing completion, irrigation schemes, reclamation of large marshy areas in the south, and settlement of the tribes, composing nearly 5 percent of the population.[12] There were many crucial questions. Despite all the long-term projects, ultimately beneficial, will the population wait patiently much longer for the attainment of a minimum of freedom? Is Iraq really maturing under pressure? Is the slight improvement in the standard of living, education, and health a sure means to temper violent nationalism? Does appeasing the Kurds by allowing them a share in the development programs and in political positions offer a solution to their national problem? Will the most oppressive conditions of land tenure not spoil the benefits of improved standards? Will national characteristics, climate, deep-rooted social mores, help or hinder gradual reforms? Will the myth of a saviour, guide of destinies to a united nation, prevail over the lesser vision of improvement and progress? Neither of these offers freedoms, but the population has never experienced them.

The revolutionary regime of July 14, 1958 did not remove

the ban on party activity. But the National Front—the only officially recognized political body—comprised members of Ba'th, Istiqlāl, National Democrats, and Communists (Free Democrats, Partisans of Peace). Following the trial of Colonel 'Arif, who sought for Iraq a close alignment or fusion with the U.A.R., the Ba'th members were removed from the government in December 1958, and the Istiqlāl members withdrew from it in February 1959. The National Democrats is the only party with open representation in the government, but its impact on the man in the street is weaker.

The Communists channeled their activity into front organizations—trade-unions, students' unions, lawyers' associations and peasants' unions. At the end of April 1959, the National Democrats saw the time ripe for the government to be reshaped so as to include Kurdish Democrats, Communists, and themselves. The Communists made the same demands. Premier Qāsim, however, who considers himself the only leader of the revolution, made it clear that during the "period of transition" the parties have to suspend their activities.

Under a new associations law, which came into force on January 6, 1960, the United Democratic Party of Iraqi Kurdistan (formerly Parti Democrat Kurd)[13] and a dissident Communist group with nationalistic leanings, were granted licenses, the latter under the name of the Iraq Communist Party. The regular Communist Party, although active, is not legalized under its own name or under The People's Unity (*ittihād al-sha'b*). In April an Islamic Party was granted license, to be proscribed in September.

In June 1960, a small faction—the National Progressives—split off the National Democrats, evidently over support of the government, and adopted a less passive attitude to it. Both parties stand for a future Arab federation, but the links between the states are to be defined by democratic decisions.

Meanwhile, all parties are at the mercy of the sole leader and the leader himself seems tossed between pressures and fears, merely keeping the appearance of balance.

Chapter Six

Glimpses of an Ideology

To discern the evolution of 'Abd Al-Nāsir's ideology seems a task both difficult and easy. To begin with, there may have been no ideological concepts at all. A sort of revolutionary mystique swayed the country, with a Revolution Command Council riding the tide. The army, that is, the junta, had been built up as a myth and identified with the people, as if embodying its needs and wishes. The army's actions had been designed, first and foremost, for the benefit of the "workers and fellahin," although cooperation between "workers and capitalists" or "capital and labor" was not lost sight of. The main objective was reformist: elimination of corruption, epitomized in the court—this evil of evils—and in the parties.[1] On January 23, 1953, a Liberation Rally, replacing the multiparty system, was founded, devised to enlist mass support for the regime.[2] Its main aims were:[3]

1. Establishment of a society based on belief in God and fatherland and on self-confidence.

2. An economic system directed towards social justice, fair distribution of wealth, and full exploitation of natural and human resources.

3. Safeguarding the basic political and social rights and freedoms; freedom of thought, belief and rite within the limits of the law.[4]

4. Moral, social and physical training of the people for the tasks of liberation and reform for the sake of a great Egypt.

The slogan of the Rally was "Unity-Order-Work."

This new system was not to identify itself with communism,

fascism, or capitalism which "gives precedence to one part of the people."[5]

On February 10, 1953, a three-year transition period was proclaimed and "rules of governing" during this period laid down. One of the stipulations of the provisional constitution was "freedom of person" and freedom of thought within the limits of the law. As "Leader of the Revolution" Naguib assumed "full sovereign powers."[6] He promised the Egyptian people that he would restore a "democratic constitutional regime" at the end of this period.[7] On June 16, 1953, 'Abd Al-Nāsir maintained that people should be free to choose a regime that suits them; the best regime must be based on "sound democratic foundations"; countries that applied the one-party system—dictatorship—had to revert to a democratic regime.[8]

On June 18, 1953, Egypt was proclaimed a republic. Naguib became its President and Prime Minister, 'Abd al-Nāsir, Minister of Interior and Deputy Prime Minister. On February 22, 1954, Naguib resigned, one of the reasons being the militarization of the government, that is, continuous identification of the Council of the Revolution with the government.[9] Other reasons: Egypt was at that time governed by "an official cabinet (Council of Ministers) and unofficial cabinet (Council of the Revolution) and a joint committee of both," but Naguib was in control of none.[10] The main issue of division was the difference of age (55 versus 36) or "that 'Abd Al-Nāsir believed in taking greater risks than I thought wise in an effort to obtain the whole loaf."[11] Or, as the Council of the Revolution put it: "despite the fact that he was nominated to be President of the Republic as well as Prime Minister, President of the Council, and President of the Joint Congress—Naguib insisted that he be given broader powers than those of the Council itself."[12] Naguib was placed under guard, and 'Abd al-Nāsir assumed the position of Prime Minister. Violent reactions of the public, including officers and men of the services, as well as pressure of a Sudanese delegation, prompted the Council of Revolution, on February 28, "in order to maintain the unity of the nation," to invite Naguib to resume office as President, on the understanding that Egypt would be a parliamentary republic.[13] On March 8, Naguib was restored to his position as Prime Minister and head of the Council of the Revolution.

These events clearly represent a struggle for power, and if Naguib's interpretation is correct, 'Abd al-Nāsir tried to destroy a foe by inflating his demands so as to produce a violent reaction against him. On March 25, 'Abd al-Nāsir announced that a constituent assembly, resulting from free and direct elections, would be convened on July 24, 1954, and would proclaim the end of the revolution. Political parties would be permitted to resume their activities. Naguib thought this change premature. The opponents of the regime naturally sought to exploit the rift and supported Naguib. In consequence of a general strike staged by the Liberation Rally, the implementation of the decision was put off till the end of the transition period. On April 17, 'Abd al-Nāsir became Prime Minister. The government became more and more militarized until it included, on September 1, all the eleven members of the Council of the Revolution.[14] The strife came to an end on November 14, 1954, when Naguib was relieved of all his official duties and put under home arrest. A constituent assembly was never convened, but on December 20, 1954, 'Abd al-Nāsir promised to restore "democratic constitutional life" on January 1, 1956.

In consequence of an attempt on 'Abd al-Nāsir's life, in October 1954, the powerful Muslim Brotherhood was dissolved, which no doubt made him feel freer in his actions, such as abolition of confessional jurisdiction in September 1955. Socialism and "positive neutralism" gained more and more currency. In March 1955, 'Abd al-Nāsir spoke of his policy as "realization of true socialism and fight against the rule of capitalism."[15] In May 1955, he announced that the new parliament would represent workers and fellahin, not parties of the past,[16] and in July 1957, he averred that the revolution aimed at democratic life in which the will of the people would decide, "not the will of exploiters and dictators."[17] No doubt, the agreement with the Soviet Union and the subsequent arms deal with Czechosolovakia, in September 1955, reverberated in this ideology too.

The new Constitution, proclaimed on January 16, 1956, purported to decide a drawn out and highly debatable problem. It declared Egypt an Arab state and the Egyptian people an integral part of the Arab nation. Islam was to be the religion of the state. A one-party or nonparty system was enshrined in the vague Constitution: a Council of National Union was to implement the objectives of the revolution.

In a plebiscite on the presidency and on the Constitution, held on June 23, 1956, 5,508,291—99.7 percent of the voters—declared for 'Abd al-Nāsir as President, and 5,496,965 approved the Constitution. The Constitution stipulates that the National Assembly has to nominate the candidate for the presidency, to be approved by a referendum.

On July 3, 1957, a National Assembly was elected. The candidates had to be selected by the National Union. The Liberation Rally was disbanded on January 26, 1958. With the merger of Egypt and Syria, the Assembly discontinued.

As seen, the Egyptian people did not declare themselves unreservedly Arabs by a free decision. There are about three million Christian Copts in Egypt. Since the time of Mustafā Kāmil, at the start of the national movement, the attitude of the Egyptians to Arabdom, more precisely their sense of attachment to the Arabs, has been ambivalent and undecided. With the upsurge of the idea of unity, following Eden's declaration in favor of the establishment of an Arab League in 1941, various concepts have been aired, all of them assigning to Egypt the task of leading the sons of Arabdom (*banū 'l-'urūba*). All of them presupposed a kind of unity of Egypt and Sudan, whose area is three times larger than Egypt's. To the pan-Islamic writer Muhammad 'Allūba, unity meant mutual help in culture, commerce, industry, defense—in everything that would not encroach upon the political and geographical sovereignty of these nations.[18] In his opinion, an Arab empire would end like the Ottoman empire. To Fu'ād Abāza, a unity of the Nile peoples—Egypt, Sudan, Ethiopia, Uganda—patterned after the United States or the British Commonwealth, is to precede an "Arab oriental Islamic unity."[19] No doubt, the failure to realize the unity of Egypt and Sudan prompted a sharp shift in attention to the Arab East.[20]

Behind a tangle of slogans and arguments, utilitarian motives may have prompted this clear-cut decision. As 'Abd al-Nāsir puts it: "The first incentive to the revolution was, in view of the increase of the population by millions in the last years, while the production is stagnating or contracting, widening of the living space (al-majāl al-hayawī)."[21] The root of the social problem is a grave disproportion between the size of the population, which increases by at least 450,000 annually, and the productive resources of the country. The pressure of the population caused the standard of living to decline. It is estimated that under the prevailing conditions half of the agricultural labor force—about 2.1 million—could be removed from agriculture without reducing the output.[22] By 1990 the population of Egypt may amount to about 40 million.[23] A solution to the population problem may be seen, partly, in pooling the resources of the oil-producing Arab countries, whose annual revenue from oil royalties exceeds $1,000,000,000, and is increasing. Here, Egypt could find a market for an expanding industry and an outlet to an increasing surplus of intelligentsia.

The resources of the Arab lands and their strategic position might ensure to the Arabs a prominent place in the world. The centuries-old trend of decline is due to be reversed. They have 11 votes out of 99 in the United Nations. An orientation of their own or in conjunction with like-minded or other interested countries may affect the balance of voting power there. This was a consideration, now enhanced, that led Egypt to accede to the Arab League. It is meditatively indicated in 'Abd al-Nāsir's *Egypt's Liberation.*

A step further in the ideology of Arabdom stresses the superiority of the Arab race and its vocation "to serve, to guide and to spiritualize the countries of the whole world," because "we are endowed with a spiritual force and a belief in God as well as a feeling of fraternity that makes us capable of opening a new chapter in the history of mankind, similar to that opened thirteen centuries ago by our ancestors. . . ."[24] "Today, a new revelation comes from our hearts to guide humanity anew towards its destiny."[25]

The pan-Islamic mode of thinking is given organizational shape in an Islamic Conference which is to forge the Islamic ties. But any Muslim government that does not conform to 'Abd al-Nāsir's concepts and policy is being defamed. An Islamic convention is far from opportune, but al-Azhar has been activated for a missionary drive in Africa.

Al-Sādāt, secretary of the Islamic Conference, sees in Egypt's revolution a turning point in the history of the East, "the land of wisdom, where revelation came down and prophecy descended."[26] Egypt is to teach the East that "logic in this world is logic of power" and that the East is "rich in material treasures as it is rich in its spirituality and humanism."[27] Here the current of civilization commenced, then moved to the West where it flourished and "showered on us imperialism and enslavement to slaves."[28] This current is to turn back to the East where it will flourish for the good of all humanity.

The vocation of the Arabs does not detract from the vocation of Egypt, whose genius has been the source of science and knowledge, the origin of monotheism, the "torchbearer of civilization since the dawn of history."[29] Egypt embraced Christianity, when it appeared, and Islam in its turn. In her shadow civilizations emerged: Pharaonic and Greek, Roman and Latin. Her relations with various civilizations were always relations of friendship and love, and "on the side of peace." Never in her history was Egypt an imperialist nation. Whoever attacked her borders came to know her strength. "Her policy today is her policy yesterday—friendship and peace, not force and revenge."[30]

The authentic attitude to communism seems to be expounded in *The Truth About Communism*.[31] A chapter in it—on communism and Zionism—might have been borrowed from a Nazi pamphlet. Communists as well as Jews strive for domination of the world. Nietzsche already touched upon the close ties between Zionism and communism. The Jews and the Russians will be the main factors in staging the expected clash of powers. A negligible minority among the Jews opposes communism and

Zionism. The vast majority of the supporters of communism support Zionism. The enmity of communism to religions is like the enmity of Zionism to the rest of humanity. The Jews stir up wars for their benefit. The Jews have invented communism in order to dominate the world and exploit its resources at will. Among Jewish communists and Zionists are counted: Beria, Shvernik, Joliot-Curie, Picasso. We are told that the wives of Stalin, Molotov, and Voroshilov are Jewish.

'Abd al-Nāsir's preface to this booklet stresses the contradictions in communism (theory and painful practice, pyramid of classes—one on top, millions at the base—loss of will and freedom, etc.). Against this, "we Arabs, we Muslims and Christians in this area of the world: we believe in Allah, his angels and his books, his prophets and the Last Day. . . . We believe that every worker is rewarded for his work. . . . We believe in freedom of work. . . . We believe in brotherhood of man, in social reciprocity. . . ."[32]

The pan-African drive has expanded from the areas bordered by the main sources of the Nile to the Congo. On the *Voice of the Arabs*, 'Abd al-Nāsir is praised as "liberator of Africa and the Middle East." The peoples of East Africa, as far as Tanganyika, are addressed in their native dialects. The many voices are necessarily contradictory, because Arab or Muslim minorities have to be spoken to differently. Recently Congo became a focal point of hectic activity.[33]

At times a sober social-democratic reformist note is struck by 'Abd al-Nāsir.

The spirit of the Egyptian revolution is represented in "a new Egyptian consciousness that believes in democratic socialism in method and spirit, so that social justice may rule—no war between classes, no one group enriching itself at others' expense, and no minority dominating a majority any more."[34] "We must equip ourselves with a philosophy other than philosophy of inertia, that ruins human existence . . . ; we have to live a life of vigor, we have to believe in reason, which is a tool of thought, in innovation, creation and inventiveness."[35] At the Cooperative Congress in 1957, he envisaged a "Socialist democratic cooperative society" in the country. "We never did and never will destroy individual initiative. Private capital is free as long as it is used for the benefit of the people. The government is participating in industry to protect the people against monopolists."[36]

The interpretative potentialities of Egypt's socialism seem inexhaustible. It stems from "doctrinal independence." "We are not Communists, nor are we supporters of western type capitalist systems, neither do we follow the various forms of socialism preached in the West. . . ." "We do not believe in the domination of nations over nations, neither do we believe in the domination of classes over classes, of minorities over majorities or of majorities over minorities, of individuals over groups or of groups over individuals. . . ."[37]

Between *sturm und drang* eras, resignation sets in, sometimes in the wake of setbacks abroad. The "implications of the President's doctrine and the basic principles that regulate it," may attest to it. Arab nationalism "being spiritual and philosophic, its tendencies are universalist." It is "a step forward from Syrian and Egyptian nationalism, in the direction of even greater union, such as the Afro-Asian, or eventually a world union." There is "no dogmatic form of union contemplated at this stage by the Arabs." At present "a truce with all political ideologies" is observed, "as long as opinions are not used to create political disturbances." "The use of force to suppress unpopular ideologies cannot be justified." Egypt's brand of socialism holds to "positive pacifism" and disagrees with "Communist or some Socialist theories, whose idea of social justice resides in elimination of some classes in the community." It stands for a "healthy competition between co-operatively run industries and those run by private capitalistic methods." The people are to decide freely on their future "when the enemy is successfully neutralized."[38]

For all the changes in word and action, the mental affinities with some defunct or submerged bodies of opinion in Egypt are striking. The spokesmen of the regime are salvation-tinged, their ultimate source of inspiration being piety. A myth of an all-pervading vocation has been built up; inevitably its concomitants are grandeur and vanity. A sense of being indispensable makes it imperative to employ all possible means; somehow they are supposed to accord with one of the professed viewpoints.

If there is much confusion in the reasoned utterings, there is even more in eruptions of oratory. To separate its sources is an arduous task: to decide what may be traced to emotionally charged verbiage, or to cherished aspirations; what stems from political expediency, a kind of ideological veneer on events under or beyond control, and what from sheer improvisation. The ruling group of today purports to represent a "popular bloc" (*kutla sha'biyya*). Under the present regime a small group enjoys freedom of speech, within the limits of an imposed internal truce. On December 5, 1957, 'Abd al-Nāsir branded as a "dirty lie" an accusation of "interference in the affairs of Arab countries."[39] After his election as President of the United Arab Republic he proclaimed solemnly that "Arab weapons will never be raised against an Arab people."[40] On Egypt's Independence Day, July 22, 1958, he asserted: "The people of Lebanon will win; free men who sacrifice their lives and are killed for Lebanon's freedom and independence will win."[41]

In the 1920's, West-European modes of thought were dominating the minds of enlightened Egyptians. In the 1950's reactions favoring a segment of Soviet concepts seemed to gain ground; at any rate they filled the air. A kind of alignment was attempted without much commitment in matters of ideology. The degree of genuineness in this attachment is open to question.* Politics is perceived as a big game, and the need to take vengeance on imaginary enemies is ever present.

The literary output stimulated from above is of course a kind of ideological superstructure. It cannot be separated from other facets of what is labeled "Nasserism." The "big lie" technique, as applied in the controlled press and on the *Voice of the Arabs,*

---

*After a spell of benevolent sufferance, Syria and Egypt witnessed in March 1959 a conflagration between the aggressive brand of pan-Arabism and Arab communism. It was touched off by the controversy between the governments of Iraq and the U.A.R.

is ever resounding. It is no more to be dismissed as the growing pains of an ebullient nationalism, supported by a proverbial notion that lying is still the salt of the earth. It is put into a straitjacket of calculation. The phantom of enemies from without must constantly be hammered at. But the same violent intolerance is applied in inter-Arab affairs. The so-called Bandung formula of self-determination may mean preservation or establishment of an authoritarian rule of a small group in the majority or even in a minority within a geographical unit inherited from colonial powers. In Egypt it implies imposition of a political creed and rule on sister countries.

A conflict of elements is inherent in this kind of paternalist dictatorship. Apparently, it started with the best intentions: elimination of graft, abolition of large estates, efforts to attack the grave social problems and to deservedly raise the nation's standing. Analysts, keen on short-cut definitions, even compared the attractive power of the Egyptian "social revolution" to the French revolution and its impact on Europe's liberals. But the real test is still ahead. This experiment rests primarily upon cooperation within a small group of men and the grip of 'Abd al-Nāsir on them. There is no genuine mass movement to support it. In the long run a more inward-looking nationalism, bent on observance of human rights, first and foremost the right to differ, is to replace this expansionist brand of nationalism. The new Egyptian ideology sought to deny this right to sister countries. This denial has been contested in the Sudan, in Iraq[42] and in Lebanon.

It is noteworthy that three authors come to share almost identical views of Egypt's regime, albeit through different approaches.

Keith Wheelock's *Nasser's New Egypt* (Praeger, 1960) seems the boldest attempt at a "critical analysis of the contemporary scene" since 1952. It may serve to destroy a myth in defense of fence-straddling historiography, often dictated by reasons of convenience or fear of becoming a *persona ingratissima*. In this case boldness is upheld in the face of exceptional treatment accorded by Egypt's leaders. Here, too, arises the pertinent question of dependability of sources, conflicting in their views as they are, and ranging from official publications and public speeches to personal interviews and foreign sources. Oddly, under the old regime, frustrating though it was, heated party polemics helped to uncover diverse causes and facets of events.

Wheelock's sympathy-rooted work draws some bold conclusions, hitherto only tentatively suggested. 'Abd al-Nāsir's "fear of relinquishing personal authority, together with his lack of political philosophy, have rendered these efforts [to build a bridge between the military and the civilian population and a new political structure] ineffective" (p. 284). "Neutralism" for him is "not a philosophy but a blanket of morality in which he has sought to shroud his aggressive tactics" (p. 282). "But Egypt has benefited little from Nasser's international adventures. Much has been undertaken in the name of lofty principles, yet Egypt has paid a high price for Nasser's tactical successes" (p. 283). After having reached the crest, "Nasserism" is "on the wane," and the "transition" period may continue "indefinitely" (pp. 264, 284).

Keith Wheelock argues, not unlike thoughtful Egyptians since the 1920's, that Egypt's emancipation could not be but auto-emancipation, namely the ability to cope with her grave social problems. 'Abd al-Nāsir "has broken the vicious circle of poverty and lethargy," and he can achieve the distinction of "one of the great personalities of the twentieth century, at least within the Afro-Asian world," "only if he tempers his personal desire to dominate the Arab world and concentrates instead on meeting the manifold needs of his nation" (p. 285). It is apparent that he is not inclined to take this advice to heart.

The restlessness of a primitive mind, overpowered by a sense of indispensability and vocation, may still have surprises in store. Here it might be instructive to trace the reactions of the great powers to 'Abd al-Nāsir's moves, how principled—at least consistent—they are, and how far they have furthered his global designs.

On the social scientist's level, Egypt's "vicious circle" is firmly grasped in D. Lerner's *The Passing of Traditional Society* (The Free Press, 1958). Semantic symbolism aside, which is sometimes redundant, many observations are compelling. It is illuminating to learn that "there was little dissent among the Egyptian élite" from the proposition that "the great need for developing a democratic Egypt is not necessarily answered, but may only be evaded, by a policy of global adventurism," and that "there was an uneasy feeling among the élite that imperial reveries might be an unworthy sort of self-indulgence at the expense of their impoverished and needy countrymen" (p. 226). "Nasser has chosen to rule with a military clique, which appeases revolutionary-reactionary fanaticism while moving toward a totalitarian model of mass society" (p. 257). Naguib "hinged the long-term success of the revolution, from the start, to popular acceptance" (p. 243). He envisioned, in his own words, "the sort of federation that . . . would begin like Benelux and end like Switzerland," but in Nasser's view Egypt "figures as the patron spirit of a nascent Africa, as the vital center of an Arab circle, as the prime ministry of an Islamic World Parliament" (p. 248). "Ambivalent affect and erratic policy will continue, probably, until Egyptians agree to do one effectively—to forget or not forget, to love or hate—instead of struggling to do both simultaneously" (p. 251). But this ambivalent attitude is also to be traced to historic tradition and to deeply ingrained urges of plotting.

"The familiar process of secularization accompanies urbanization in Egypt as elsewhere" (p. 230), and "the symbols of Nation now confront a much more potent adversary than the British—namely, the symbols of class" (p. 231). "This and any future government, confining its attention to the easier terrain of international maneuver, will sooner or later be forced to recognize that a potentially powerful class at home keeps its gaze firmly riveted on the primacy of social reform" (p. 261).

As to the intelligentsia, "oriented toward secular modernity, they find themselves torn by the imposed need to define Egypt's course in terms acceptable to traditional Islam" (p. 239). "They look outward for help—often to the same Western world against which, on other grounds, they invoked the routine slogans of petulant self-indulgence" (p. 240). They "find no guidance in Koranic fundamentalism. Nor is the Nasser way their way. . . . Psychic displacement of the élite between the ancient world of piety and the modern world of ingenuity is possibly the most fundamental problem of stable governance in Egypt" (p. 259). They look for a "participant society," that is, for free identification with the social and cultural aspects of a regime.

As to the pyramidal "training school of democracy" instituted by the regime, E. B. Childers admits in his apologetic essay *Common Sense About the Arab World* (Macmillan, 1960, p. 164), that "no new 'gradualist' approach to genuine democracy can succeed unless the executive is enlightened, capable of tolerating and heeding criticism in the press and elsewhere, and able to win the confidence of the Western-inspired educated minority. . . . Broad external-nationalist slogans will not satisfy this intelligentsia; the sterility of a controlled press and the prohibition of political controversy will not stimulate that very intellectual vitality on which Arab civilization depends."*

---

* The recent measures designed to further reduce, by compensation, the private sector of Egypt's economy, and thus proceed on the "endless road" of "Arab socialism," may affect the militant policies of the regime in other spheres of activity. It may be asked whether this "pragmatic socialism," with no social philosophy to feed and no popular movement to rely on, is to release the creative energies in a people. It may degenerate, as elsewhere, into barren étatism.

Chapter Seven

Syria in the Shadow of Coups d'Etat

A Chronicle of a Decade

At the end of 1948, Syria stood, as it were, on the brink of an abyss. The various causes which combined to bring her to this predicament culminated in the outcome of the Palestine war. The presidency of al-Quwwatlī and the government were openly derided by the public.[1] A group of land-owning families and large merchants treated the country as if it were their own property. It controlled the high offices of state and extracted from it open and concealed benefits, while a small inner circle all but monopolized the foreign trade. Throughout the country charges of peculation against government departments were rife. The war had impoverished the treasury; prices rose and unemployment increased. On the other hand, the country was flooded with foreign goods which consumed the fiscal surpluses accumulated after the entry of the Allied forces into Syria. The Druzes and 'Alawis bore a grudge against the government because they were denied due influence in public affairs.

In August 1948, Jamīl Mardam tried to broaden the basis of his government by taking into it three members of the group of al-Haffār, a section of the National Bloc which had been expelled from office by al-Quwwatlī, and some non-party men. He failed, however, to secure the adhesion to it of the Constitutional Bloc, comprising about forty deputies, mostly rich landowners from Aleppo and the Jazīra.

In November the government began to break up. Demonstrators called for an investigation into the course of the Palestine war, the dissolution of the Chamber, and a reduction in the price of bread. Riots took place in many towns, and people were killed and wounded in clashes with the police. On December 1, the government resigned. The army was charged with maintenance of order in the country. On December 16, Khālid al-'Azm, a wealthy businessman from Damascus, formed a government, which comprised members of the National Party and non-party men, including Muhsin al-Barāzī, a landowner of Kurdish origin. A currency agreement was signed at that time with France and a preliminary agreement with the Trans-Arabian Pipeline (Tapline) Co. The Populists, the Muslim Brotherhood and al-Ba'th opposed the agreements, and at the beginning of March 1949 demonstrations took place in various towns. The government planned an investigation into the disaster of the war, and the army chiefs, who regarded the corruption of the regime as the root of the evil, were angered by overt attempts on the part of the government to shift the blame for the defeat onto the army, and by detention of officers charged with embezzlement. In a new military law, the Chamber paid no attention to the army's demands.

Ten days before the coup, officers met at Qunaytra to discuss the events to come.

First coup d'état.

On the night of March 29-30, armored cars were posted at key points in the capital. A state of war was proclaimed in the country, and al-Quwwatlī, al-'Azm, and a number of other persons were placed under arrest.[2] In his first statement, Husnī al-Za'īm declared his intention of establishing a "genuine democratic government." He reproached the previous regime with corruption, infringement of liberties, and violation of the constitution and the laws. Negotiations with party leaders on a constitutional solution failed. The majority of the Chamber was inclined to cooperate with al-Za'īm, but there was much confusion and indecision. To many, sitting on the sidelines seemed to be preferred. The Chamber was dissolved on April 1; a committee was to draft a new constitution. As early as April 5, the regime was overtly supported by al-Ba'th; on April 9, by the Muslim Brethren. Both parties hoped to see constitutional life properly restored. On April 10, Hāshim al-Atāsī pronounced in favor of the coup as an "inevitable event" and asked the deputies to cooperate with it. Akram al-Hawrānī became a member of a committee for investigating the procedures of the old regime.

On April 16, a government was formed by al-Za'īm himself, including among its members Faydī al-Atāsī, representative of al-Sha'b. After three days, on learning of Za'īm's attitude to the project of a Greater Syria, al-Atāsī resigned. Thereupon some of the leaders of al-Sha'b and al-Ba'th were detained for a short time. Thus in the course of nineteen days al-Za'īm lost the favorable attitude of elements which had been united with him in hostility to the old regime. And in the government itself four members out of five came from minorities (Kurds, Druzes, 'Alawis, and Christians).

It is admitted on all sides that at first the *coup d'état* was received with satisfaction. The fact that the old regime had been overthrown without any sign of violence enhanced Za'īm's prestige. In the very first days legislation was promised which would aim at "social justice," at abolishing the feudal system, and at settling peasants on state lands. On the other side, al-Za'īm was averse to "social creeds like communism and others." There was some immediate relief: the prices of bread and meat fell, partly due to that year's good harvest, and prices were fixed for foodstuffs. Army pay was increased. Government officials were forbidden to belong to business companies. Some newspapers, the majority of which practised blackmail, were suppressed. In May, a modern civil code was drawn up by Dr. al-Sanhūrī of Egypt; it restricted the powers of the *sharī'a*. The family waqf was abolished, and the charitable waqf was reorganized. The draft constitution would have abolished confessional representation and given the vote to literate women. Apparently al-Za'īm was attracted by the étatist tendencies of Ataturk. He hoped to see Syria, within five years, "prosperous and civilized like Switzerland."

There was no immediate sign of a new trend in relations with the Arab countries. Al-Za'īm expelled a group of men who in general opposed the Hashimite projects, a step which was calculated to upset the balance of power within the Arab League. However, King 'Abdullah and Nūrī al-Sa'īd thought that the time for realizing their projects had arrived. 'Abdullah commenced at once to declare for a Greater Syria and for a joint kingdom of Iraq, Syria and Jordan.[3] He was at once told by Ibd Sa'ūd that any aggression against Syria would be considered as aggression against Sa'udi Arabia. On April 16 Nūrī al-Sa-'īd visited Damascus, and on the next day Iraq recognized Za'īm's government.

Za'īm's attitude had not yet become clear. On this point there is room for various conjectures. At first he did not take up any definite attitude toward the projects which were being mooted, and even gave hints in favor of a confederation of Syria-Jordan-Iraq. The paternalist attitude of the heads of Iraq and Jordan, who proposed to treat him as their *protégé*, aroused his indignation. What was more, he was all the time subjected to a corresponding pressure from Egypt and Sa'udi Arabia. In his diplomatic devices to induce the Arab states and the Big Powers to recognize him, he could not but be ambiguous. Following a visit to Fārūq, on April 21, the new regime was recognized by Lebanon, Egypt, and Sa'udi Arabia. On April 26, al-Za'īm announced that Syria did not desire either a Greater Syria or a Fertile Crescent scheme; and as for Jordan, it was a Syrian district and one day would be joined to Syria as a tenth district.

In May, various factors brought about an easing of the tension. In declarations from Baghdad and 'Ammān, the matter of union was left to be decided in accordance with the wishes of the population. By June relations with Iraq had become strained again, principally on account of reports on concentration of Iraqi units on the Syrian border. Thereupon al-Za'īm saw fit to suggest a triangular bloc—Cairo-Damascus-Riyād—and Nūrī al-Sa'īd informed the representatives of U. S. A., Great Britain, and France that his government would not recognize the procedure of a referendum in Syria.

In the field of international relations fortune seemed to smile on al-Zaʿīm. On April 21, his government ratified the currency agreement with France, and the French raised the embargo on sale of armaments to Syria and Lebanon. In a very short time arms were sent from France, a step which adversaries utilized to spread rumors that the French might return. On April 27, France, U. S. A., and Great Britain recognized the new regime. The influence of the U. S. A. seemed to grow stronger and stronger, to the extent that the American government announced that it would oppose any change in the geographical map of the Middle East. Relations with Turkey underwent an improvement. A military mission was sent from Turkey to train the Syrian army, but the Syrians could hardly be reconciled to the loss of the Alexandretta region. Al-Zaʿīm sought economic aid from the U. S. A. and promised to stand behind Turkey in the fight against communism.

Government circles in Lebanon were apprehensive of the seeming growth of Syrian strength. There was practically no cessation in the tension between the two countries. The note of aggression in some Lebanese newspapers contributed to it. In June an ultimatum was presented to Lebanon in which a choice of three plans was offered for regulating the economic relations between the two countries; a provisional agreement was reached only in July. In June the Syrian National Party in Lebanon was dissolved, and its leader, Saʿāda, fled to Damascus. Members of this party alleged that they were also allowed to convey weapons from Syria to Lebanon. The Lebanese government invoked effectively the good offices of the Egyptian government: Saʿāda was extradited and executed. Handing over a man who had received protection was a grave violation of traditional practice.[4]

At the end of May the political parties were dissolved. Party leaders escaped to the neighboring countries. On June 25, al-Zaʿīm was elected president by 730,731 votes to 1,784. It was simultaneously decided by a referendum that the president should be empowered, on the proposal of the government, to issue decree-laws and to draft a constitution which ought to be ratified by a referendum or by an incoming legislature. On the next day a government of Muhsin al-Barāzī was formed.

On the night of August 14, al-Za'īm and al-Barāzī were assassinated by officers from the group of Sāmī al-Hinnāwī[5] who had cooperated with al-Za'īm.

The personal traits of al-Za'īm seem worth mentioning. Born of a Kurdish mother, he studied in a military academy in Constantinople and also served in the Turkish army in World War I. He later served the mandate authorities in Syria and attended a military school in France. On the entry of the Allied forces into Syria, in 1941, he was jailed for having refused to stop fighting against the Free French forces. In 1947, al-Quwwatlī appointed him general inspector of police, and at the end of May 1948 he became chief of staff. It can hardly be assumed that he had any clear notion as to the direction in which the ship of state should be guided. From the stream of proclamations he poured out, and partly from his actions, one may judge that he was not of a stable character, that he was fond of display, easily excited, at times childishly self-confident. The attainment of office awakened ambitions in him, e.g., for a marshal's baton, which made him the laughing-stock of the people.[6]

Last but not least, he estranged his ministers by surprising them with a referendum ordinance. They found it strange that a president was to be elected before a new constitution and a new electoral law were framed. In their opinion, a new parliament would gladly place him at the head of state. In this matter al-Za'īm hid behind his councilor al-Barāzī and foreign states demanding a constitutional government.

Za'īm's fall was as sudden as his rise. From the outset he ignored the subtleties of public opinion. The first arrests were made by a foreign unit, a motley group of refugees. Early in his rule he was abandoned by the opposition which had supported him. At the same time he was intoxicated by the rapidity of his success; he made boasts which he seems to have regarded equivalent to deeds, such as that the Syrian army would be second in strength after the Turkish army, and that its air force would be stronger than those of Iraq and Israel combined. The minority units on which he sought to rely did not stand by him. He removed from the army some of the supporters of the previous regime, but the storm broke on him from the midst of his comrades-in-arms.

The coup d'état of al-Hinnāwī

On August 14, an announcement was broadcast that a Supreme War Council had been formed with Sāmī al-Hinnāwī at its head. It stated that al-Zaʿīm and his faction had brought the country to the brink of an abyss. Some of the charges against him were those levelled against the former government: infringement of the rights of the individual, squandering of public funds, and forgery of votes. Others, however, referred specifically to him: disrespect of the army, lack of responsibility in foreign affairs and insults to Arab neighbors, restoration of imperialism in order to break up the Arab nation, hatred of every nationalist of distinction and "every Arab principle." Furthermore, he was accused of having opened his headquarters to numerous foreigners, and of being false to the objects of the revolution.

On the same day a civilian government was formed, headed by Hāshim al-Atāsī, the doyen of the country's leaders. Most of its members belonged to al-Shaʿb; it also included a member of al-Baʿth, representatives of the National Party, and Akram al-Hawrānī. The government was meant to be merely a stopgap, for the purpose of convening a constituent assembly.

The lesson of al-Zaʿīm deterred other countries from recognizing the new government immediately. Only on September 19 was it granted recognition by Egypt, Lebanon, and Saʿudi Arabia, and next day by France, Great Britain, and the U. S. A. Iraq and Jordan, which had contributed to the change by various means of persuasion, did not consider recognition necessary. Iraq at once sent a military mission.

With the *coup d'état*, propaganda for union with Iraq was renewed. The question of union became the focus of an acute struggle between the parties and within them. The inducements to union were: weakness of the country, fear of Israel, bankruptcy of the ruling caste and the vacuum which it left behind, fear of a perpetual dependence on an officers' clique. Against these were set: the attachment to the republican regime and the newly won independence; dislike of the Anglo-Iraqi treaty, which involved military obligations; and fear of the ruling caste for its privileges. Similarly, opinions were divided on the form of union: most of its supporters thought of a kind of partnership, not of a fusion. Already in 1946-47 emissaries of 'Abdullah had established a close contact with the Druzes and the 'Alawis, with Bedouin chieftains, with some spokesmen of the clergy. The adherents of 'Abdullah urged a union with Jordan first. Unquestionably, in this matter there was some rivalry between Iraq and Jordan. Other proposals were mooted: a dual monarchy; the accession of 'Abd al-Ilāh to the throne of Syria after he should have ceased to function as regent of Iraq; a federal union with the retention of the republican regime; a referendum on the form of the regime. Only in the slogans of the Populists was there any clear hint of a trend toward union with Iraq. The Religious Socialist Front advocated a "union of the Arab countries" free from all contamination of Western imperialism.

The elections to the Constituent Assembly, held in November 1949, produced a solid bloc, even a potential majority, favoring union with Iraq (out of 114 members, forty Populists and some other supporters). A provisional constitution was drawn up, and al-Atāsī was elected Head of State for three months. By a small majority a form of oath for the president and the deputies was drawn up by three partisans of union. Those who took it bound themselves to defend the independence of the fatherland, and to work for the union of the Arab countries. On the other hand, the Assembly rejected the motion of al-Hawrānī that they should bind themselves to preserve the republican regime, on the ground that Syria should not join Iraq so long as its regime was monarchical and contained an alien factor. This was a sign that the majority was prepared to ratify a plan for union with Iraq.

Al-Hinnāwī was in full agreement with some political leaders that the union should be effected by a sudden stroke.[7] He had been warned that resistance to this was being planned in the army and in civilian circles. On December 19, a unit of armored cars was ordered to close the approaches to the city, so as to prevent any military interference from without. But the opponents took their measures first.

The coup d'état of Adīb al-Shīshaklī

On the eve of December 19, 1949, by the order of Lt. Col. al-Shīshaklī, al-Hinnāwī and some high officers were arrested. A number of soldiers were killed in frays. Al-Shīshaklī was supported by al-Hawrānī. It was announced that al-Hinnāwī and some politicians were plotting, along with foreign groups, against the security of the army, the fabric of the state and its republican regime.

On the night of December 27-28, the government of Khālid al-ʿAzm was formed. It contained four representatives of al-Shaʿb, al-Hawrānī, who was placed in charge of defense, one of the Religious Front, and some non-party men. In the Constituent Assembly the premier promised that he would act in the spirit of "republican democratic traditions."

From the very first the position of the government was precarious. On account of the opposition of the army the al-Shaʿb did not have a majority in it, and conflicts immediately arose within the government itself and between the government and the Constituent Assembly. Al-ʿAzm tried to revive the policy of rapprochement with Egypt and Saʿudi Arabia. Following a visit of al-Shīshaklī to Saʿudi Arabia, Syria was granted an interest-free loan of six million dollars. In May 1950, al-ʿAzm voted in the political committee of the Arab League along with the representatives of Saʿudi Arabia, Egypt, and Lebanon for acceptance of a suggestion of the Council of the League which would have involved the removal of Jordan from the Arab League for having annexed a part of Palestine. In contrast, the majority in the Constituent Assembly looked with approval on this action; at any rate, there was no hostility to it.

At the end of April, al-Hawrānī resigned, allegedly on account of lack of unity between the government and the Constituent Assembly. His group in the Assembly worked as a Republican

Front, and outside of the Assembly he established an Arab Socialist Party of which the main principles were abolition of communalism, emancipation of women, and elimination of feudalism. This group, al-Ba'th, and the Religious Front urged neutrality.

On May 29, al-'Azm resigned. Six days later the government of Nāzim al-Qudsī was formed. The great majority of its members, including the premier, came from al-Sh'ab. In his government Fawzī Sello, a representative of the army, began to serve as defense minister.

The new government brought no peace to the country. The old opposition parties, including the Socialist Cooperative Party, formed a Patriotic Front which contested the legitimacy of the new government and demanded the restoration of the old constitution and of the old parliament. The struggle between al-Shīshaklī and the government, which tried, in vain, to neutralize the army, came into the open. In August al-'Ajlānī called the attention of the Assembly to the interference of the army in the internal affairs of the country. Al-Shīshaklī thereupon felt compelled to promise that the function of the army would be confined to defending the country.

In September the draft of the new constitution was approved. The third paragraph of the old constitution which stated that Islam was the religion of the country was amended so as to make Islam mandatory as the religion of the president. The Constituent Assembly converted itself into a Chamber of Deputies, and Hāshim al-Atāsī was elected president. The new government of al-Qudsī, mostly members of al-Sh'ab, contained two non-party men with pro-Hāshimite leanings, and Fawzī Sello.

The army itself was riven by dissension. At the end of July Col. Nāsir, the commander of the air force, was shot and killed. This aroused the anger of the 'Alawi community to which he belonged. On account of this, the head of the intelligence, Ibrāhīm al-Husaynī, and his assistant were jailed. A military court released them for lack of sufficient evidence.

In September the military authorities arrested a number of officers, among whom were Col. Bahīj al-Kallās, who in his time had assisted al-Zaʿīm and afterwards al-Hinnāwī, and some civilians, including the deputy al-ʿAjlānī, on a charge of conspiring with some Jordanians toward bringing about a union between Syria and Jordan. It was stated that Col. Nāsir was in league with agents of ʿAbdullah, although he was suspected of plotting also with the faction of al-Quwwatlī.[8]

On October 12, 1950, an attempt was made on the life of al-Shīshaklī. Among those detained was Nash'at Sheikh al-Ard, director of the Saʿudi airlines. The military investigation brought to light the existence of Phalanges of Arab Redemption (katā'ib al-fidā al-ʿarabī), which had been founded at the end of 1948 by young men from Damascus, Beirut, Baghdad, and Egypt, with the object of uniting the Arab countries and taking vengeance on the Jews. The Phalanges had been charged with terrorist activities since 1949—throwing bombs at the Jewish quarter in Damascus, at the British embassy buildings in Damascus, Baghdad, and Beirut, plotting the murder of ʿAbdullah and al-Shīshaklī, and other offenses. According to the indictment, they had been incited to murder al-Shīshaklī by Dr. Amīn al-Ruwayha; Sheikh al-Ard had placed means at the disposal of the latter from funds of the Saʿudi government.[9] At that time al-Qudsī and Fawzī Sello returned from their visit to Riyād where they had failed to receive the second and third installments of the loan. The attention paid in Egypt to al-Quwwatlī and his group also caused displeasure in Syria.

Syria was swarming at that time with agents from Arab countries. On account of the pressure of the two Arab blocs the official attitude of the government was inevitably evasive or contradictory; it could be construed as a support for some kind of union without impairing Syria's independence. Shīshaklī's attitude was calculated to allay the misgivings of Egypt and Saʿudi Arabia. Syria, according to him, did not want to be made an arena for the ambitions of those who desired to set up their throne in it. Arab unity should be brought about by equalization of the status of the Arab peoples; and a republican regime suited Syria.

To increase the confusion, the question of the "Defense of the Middle East" then began to be discussed by the Western powers.

Al-'Ajlānī and Hasan al-Hakīm, formerly supporters of Hashimite projects, opposed the neutralists and advocated joining the Western bloc. The premier was in favor of deriving the maximum advantage from the existing situation, and of taking no definite stand save on assured conditions.

In March 1951, the government of al-Qudsī resigned. His party maintained that the duplication of powers in the state—military and civil—was not in accordance with the Constitution. His attempt to form a government from his own party alone came to grief through the refusal of Fawzī Sello to join it.

On March 27, the non-party government of al-'Azm was formed, again with Fawzī Sello as a member. The government newspapers reproached al-Sha'b for planning to hand over Syria to the Hashimites and Great Britain, while the papers of this party charged the premier with designs to sacrifice the country's political and economic interests to France. The truth was that, after the cessation of the mandate, France was inclined to support those who aimed at retaining Syria's independence.

The incidents in the demilitarized zone between Syria and Israel in March-May 1951 were grease to the wheels of those who aimed at union. Syria asked for arms from Egypt and Iraq. Arms bought in Egypt—other than aircraft—were sent in June, while Iraq dispatched military units and aircraft, a step which enhanced the prestige of the Hashimites.

On July 30 the government resigned. It had had no secure majority in the Chamber. A strike of government officials against material hardships hastened its resignation.

With the murder of 'Abdullah, on July 30, 1951, a shift took place in the balance of power between the two Arab blocs. It is safe to say that it caused satisfaction in the camp of the opponents of the Hashimites. The attitude of al-Shīshaklī was not dissimilar to that of Ibn Sa'ūd: that the people of Jordan ought to decide their own fate by a free plebiscite. Ibn Sa'ūd at that time ordered the balance of his loan to Syria to be released.

On August 9, the turn of al-Hakīm, an office-holder during the mandate, arrived. His government included five members from al-Sha'b, Sello, two from the Republican Front and one from the Religious Front. Al-Sha'b looked on this as its last attempt to join in a government; and it announced that if the Constitution was not brought into force and if the dual regime was to continue, its members would withdraw even from the Chamber. It held that the present government pledged itself to bring under its direct control the forces of internal security. It was then stated in the Chamber that the interference of the army was open and explicit: the Chamber was silenced, and governments were made and unmade without its consent, and even against its will.

The resignation of al-Hakīm, on November 10, was brought about mainly by divergence of opinion between him and some of his colleagues regarding the plan for a Middle East Command, which was suggested to Egypt, in October 1951, by the U. S. A., Great Britain, France, and Turkey. To make this project palatable, al-Hakīm commended it as an opportunity for wrecking the Anglo-Egyptian pact, for getting rid of the British bases in Iraq and Jordan, and for deriving economic advantages.

The deadlock lasted till November 28. Al-Sha'b demanded, among other things, that the portfolio of defense should be entrusted to a civilian. The government of al-Dawālibī, a notorious colleague of the Mufti of Jerusalem, was preponderately Populist. Sello was not included in it. On November 29 the government was dissolved by al-Shīshaklī, and a number of al-Sha'b deputies and independents were detained. The army publicly laid on al-Sha'b the responsibility for the three *coups d'état*. Through sheer slackness, it said, they had pushed al-Za'īm into a dictatorship. It was they who had taken al-Hinnāwī to their hearts and dragged him into a plot which had almost put an end to the country's independence. In the third *coup d'état* the army leaders had treated this party with consideration, so as to prevent the suppression of parliamentary life. It was the al-Sha'b leaders who had brought about the last governmental crisis. For the purpose of coming elections they had put forward the demand for the transference of the internal security forces. The aim of this party was to establish a monarchy in Syria.

After al-Dawālibī (a firebrand attached to both al-Sha'b and the Religious Front), had been forced to offer his resignation from prison, the President charged Hāmid Khōja of the Republican Front with the formation of a government. According to the army leaders, he ought to have prepared new elections, but al-Sha'b deputies refused to dissolve the Chamber. Hāshim al-Atāsī thereupon resigned on the ground that the Constitution had been broken by an unconstitutional authority. On December 2, al-Shīshaklī assumed the office of Head of the State and dissolved the Chamber. On the next day Sello replaced him as Head of the State.

In speeches delivered on this occasion "fellahin and workers" took precedence over "merchants and officials," and promise was made of protection from "exploitation inside and imperialism outside." Since the uprising in Egypt the magic term "revolution" had frequently been used. It was promised that a civil government would be set up as soon as the army was satisfied that elections would result in a "true representation" of the nation.

At the start al-Shīshaklī was supported by Hawrānī's Arab Socialist Party and al-Ba'th, on the one side, and, curiously, by the Syrian National Social Party on the other. But the first two parties soon turned against him. They may have been frightened by the students' demonstrations, and the many dead and injured. On account of a steady rapprochement with the West, especially the U. S. A. and France, al-Hawrānī charged al-Shīshaklī with relying on officers trained in France and of being supported by the Bank of Syria and Lebanon and "American circles."

In April 1952 political parties were disbanded. A multitude of decree-laws descended upon the country. One decree banned politics from sport groups such as the boy scouts; another decree abolished Ottoman relics like the fez and titles; yet another placed foreign establishments (companies, schools) under strict supervision. The press was subjected to severe control. A number of decrees restricted the communal activity of the minorities, no doubt with a view to doing away with relics of their autonomy. Clubs and associations were obligated to assume Arabic names. The clergy was ordered not to speak publicly outside of the prayer house. The decree on parties banned groupings with regional, communal or racial aims.

In August, an Arab Liberation Movement was inaugurated, stemming from a "revolt of conscience of Syria's Arabs." In November, al-Shīshaklī saw in Syria's people "one party, one community." The press extolled Saladin and the "days of happiness in the middle ages"; Damascus was praised as the Arab capital and the heart of the nation.

Meanwhile, the officers' corps itself was not free from subversive activities. A number of officers were relieved from their posts or transferred to the desert. On the first anniversary of the coup, bombs were thrown at the offices of the Liberation Movement. Hundreds of citizens fled to Lebanon, to return only after the new Chamber was elected.

In June 1953 a draft constitution was announced. It envisaged formation of parties, if their aims were within the limits of the constitution. Franchise was to be granted to both men and women. A group of more than a hundred leaders denounced it on the ground that it was not drawn up by a constituent assembly. In July a referendum approved it by 861,152 out of 864,425 votes. By the same referendum al-Shīshaklī became president. In October, elections were held for the Chamber. The main opposition parties boycotted them. Out of 82 members 72 were nominated by the Arab Liberation Movement and one by the Syrian National Social Party.

The government of Iraq never recognized Shīshaklī's regime and asked for renewal of parliamentary life in Syria. Shīshaklī's attitude toward inner Arab affairs was adjusted to that of Egypt and Sa'udi Arabia; he saw in the Arab Collective Security Pact a proper frame for regional defense.

In January 1954, prominent leaders of the National Party, al-Sha'b, al-Ba'th, and the Arab Socialist Party were arrested. Armed clashes occurred in some places, particularly in Jabal al-Durūz, where, according to Sultān Atrash, more than a hundred civilians and some soldiers were victims of a punitive expedition that besieged his residence.[10] Atrash himself fled to

Jordan. For all this, al-Shīshaklī sought to negotiate with the jailed leaders of the opposition. This punitive expedition seems to have set off the spark of rebellion.

On February 25, 1954, commanders of the military areas of Aleppo, Latakiya and Deyr al-Zor broadcast from Aleppo an ultimatum to al-Shīshaklī to leave Damascus within twenty-four hours. The commanders of the central area (Homs, Hamā) and of Jabal al-Durūz joined in. Some of the officers in Damascus tried to uphold the regime. The rebels announced that the fight would go on until the regime and its constitution were done away with.

The leaders released from prison met in Homs and decided to renew the 1950 Constitution. Hāshim al-Atāsī resumed his functions as president.

On March 1, a stopgap government under Sabrī al-'Asalī, secretary of the National Party, was formed, consisting of four members of the National Party, four of al-Sha'b, and four independents. The newly constituted Arab Socialist Resurrection Party, led by al-Hawrānī, demanded, as a condition of participation, control of the defense and interior ministries, at least a three-party control of the latter. Meanwhile, government services were purged, officers removed, or returned to service.

The A.S.R.P. kept agitating against the government, by accusing it of paving the way to a Syria-Iraq federation and accession to the Western defense projects. It gained a strong foothold among peasants, especially in the Hamā region. On account of internal friction within the government and interference of the army, a non-party stopgap government of Sa'īd al-Ghazzī was formed on June 19.

The elections were comparatively the freest ever held in Syria. The composition of the Chamber changed considerably (28 al-Sha'b, 16 A.S.R.P., 12 National Party, 5 Islamic Party, 2 National Social Party, 2 Cooperative Socialist Party, 1 Communist, 9 tribal sheikhs, and the rest independents, including some from the ex-Liberation Movement).

The success of the dynamic and vociferous A.S.R.P. marked a potential shift in foreign policy and in inter-Arab relations. The government of Fāris al-Khūri, formed on October 30, was divided on foreign policy and ambitions of superiority within the coalition (National Party, al-Shaʻb, independents), and on February 13, 1955, gave way to a cabinet of al-ʻAsali, a coalition of the National Party, A.S.R.P., and a Democratic Bloc of al-ʻAzm.

The trend not to join any non-Arab defense pact became more and more accentuated on account of the Iraqi-Turkish Defense Treaty, concluded in February, 1955. In March an "Agreement defining the principles of defense alliance" was signed between Egypt, Saʻudi Arabia and Syria. In August al-Quwwatlī was elected President by 91 to 41 votes. The election meant a further move toward the Cairo-Damascus-Riyād axis. On October 20, an Egyptian-Syrian Mutual Defense Alliance was concluded, providing for a joint command in peacetime as well as in wartime. This step was effected by a cabinet of al-Ghazzī (September, 1955–June, 1956), which comprised al-Shaʻb, the Democratic Bloc and independents.

In an all-coalition government of al-ʻAsali, Salāh Bītar, a leader of A.S.R.P., became foreign minister. On July 5, 1956, the Chamber initiated a discussion of a federal union with Egypt. Meanwhile, the relations with the U.S.S.R. continued to improve. Quwwatlī's visit there, in October, 1956, was followed by additional arms shipments in November.

The way to a union had to be forcibly paved. In November an alleged plot against the security of the state was uncovered; Iraq, Great Britain, Turkey, Lebanon, and Israel were said to have been direct or indirect participants in it. On December 22, al-Shaʻb was ousted from the government. Members of the Chamber (from al-Shaʻb, the Socialist Cooperative Party, and independents) left the country. Forty-one leading citizens, including seven former ministers from al-Shaʻb, and some members of the Syrian National Social Party, were court-martialled on charges of plotting a revolt to set up a pro-Iraq government. Opponents of the ruling faction were denounced as traitors, eager to side with Israel; army officers were ousted or arrested. The remnants of al-Shaʻb had to readjust their program toward "positive neutralism" and worship of ʻAbd al-Nāsir. Many members of the National Party chose silence. The economic and cultural rapprochement with the Soviet Union grew apace. By August, 1957, the army seemed to be firmly in the grip of al-Sarrāj and al-Bizrī, the former owing allegiance to al-Ba'th and the latter to the Communist Party. In November, 1957, the Chamber and forty visiting Egyptian Assembly delegates met in joint session and passed a resolution recommending the establishment of a federal union.

On February 1, 1958, the formation of the United Arab Republic was announced. On February 21, a plebiscite on the merger was held, and at the same time 'Abd al-Nāsir was elected President by 99.99 percent of the votes in Egypt and 99.98 percent in Syria. Legislative authority in the new republic was to be vested in the National Assembly (three-quarters Egyptians, one-quarter Syrians), whose members were to be appointed by the president.[11]

One is tempted to see in this fateful step self-denial of the highest degree. Syria renounced her claim to sovereignty. The merger is by no means the outcome of a free decision. Society and army were deeply split on this question. Unanimity had been displayed, in behalf of the various rulers, at every referendum held since 1948. No doubt a large measure of fear, coupled with a sense of adventure, prompted the voters to take part *en masse* in this game. It had been argued that this step was designed to prevent the Soviet-oriented officers in the army from gaining the upper hand. But this argument may also have been launched in order to sooth the West. The Turko-Syrian tension may have been a supplementary cause. The growing influence of al-'Azm, ever an aspirant for the presidency, and his tactical alliance with the Communists, may have prompted al-Ba'th and al-Quwwatlī in their drive toward merger. Al-Ba'th may have cherished a hope that Egypt's regime would be liberalized and that they might provide the ideology of the new state.

The real test may come in social and economic fields, such as integration, free migration and settlement. But the questions remain: Is unity to be effected by force? Does it imply abolition of diversity? Do complementary relations necessitate compulsory uniformity of institutions and beliefs? Is unity in Egypt's image the proper one? In short, is there one road to Arab nationalism?

Three years after the merger, Egypt's system is being introduced in Syria, and 'Abd al-Nāsir promises that in the future society of Syria "all individual egoism will be abolished." The country is being rushed into a state-controlled economy. The leaders of al-Ba'th ponder the benefits of merger in exile, while the country is run by young officers.

Part Three

CRAFT OF THE WORD

Chapter Eight

Renewal of a Language

The perennial struggle between "old" and "new" in a language is most acute at times of revolutionary upheaval.[1] This struggle has had a part to play in recent Arabic literature. Owing to some four centuries of stagnation, the written language had lost much of its literary quality. During the initial stages, in the second half of the nineteenth century, the sponsors of the enlightenment looked for inspiration in the early literature—in the youth of the language or in periods of its renascence. Purism seemed a vehicle to eliminate the dross which had accumulated under the impact of Persian and Turkish and colloquial Arabic, as well as a shield against the pressure of European languages. Unfortunately, the purists preferred the rigid forms of rhymed prose to patterns of personal and direct style. By degrees, this movement, fed on romantic esteem for the past, became more and more public-spirited and prepared the way for the national movement. Literature gradually moved away from didacticism, engaged in translation or adaption of foreign works, into the field of creative effort, which was to no small degree stimulated by imitation of foreign works. Nevertheless, the written language lagged behind the currents of life and thought which forced their way into literature.

The national upheaval of 1918 marked a new and forceful stage in the development of the Arabic language. As a result, a vehement strife over "old" and "new" commenced. Haykal sees its nature as follows:

> The supporters of the old school are of the opinion that the modernists have foresaken the Arabs and their literature for the West and its literature, and therefore do not ap-

preciate Arab style which is verbally lucid. . . . In the opinion of the defenders of the "new," however, the point at issue is that the conservatives have allowed themselves to sink into the depths of the past, and their attitude toward words and their meaning and to sentences and their structure is the same as that of the ancient Arabs. Language is a manifestation of life, and must necessarily be able to express thoughts and concepts in the manner that people desire.[2]

There is no quarrel between "old" and "new." . . . The quarrel is between literature of the word and literature of thought.[3]

For Haykal, it is not the fault of Arabic that it cannot sustain many of the forms of modern culture. Written language is only a tool, and if it is not kept polished it grows rusty. And possibly this very "war of pens" between conservatives and modernists is one of the steps making Arabic capable of containing world culture. The former wish to slow the modernists down lest they go as far as the Syro-American writers Amīn al-Rayhānī and Khalīl Jibrān, who disregarded the individuality of the literary language. The modernists, however, wish to carry the conservatives with them into the present.

The fate of the literary language will not be decided by this battle. This lofty objective requires the efforts of some outstanding individuals—guides of their people. They must be thoroughly at home in the whole range of culture. They will impress their spirit on prose and verse. When they gain the allegiance of both conservatives and modernists, the battle will pass from the sphere of "old" and "new" to that of wholeness.[4] Writers representing their generation are the masters of language. Grammars and dictionaries will submit to their judgment and linguists will admit their authority, even those who would prefer stagnation.[5]

The protagonists of the "new" style could employ the argument that the "old" also consists of many layers. Those demanding an Arab style did not specify what it had to be. Al-'Aqqād listed a succession of classic prose writers who had belonged to different periods, no two of them resembling each other in their manner of writing.[6] Taha Husayn, furthermore, insisted that the traditional language had itself been influenced by translations of foreign works. But for the translations of the Abbasid period, Arabic would not have known the prose of Ibn Muqaffaʿ and al-Jāhiz, and without the contemporary translators the forceful life of Arab prose would never have been restored.[7]

The Egyptian writers felt clearly that Arabic was in the midst of a unique movement. The woman writer Mayy regards it as the beginning of a resurgence such as had never been known in its history. It was liberating itself from prolixity, and making the transition to the more clear and comprehensible sentence of contemporary writers. It was difficult to coordinate the influx of new concepts with rigid and obsolete means, so that there was bound to be confusion. But the new form of expression was the commencement of "walking on both legs." "And no matter how much negligence there may be, these are legs of human beings, and not stilts made of carved wood."[8] There was an unceasing exchange between thought and language to their mutual benefit: education of thought through expression and education of expression through thought.[9]

Taha Husayn holds that the national movement which gathered strength from youth and gave vitality to the press was among the primary factors in the renewal of the language. Newspapers have no time to spare for excessive attention to linguistic purity, and youth cannot be persuaded to use standard dictionaries. The craft of writing, which had previously been the domain of a specific social stratum, now became the possession of new strata. The political upheaval following World War I, together with party strife, left deep marks on prose style. Incessant polemics made it keen and violent.[10]

The struggle between "old" and "new" Arabic is, to Taha Husayn, the affair of a negligible minority. The upholders of the "old" indulge in philology and verbosity, and the public disregards them for it does not understand them. The others depreciate words, and "their Arab personality wilts in the shadow of Western writers"; for this reason, the public ignores them, too. Readers are concerned both for the past, in order that their individuality may not be obliterated, and for the new, because they do not wish to be in any way behind the West.[11]

This estimate of Taha Husayn seems overly optimistic. Various factors were slowing down the pace of progress: the religious tradition which sustained an enthusiasm for the "old"; the social tradition; the structure of the language itself and concepts enshrined therein.[12]

The weakening of the link with traditional ways of expression involves a weakening of the link with a pattern of civilization. Eloquence through poetry has been considered a virtue since pre-Islamic times. Arab tradition had fostered an attitude towards *'arabiyya* (grammar and lexicography) which was almost worship. Arabic was thought to have had its beginnings at the time of Creation, and the language to have been placed in the mouth of Adam or Ishmael. Linguistic purity was valued, such as was bestowed by the Prophet.[13] Meticulous use of the language was required, particularly as regards the correct reading of the Qur'ān, and the comprehension of *'arabiyya* was placed on a level with acts of charity ("Hold fast to charity, the understanding of *'arabiyya* and its felicitous lucidity").[14] To the Arabs it was their most characteristic trait ("The wisdom of the Romans is in their brains, the wisdom of the Indians in the imagination, the wisdom of the Greeks in their soul, and the wisdom of the Arabs in their tongue").[15] Linguistic prowess was a method of settling disputes, the two rivals meeting in public competition. Poets would dispute and tribes prepare for battle. The "science of *'arabiyya*" was carefully fostered, its aim even being regarded a moral obligation.[16] The poet was not the only person to hold a distinct position in public life. Down through the centuries the preacher-rhetorician in his differing or changing functions (*khatīb, wā'iz, mudhakkir, qāss*) exercised a considerable influence.[17] The status of *'arabiyya* was enhanced by the very fact of having been, for nearly twelve centuries, divorced from everyday speech and to a great extent confined to spheres of exalted life (literature, religion, oratory).

Salāma Mūsā applied a social criterion: Linguistic wealth had a social function, because mastery of Arabic was a monopoly of a specific class. It is characteristic of Arabic literature that it overrates the craft of expression, being a literature which sustains the taste and requirements of aristocrats by birth and office instead of satisfying the needs of those who advance by force of their own toil and effort. Study is the privilege of the wealthy and powerful. Hence their literature was a decorative and mosaic one. Arab society never was a democratic society, and the archaic Arab style resembles the furniture of the wealthy, the purpose of which is ornament and not utility. This classicist attitude to the language is a deterrent to Egypt's literary and social evolution.[18]

Until recently, hyperbole and euphemism abounded even in the style of forward-looking writers. Emotionalism is well served by high-flown metaphors, causing the writer to touch off a dreamlike world. Passionate eloquence marks even the latest political speeches.[19]

Clearly the struggle for direct expression cannot be other than painful. The literary tongue of our own times is a direct continuation of 'arabiyya. Pride in this immense heritage barred critical approach by means of historical evaluation as well. The myth that purism was feasible was upheld through all generations. Elements from pre-Islamic poetry and from *hadīth* (religious and historical tradition) are found even in the writings of the protagonists of modernity. This continuity has also produced the *embarras de richesse*—which is almost beyond the power of our contemporaries to master. Arabic is invested with immense power of transference of meaning sustained by senses attuned to nature.[20] As far as its origins are traceable in the pre-Islamic poetry, it absorbed an astonishing set of elemental reactions of the Bedouin—an image of his soul and world outlook. The onomatopoeia is still widely discernible in it. The evidently massive mutation of consonants is due, in part, to the impact of the idioms (*lughāt*). The movement of content in an Arab word, in the hundredfold ramifications of its root, in which the order of the consonants was not necessarily observed and the third radical not essential, is varied and tinted. The associative power of identifying objects and activities, either concretely or metaphorically, led to countless synonyms, which serve to define stages of growth, qualities, shapes, gradation of color, voice, and so on. A second aspect of inclusiveness, deriving from the common features or qualities, is found in homonyms. This unbounded power of suggesting analogy has also made it possible to unite two opposites in a single word. This powerful trend toward association has transformed the Arab language into an idiomatic treasure house.*

With all the shakiness of generalization, it is nevertheless necessary to point to a specific psychological tint coloring many of the varieties of earlier literary production. The wealth of grammatical forms, especially of particles, provides, on the one hand, for subtle and precise expression, and, on the other, helps to diversify and even obscure a meaning, often leading to the opposite. Even the very place of a particle may determine the whole situation. The capacity for concealing intention or merely hinting at it seems a characteristic of the language. The unspoken aim finds expression in epigrammatic conciseness. Wordplay makes it possible to go round and round the subject. The wit in what is left unsaid has outlets in various forms running from badinage to keen and biting mockery. This is to be found in proverbs and sayings, in historical narrative and poetry, and in folk stories. It serves a Muslim idealist and a conqueror, a poet and a Bedouin alike. Light humor can be found in *hadīth* in particular, and this is what opens the door to deeper understanding. The vast *adab* literature is permeated with an urge to bypass, allude, and puzzle.[21]

---

*Much is to be said about the metaphorical quality of the Arabic word, i.e., to what extent there prevails in it transference of attributes of inanimate things into human notions, or vice versa. Of course, both ways of representation originate in the human mind, be it "primitive" or "sophisticated."

In dealing with metaphors and images, Herbert Read, in *The Nature of Literature,* could have profitably referred to special characteristics of the Semitic word and to Arabic imagery handed down from generation to generation.

Another controversial ground is the impact of a language on a people. The question arises: how far is the Arab writer bound by words and phrases which are part and parcel of his memory? The pressure of the linguistic burden is so heavy that it may affect the free movement of thought.[22]

The intrinsic qualities of Arabic would at first sight appear to facilitate its adaptation to the needs of modern society. The incursion of foreign words is a relatively minor phenomenon. It seems that modern Arabic has absorbed, by way of Arabization (*ta'rīb*), fewer loan words than Hebrew did; and even so the latter, which is less rich in roots and forms, makes little use of them. The strong opposition to loan words on the part of Arab academies of language goes back to the myth of purism. The ease of metaphoric approach makes it possible to adjust existing words by expanding, contracting, or modifying their meanings (*tadmīn*), or else, by various derivations from existing roots (*ishtiqāq*). Borrowing, by way of translation, of words and phrases, that is, ideas and notions behind them, is a powerful influence on a language.

With all the differences deriving from personality and literary influence, there are common characteristics in the new style. No doubt, the French and the English languages have a salutary share in it; their impact can also be traced in the greater lucidity of the Arabic sentence. Because of divergence of criteria, let alone tastes, even classification of the styles— from ultraconservative to ultramodernist—rests on shaky ground. It may become obsolete all around, or overtaken by a new stage in a writer's literary activity. Al-Manfalūtī and al-Shawqī sponsored a kind of neoclassicism in protest against the conservatives, and now Taha Husayn, once considered modernist, is labelled neoclassicist. But within the common bounds of the new style there are immense creative possibilities, partly bound by the degree of attachment to the tradition of expression. The easy, tradition-fed style of Taha Husayn, reminiscent by its rhetorical cadences of public speaking, differs widely from the sober and factual manner of Haykal in his earlier days of activity. As against this, 'Aqqād's way of writing appears archaic, and, perhaps owing to his labored way of thinking, obscure. Neither of these resembles the precise prose of Maḥmūd Taymūr, nor the deliberately austere one of Salāma Mūsā.[23]

The battle is being won by the "new" style day by day. Even among the conservatives there are wide differences; suffice it to mention the previous rigidity of al-Zayyāt and the stylistic vitality of Mustafā al-Rifāʿī. It is a simultaneous process of shrinking in volume and concepts and of natural growing or absorption from outside. In fairness, it is not merely conservative stubbornness which impels an *arrière-garde* fight. It is anxiety about a pattern of civilization, enshrined in the language, that is passing forever, about a world of ideas that at best may become an object of study. It may be consoling to reason that Ibn Khaldūn would have been on the side of the evolutionists.

Arabic and Hebrew

The refining process of Arabic must inevitably differ from that of Hebrew. Unlike Arabic, Hebrew ceased to be spoken about eighteen centuries ago; but as a language of prayer, a lifelong study and a comprehensive literature, it served for centuries chiefly religious needs which nearly covered the cultural needs of a literate community. It wandered with the wandering people, absorbing influences in form and content.* Hebrew, too, knew some centuries of impoverishment and exhaustion in the rabbinic literature. The Hebrew enlightenment (*haskala*) in the second half of the last century, being in the main secular, was deeply attached to the prevailing social currents in Europe and enjoyed, to a far greater extent than Arabic, freedom of thought and expression. On the other hand, the

---

*Hebrew maintained close symbiotic relations with Jewish vernaculars. Hebrew elements lived on in them, often taking on new meanings. By strange ways, some of those pertaining to sublime or solemn life became profane, and a touch of humor made them colloquialisms, sometimes bordering on the frivolous. Nowadays, these "exiles" are being ingathered, too. As against this, Yiddish, whose literary renaissance coincided with that of Hebrew, lent some of its vigor and vitality to Hebrew and moved it towards directness and simplicity.

Hebrew writer had also to force his way under the heavy impact of inherited imagery, sayings of ideal personalities, or terms of argument and reasoning. This movement started from stylistic and also thematic attachment to the Bible.

In the 1870's, the *melitza* (Hebrew rhetoric of the late eighteenth and nineteenth centuries) had been gradually subdued, or forced to bear the full weight of modes of thinking and feeling then current. Thanks to the outstanding activity of some writers the various layers of Hebrew have been revitalized. Talmudic elements came again into use, and a kind of new mosaic style evolved. With Mendele Mokher Sefarim and Ahad Ha'am, the language moved from artificial coexistence of its various elements towards fusion. Bialik, Czernikhovsky, Berkovich and others advanced this process of amalgamation. A band of writers carried this activity further in the direction of sense and simplicity, even puritanical simplification. For all this, one or another layer may have prevailed in the language of an individual or group, sometimes not without confusion, involving morphology and syntax. In our days Shlonsky, chiefly by his classical translations, and Alterman, mainly through his topical poems, invigorated it immensely. All these linguistic exploits were closely related to the national movement and to the constructive efforts in Palestine.

In the last forty years or so, two outstanding writers with a genius for Hebrew—'Agnon and Hazaz—have almost revolutionized the Hebrew style. 'Agnon conjures up a seemingly primitive mosaic of word associations from a multitude of sources, the setting being that of the religious folk literature of the last centuries. The prevailing element in it fits the era, situation, or character. There is a quasi-settled atmosphere about 'Agnon, which in its subtlety recalls a refined strain in German literature of 1900-10, but it is a subdued one; superb humor is often replaced by plain mimicry. His writings may well be linked with Tyll Eulenspiegel or Colas Breugnon. His later work is a mine of allegory, becoming more and more rarified. Hazaz is elemental in forcing archaic words and unusual derivations of roots to his purpose—uncovering chaotic processes of the human soul and the perennial interplay of good and evil. There is an affectionate mood in the tense atmosphere effected by the stuttering, pieced-together style, ranging from deepest compassion to cutting satire, often carried to a grotesque extreme—be it about the early days of revolutionary Russia or about the nostalgic outlook of the Hasidim as displayed by their pioneering descendants in Israel. Style seems inseparable from content. The test of translatability can hardly apply to them. Under their spell stood a group of writers. Their style, being mainly related to the *aggada*, agreed with the utopian and venturesome mood of a time committed to a great task—a time when every task seemed great.

Added to the confluence of styles, Hebrew is exposed to pressure from a variety of linguistic backgrounds, namely, idiomatic impact by means of translation or metaphorical transference. Various cultural and mental levels leave their mark, too. In some ways this situation is similar to that in the United States. And all this takes place amidst tension between communities, many strata of immigrants, and in a country that is all but a frontier.

The late 1930's, and more so the 1948 war, seemed to end a period in the evolution of Hebrew. The more intense and chaotic life became—with waves of refugees, Arab-Jewish strife, argument with the British—less inhibited did the modes of writing become, and the vernacular gained more and more of a foothold in the novel. Stylistic carelessness seemed to match the anarchic mood of young writers who were endowed with a more open sense of nature; perhaps it stemmed also from a poorer mastery of the writer's craft. After the war of 1948, Hebrew had to accommodate the thousandfold new manifestations of life. To a purist the "war Hebrew"—sprinkled as it was with Anglicisms, Arabisms, Yiddishisms, and slang elements of Hebrew provenance—seemed sheer profanation.

In the 1950's a strange term—Israel Hebrew—came into use. At first it was meant to mark a literary Hebrew which represented, so to speak, the country's new life. Later on, it indicated the existence of a stratum in its own right, comparable to biblical, mishnaic, medieval or new Hebrew. It bears the imprint of a vernacular in more than an embryonic stage. It commits narrative garrulity to writing. There is more color in it, vigor of spontaneity, but it lacks the building elements of culture. Ostentation and pose may be given free rein in this mode of writing.*

To be sure, a rapid pace of evolution is not unusual in Hebrew. It experienced a startling transformation in its mishnaic period, in medieval prose and poetry, in the near-colloquial of Hasidic literature. The impact of other languages on it was great, too. But these changes had solid brakes—all-pervasive tenets, comprehensive learning or "duties of the hearts." Traits of a language can be preserved even without exhibiting attachment to the past. Shofman and Rahel bear testimony to it. But the moment one renounces the claim to creative continuity by failing to foster the language, it is bound to lose its individuality.

Hebrew seems to be heading for a crisis, maybe the severest since the Spanish period. At that time occurred, as Abraham Geiger put it, an *"Arabisierung der hebräischen Sprache und Judaisierung der arabischen Kunstanschaung."* The linguistic genius of Maimonides linked Hebrew again with native tradition and molded it into a style representative of all periods in its development. In a sense this process repeated itself at the turn of the last century.

At present it is felt that the survival of Hebrew as a Semitic language is imperiled. It has to contend with all the disruptive forces of a transition period. Nowadays it has the means to safeguard its qualities: schools, the theater, a stable philiosophic terminology, and some institutions that provide for recreative translations. To a great degree its future lies with the creative writer.**

---

*Derivative affluence of Hebrew is a problem in itself. It assumes menacing proportions in Izhar's prose, reminiscent of the penitential *piyyutim*. Critical edition of earlier sources helps revive words and idioms, but there is no guarantee against the tyranny of the colloquial.

**In the last century, the Russian language had to withstand the heavy impact of foreign languages, especially French, but great writers guarded it.

After the war of 1948 a constructivist trend, perhaps toward some kind of neorealism, seemed to set in. But Hebrew may be threatened from within the literature, too. A rambling style, a kind of monologue of the subconscious, marks the works of Izhar. A prototype may be searched for in Gnesin, a dawn-of-the-century novelist, elegiac and nostalgic, a mood that suited well the despondent Jewish intellectual of that time. The Chekhovian mood in its integrity was then supreme. It takes Izhar's characters, like those of Hemingway, a few days or hours to discover their destiny at a tragic moment in Jewish history, when martyrs of centuries forcibly became successful warriors. Slang and colloquial, real or imagined, weigh heavily on these rigged records, and it seems difficult to comprehend how a highly revered language evolved to accommodate them within some fifty years. It had to respond to the transition of the generation of the 1920's which made its way from despair and frustration to a social and moral uplift, to a warring generation at its finest and its toughest. But are there creative limits to this response: sense of proportion, harmony in blend, precision, stimulating allusion?***

U. Z. Greenberg, a poet with a gift of a rhetorician, fights a one-man battle against the world of the Gentiles for the tragedy that attended his people. The tragedy is beyond proportions, but is an eruptive style to follow suit? One may contend that rhetoric served Bialik, Whitman, and Hugo as well. They had humanity on their side; only Nietzsche aimed at superhumanity. There is much of indiscriminate blending in Greenberg's style by vindicating the potential of verb and noun and by closely associating words into conceptual units. Repetitive topicality, projecting ecstatic self-centeredness, often gives way to fine lyrical perception.

***C. S. Lewis, in *A Preface to Paradise Lost,* calls to attention that this "disorganised consciousness" is "discovered by introspection," that is, "by artificially suspending all the normal and outgoing activities of the mind," by stopping concentrated will, logical thought, morals, stable sentiments. Consciousness "ceases when selection ceases."

Two processes, seemingly contradictory, are discernible in Hebrew. The written language still leans heavily on the old sources that are being revealed more and more; at the same time it is withdrawing from them in the domain of morphology and syntax. On the other hand, the spoken tongue is being estranged from the literary language, although even old elements of it may become colloquialized. In Arabic, however, the linguistic sources are being increasingly locked away, partly because of the lessening of interest in religious literature. Without a historical dictionary and critical editions of at least the main works that reflect the literature in its various periods and branches, it seems impossible to put to use the hidden treasures of the language, which had certainly been the creative work of many centuries of shared human comprehension. Given freedom of quest and discussion, the refining process of Arabic may help to preserve its continuity. No doubt, as a result of a careful scrutiny of words and meanings, a part of the material may become valueless.[24]

The present is an interim period for Arabic, to use the words of the Hebrew poet Bialik: "A period when last and first are confused, a time of breaking down and building up, of age and youth." Mahmūd Taymūr sees the Egyptian writer as residing in a strange universe which can only be regarded as a temporary halt. Around him are various schools, and he does not know whether to confine himself to the Arabic heritage and express himself accordingly, or whether to pay attention to the latest novelties of Western literature. Sometimes he will feel nostalgia for forsaken words and stylistic toys; at other times he will affect the speech of the common people; or else he will choose a middle path and use a mixture of both. The literary atmosphere is like a pot in which scattered aims and cultures are cooking together.[25]

Taymūr, like Haykal and Mayy, is looking for individuals of rare quality. Yet under the conditions in Egypt, and, for that matter, in other Arab countries, they cannot function effectively. Here, no one has ever been permitted to develop his thought freely. Discussion of extensive fields of thought—religion, religious literature, various aspects of social and psychological problems—is banned. Non-Muslims are even more restrained in their zest for inquiry.

During this period Arabic has had two stages of advancement, both inspired by the prevailing mood in the world. These were during the 1920's and the second half of World War II. During the late 1930's, the linguistic polemics lessened, and some of the "modernists" laid down their arms. At the same time, partly owing to the impact of fascism, emotional verbosity held sway. It is almost a rule: the language rose and became clearer whenever and wherever the opportunity for freer inquiry was provided.

The recent upheaval in Egypt could not fail to leave its mark on the language. Party strife has been silenced, and aggressiveness diverted to a severe—at the start torrential—criticism of the recent past, both from religious and secular circles. A kind of stylistic grandeur, resounding a deep desire for national redemption, became dominant. But the inward-looking mood subsided soon, supplanted by adventurous power politics which extended to the east, south, and west; the urge for over-all reconstruction is necessarily narrowing. Silence out of fear and verbosity in eulogy and attack, both in new guise, recaptured their old positions.

The sense of the future seems not to have misled those opposed to linguistic innovation, for it is not the tradition of expression alone that is imperiled. Decline in knowledge of *'arabiyya* means decline of tradition in general. Religious and social tradition functioned for centuries within one and the same world-outlook with which the language is also imbued. These polemics must also be understood from the viewpoint of the struggle between "old" and "new" in society.

Common Language and Vernacular

In the period just dealt with, the discussion also centered on the future of the dialects.[26] The unifying forces here are very strong—and yet they seem to work in two directions: weakening the dialectal differences within each country, but without a tendency to eliminate the dialect, and, against this, the steady penetration of more and more domains of life by the *fushā* (literary language). The cultural awakening was bound with the renewal of the literary language. The purists at the end of the last century had no use for dialect. At the beginning of this century there was even a social novel—*Hadīth 'Isā ibn Hishām* by al-Muwaylihī—written in rhymed prose. In the 1920's, however, the vernacular already served the dialogue in novels by Taymūr and plays by Tawfīq al-Hakīm. Its influence widened as theater, gramophone, and radio made use of it. It permeated the press, especially the comics and columns of political strife combined with personal rancor. A kind of literary dialect arose in stories and poems, although its creative scope is limited; as a written language it is necessarily bound to develop away from its sources, including the oral literature, and in a sense may become a dead language. On the other side, as the people's range of interests widens, the vernacular is being saturated more and more with the *fushā*, but it cannot aspire to serve the higher, sublime interests of the human mind.

Various factors may raise the status of a dialect: a romantic current, encouraging the study and compilation of folk literature, a naturalistic trend, or political considerations. In Switzerland the main dialect, being written as well, is regarded as a national possession, in many respects scarcely less valuable than the German literary language. This linguistic independence was particularly stressed there as a matter of self-defence against German National Socialism. A main dialect raised to a status of literary language, alongside of oral literature, may well serve as a spiritual basis to a nascent nationalism. But, under other conditions—such as renascent nationalism—the fostering of the written language serves to promote the sense of national entity. A self-assured nationalism may then turn to the spoken tongue as a source of strength and pride. Yiddish, for centuries mainly a spoken tongue, and as a language of instruction merely an auxiliary to Hebrew, became at the turn of the last century the vehicle of remarkable literary activity.

One of the reasons against raising the Arab vernacular to the status of a literary language is that it would distract from the cultural heritage and weaken the bonds between the Arab countries. Besides, in every country there are many dialects, let alone the dialectal differences between the Arab countries: in phonetics, vocabulary (especially old Arab roots and relics from replaced languages), and morphology. An Egyptian film may contain hundreds of words strange to an Iraqi.

Recently the tide turned against the use of vernacular in print because it supposedly lessened the dignity of literature. The urge to use it in dialogue is diminishing. According to al-Hakīm, it tends to lower the morale on the stage and cheapen it. Only the literary language, reflecting the genius of the nation and its past, serves its cultural life.[27] There are even voices calling for unification on the basis of popularizing the literary language and enriching it with elements of strength from the colloquial idiom, without distorting its essential characteristics.[28]

Meanwhile, the literary language is constantly being revitalized. It is expanding beyond the spheres of exalted life, gaining in simplicity and naturalness, and, in this respect, approaching the vernacular. It is colored by local dialects and cultural standards, and shows differences in the use of technical terms. But it is being unified by press and radio, by literary contacts, and paradoxically, by the fact of being more and more detached from *'arabiyya*.

The problem of this kind of bilingualism may be nearer to a solution when the written language becomes the possession of the entire nation and comes to influence the vernacular at every point. In the meantime, though, the vernacular governs street, home, and office. In a sense, even a writer has to translate himself from the vernacular, which cannot but impede the power of expression. Moreover, the vernacular is a more spontaneous means of expression, forceful even in its gamut of vowels. It even gains in strength and converges into the literature.

Chapter Nine

Some Trends of Thought in Egypt

In almost all the stages of her awakening, especially since the rule of khedive Ismāʿīl in the 1860's and 1870's, Egypt's position in the Arab world has been a matter of uncertainty. To a great degree it has always been politically conditioned. The Arab conquest in the seventh century imposed a language and a religion, but it was not able to efface the identity of the country. Egypt's contact with the West, from the beginning of the last century, stimulated a slow cultural awakening, the basis of which was the revival of Arabic by means of lexicographic and didactic activity and through bringing it into touch with Western literature. From the first this went hand in hand with the struggle for self-rule, and, when the opportunity arose, for expansion wherever possible (south, east, and north). This was bound both to strengthen in Egypt the feeling of attachment to the Arab heritage (which was also stimulated by the intensive study of Arabic in Europe and by the emphasis that Western nationalism placed on the language) and to estrange her from the Arabs through the superior attractions of the West.

Muhammad ʿAlī and his son Ibrāhīm sought to establish an empire, and for this purpose tried to entrench Egypt's position in Syria, or, as it seems to some interpreters, to launch an Arab movement there. Instead they succeeded in securing for Egypt a kind of domestic independence within the Ottoman empire; accordingly, a patriotic feeling of attachment to Egypt evolved into a national feeling, in which the Arab element was only one of the components.[1] The struggle which followed the British conquest sharpened the consciousness of national unity. The independence movement inevitably sought vindication in the spiritual field by nursing the idea of Egyptian nationalism. The Arabs were at that time a negligible factor in political life. The first shoots of political awakening, in the form of secret societies, appeared in Lebanon in the 1880's, while the beginnings of a political movement, with its centers in Cairo and Paris, did not emerge until the eve of World War I. The Arabs sought to see the Ottoman empire weakened, whereas the leaders of the national struggle in Egypt at that time preferred, with varying emphasis, to place their reliance upon it and on the pan-Islamic idea which it sponsored. At the same time, however, Egypt exercised a joint influence with Lebanon through the agency of hundreds of graduates of the schools of Beirut and thousands of other Lebanese and Syrian immigrants to Egypt. It was chiefly they who established in Egypt a manifold press and who thus stimulated the Egyptian national consciousness and, indirectly, the Arab cause. They also helped to adapt the language to the needs of the time, especially as the national struggle implied attention, within the limits allowed to literary work, to social matters such as conditions of the fellah, and women's rights. It was they who labored to train the young generation to understand the theory of evolution and who raised the standard of freedom of thought (Ya'qūb Sarrūf, Farāh Antūn, Dr. Shumayyil, Jurji Zaydān).

After World War I, the political importance of pan-Islam declined, chiefly on account of the break-up of the Ottoman empire. Its position had been precarious from the first, among other things because of its conflict with the national aspirations of the Arabs and of opposing currents of power politics in the Islamic countries. On the other hand, the East began to come into greater esteem, especially on account of the moral and social trends of the national struggle in India and China, which evoked responsive echoes in the West, also. The reforms of Kemal Ataturk also had repercussions. With the first achievements of independence among the Arabs, their political stock, too, went up. For all this, and in spite of the policies of Western governments in Asia and the sharp controversy between Egypt and Great Britain, the active contact with the West was then the driving force in the development of thought in Egypt. A band of bold writers came to the fore.

The need for revolutionary reforms was at that time widely recognized. Haykal, who might have been prophesying about himself, says:

> The people need continuous efforts on the part of hundreds and thousands of its sons in order to gather the fruits of the other peoples' efforts and to disseminate them in the Arab countries. Those hundreds and thousands will endure toil and suffering, some of them will fall exhausted and some will flee in despair. . . .[2]

Taha Husayn was of the same mind:

> Egypt is in need of trials, she has not yet suffered as she ought, troubles have not yet sufficiently accumulated on her. Egypt needs knowledge, Egypt needs a revolution, the worst of her enemies is rest.[3]

On the whole, in the 1920's, which was a period of hope in Europe, the Egyptian intelligentsia turned its face to the West. In literature an endeavor to apply modern criticism could be discerned. A bold critique was written by 'Alī 'Abd al-Rāziq on *Islam and the Bases of Government*, contesting the sanctity of the caliphate and advocating separation of religion from secular rule. In 1926, Taha Husayn wrote an essay on Arab pre-Islamic poetry calling into question most of its antiquity.[4] Ismā'īl Mazhar, continuing work already done by his predecessors, expounded the theory of evolution and sought to illustrate from it the history of Arabic thought. Later on the writings of Bint al-Shāti' on the condition of the fellah aroused great concern in the public. Whether from the pressure of the authorities or because of the stifling atmosphere, silence was soon enjoined on these attempts at modern research.

Actually, at that time there was much confusion in the trends of thought, even within the sphere of rationalist approach. Haykal attempted to find a common measure for them, but only by placing the primary source of cultural revival in the West.[5] Taha Husayn[6] and Salāma Mūsā[7]—this Fabian offshoot on Egyptian soil—argued for Western predominance in the Egyptian mentality. Neither they nor Haykal sought to depreciate the cultural links to the pre-Islamic period. Widespread too, not unlike the Phoenician trend in Lebanon, was the tendency—purely literary—to place emphasis on the first link in this chain of descent, that is, the Pharaonic period, when the country was "the cradle of human culture." This notion may have been stimulated by the expanding Egyptology. Partisans of this line imagined traces of this period in the soul of the fellah of our own day, in linguistic remains, and social mores. A somewhat modified attitude was adopted by al-'Aqqād, and also by Mansūr Fahmī, both of whom were more anxious to foster the link with the East. Those, however, who sought to expound Islam on rational grounds—the brothers 'Alī and Mustafā 'Abd al-Rāziq—saw in the culture of Islam a basis for the culture of Egypt, which the creative link with the West ought not to displace. In this period the course of modernist thought, with all its conflicting variations, was on the side of synthesis.[8]

Egyptian literature at that time seemed to be passing through a period of enlightenment, first and foremost in view of its mood of expansiveness. Its exuberance of language was not due only to the inherited wealth of expression or to a leaning to chatty picturesqueness. Salāma Mūsā in his essays and Mahmūd Taymūr in short stories urged self-control on their gift of language. This expansiveness was chiefly due to that youthful straining after new horizons, out of eagerness to impart to others ideas that have been revealed to the writer. This explains the predominance of collections in literature—collections of articles and essays and stories first published in magazines. This, too, explains the versatility of some writers; in many cases feuilletons and essays, poetry and criticism, novels, biography, and research issued from a single pen.

The influence of the Enlightenment literature of the West, especially that of the French, turned out to be in the main only formal. In a movement of enlightenment that is essentially literary, criticism by its nature tends to be polemical, even excessively violent.[9] But in the corresponding period of Egyptian literature, criticism moved within a narrow circle. Scrutiny of the sources of religion was practically forbidden, unless for the purpose of asserting tradition, and so, too, was criticism of religious literature; anyone who attempted to speak his mind openly was penalized. Social criticism was more of a routine character and proceeded mainly from a philanthropic approach; it was not allowed a free hand to deal with causes and developments. Needless to say, it was not allowed to anchor itself to a social idea and, in virtue of that idea, to a program worthy of the gravity of the situation.

For all this, it was a period of upsurge. Imaginative literature in the form of novels and short stories, plays and even essays, had been introduced during and after World War I. In discussing the possibilities of Egyptian literature, judging merely from Egyptian achievements, H. A. R. Gibb even looked for an analogy in Russian literature, which "has expressed the distinctive contribution of the Russian genius" to modern civilization.[10] True, the resemblance between the social problems in pre-revolutionary Russia and those of Egypt is striking, but one should not overlook the difference in the nature of the link with Western culture, which became very soon—from the second half of the last century—one of creative reciprocity. Russian literature in the last century, invested with an immense gift for human sympathy, was occupied with a message of freedom. In spite of its contact with the heritage of European Enlightenment, Egyptian literature did not receive revolutionary impulses from it, and thus the impact which it made on society was extremely feeble.[11]

In the 1930's, literary activity took a sharp turn toward a religious, in a way, conservative mode of thought. In 1933, Taha Husayn, prompted by a French work, opened with his biography of the Prophet a series of life stories of the early heroes and men of genius in Islam. Into this vessel, which may have served as a protection against charges of heresy, could be poured matters of topical interest. This pattern, headed in Europe by Emil Ludwig, was taken up by Haykal, himself inspired by two French writers, by al-'Aqqād, al-Hakīm and young imitators. They differed widely in method and approach (analytical, apologetic, reflective, or imaginative). This kind of writing was liberally supported by the authorities. Taha Husayn sees in these works, produced in 1933-1946, after the pressure of *"despotisme politico-clérical"* had been relieved, a literature of religious inspiration.[12] The temper of the 1930's also lent itself to it: values of the West fell out of favor, hero worship gained ground, and the past was extolled. In fairness, a humanist trend was pursued not exclusively in guise of the past. Suffice it to mention works ranging from realism to symbolism by Taymūr, Taha Husayn, al-Hakīm.

Contrary to expectations, the Treaty of 1936 did not introduce any constructive period in Egypt. Quarrels soon sprang up between the Wafd and the young king, around whom rallied religious leaders who favored Muslim unity and the heads of the opposition. Ambitions for the caliphate hovered around the royal court. From 1936 the government turned more and more to Arab affairs, but still without identifying itself unreservedly. The impact of fascism showed itself in the dissemination of pan-Arab slogans of grandeur—from one ocean to the other, all-Muslim unity—adopted by Young Egypt, the Young Men's Muslim Association, and the Muslim Brethren.

With World War II the idea of Arab unity gained currency in Egypt to an unprecedented degree. As far as Egypt was concerned, this may also have been a manifestation of independence which could not come to fulfilment in a great constructive action. There was the prospect of joint defence against various enemies, among them Zionism, French and British *isti'mār* (imperialism or colonialism), and of joint activity in the international forum. Very soon this became the great theme for publicists and was acclaimed by many, including opponents and doubters. Attractive, too, was the idea of cooperation, of an attachment to a cultural entity, prospects of economic and cultural expansion. Stress was laid on the community of language as the chief mark of kinship, or as the main factor for producing unity. For all this, there were definite limits to this ferment. Through the improvement in the prospects of the Arabs to attain independence, various federative solutions gained currency. There was no thought of curtailing the political independence enjoyed or striven for by each state, and certainly few, if any, were seduced by the vision of an Arab empire. On the other hand, the leadership of Egypt was regarded as self-evident. Its numerical and economic superiority placed it in the relation of guardian to the weak, with a natural inclination to guide, and alongside of this a kind of political reserve was discernible, which suggested that the improvement of Egypt lay first and foremost in self-improvement. In any case, the feature common to all the intellectuals of Egypt, whether traditionalists or rationalists, was that they all took for granted a spiritual predominance in the Arab world.[13]

The years 1943-45 were a period of comparative freedom of thought, and consequently of the written word. Owing to the ideas that were current then in the democratic camp, and to the certainty of the defeat of fascism, the reins were slackened somewhat. Projects of reform and planning were in the minds of all. For the first time in the history of the country, there appeared some periodicals and popular works of a socially inspired bent and of some analytical value, mostly left-wing or Communist-sponsored.

After the war the struggle over the Suez Canal, the Sudan, and Palestine became a focus for the political emotions of the intelligentsia, the social problem acting as the leaven. There was a widespread belief that the ruling elements were not willing or even competent to grapple with it. Nearly all at that time used socialist phraseology and adapted their premises to it— from the Wafd and Young Egypt in its latest metamorphosis to the Muslim Brethren. The essentials of British policy in Egypt made it easy to give a Socialist coloring to the national struggle. Since Western social-democracy was identified with British Labor policy, alignment was sought with the Soviet Bloc by way of neutralism, or openly taking sides.

Salāma Mūsā distinguishes in some sweeping generalizations three currents in Egyptian postwar literature. Among the classicists, who are captivated by the greatness of the Arab stock, he includes—in spite of sharp differences in their attachment to the past and all the metamorphoses of their own intellectual past—Haykal, who in his books on the pillars of Islam also applies standards of Western criticism; al-'Aqqād and Ahmad Amīn, who adopt, each in his own way, a kind of middle attitude; and al-Zayyāt, the staunch adherent of tradition and its style. The second current is represented by Tawfīq al-Hakīm and Taha Husayn. The trend of their thought is Western, but still they "tend to be conservative in their outlook." Finally there is a current of the progressives, partly Socialists of the Fabian type. The main sphere of their interest is Western civilization. The most gifted among them was the poet and critic Abū Shādī. Most of the Coptic writers can be ranged with them.[14]

The literary scene, as it is revealed by Abū Shādī, perhaps the most unconventional poet, is even gloomier. A number of essayists of repute, including Salāma Mūsā and Taha Husayn, sought to foster humanism. But a strict censorship, servile criticism, and party favoritism deprive the beginner of security, and only a few are able to rise above the depressing environment. Poetry makes no contribution to human sublimation. Every attempt to penetrate to a higher level of thought provokes a storm. The story-writer has a rather larger measure of freedom, but with the exception of one or two, they do not turn this opportunity of expressing humanistic ideals to the best account. The story as a rule barely touches the crucial problems of the people.[15]

Fear of economic extinction forced the writer to bow before the powers that be, even though with mental reservation. Many writers had to embark on party journalism, but even economic independence could not make them free from social fear, fear of the powerful and the public alike.[16]

The new regime did not remove the millstone that weighed on intellectual life; in some respects it replaced it with a new one. At first, there was a good deal of spontaneous acclaim for it; in the eyes of many—both orthodox and reformers, workers and fellahin—the initial promises and performances seemed to be the first signs that heralded liberation. The spokesmen of this paternalist regime seemed to steer without ideological guidance, that is, without a clear vision of a new social edifice. At first, the Liberation Rally argued both against socialism, as infringing on the liberties of the individual, and against capitalism, although the regime tended to promote it, even with the aid of foreign capital, on a nonmonopolist basis. Later on, 'Abd al-Nāsir adopted a vague Socialist attitude; working for the good of people, not through the people, was the line of argument. The last version of his aim is a "democratic Socialist co-operative society." True, this regime opened channels to constructive planning, but against this it shut sources of free intellectual argument. It necessarily failed to create a genuine popular movement in support of its aims. An atmosphere of flattery and fear in a one-man show is hardly conducive to it.

Ever since the *isnād* literature, based on a chain of transmitters, emerged in the early centuries of Islam, authority has dominated literary activity. The real test may come when authoritarianism has, humanly speaking, come to an end, and the individual will be able to move freely within the entire compass of his thoughts. The upheaval of 1952 opened to literature areas of human concern but, against this, narrowed the scope of other areas.

In retrospect the creative effects of one and a half centuries of intellectual contact with Europe seem negligible. Commencing approximately with the British conquest, the European impact on cultural life is clearly discernible; the thought of the intelligentsia was dominated by the evolutionary doctrines and political philosophy of the West. In this spirit, Mustafā Kāmil and Qāsim Amīn sought to give effect to the national awakening. Religious reformers—al-Afghānī and Muhammad 'Abduh—sought in arguments with the West to point to the creative faculties of Islam. The ideas of Spencer and Darwin vied in men's minds with those of Voltaire and Rousseau. After World War I, signs of a tentative advance toward an outspoken humanistic attitude could be seen. In the period of independence the process of westernization in science and technique was accelerated, but correspondingly, as H. A. R. Gibb has pointed out, the process of "easternizing" the achievements of westernization, that is, of divorcing them from the social and moral ideas behind them, set in.[17]

The negative elements of Arabism, elements of protest (against internal enemies, against Western imperialism, which, after all, set a score of Arab countries free from their centuries-old yoke) still dominate the air. The far-sighted already point to the real test to come, that is, the vitality of positive aspects. One of them is a keen need of social justice. The prevailing mood is that of paternalist populism, with all the trappings of "street democracy" and with socialism as its extreme coloring. Within the limited scope of questioning, a ferment of tendencies in literature is noticeable (from a humanist approach in the image of Taha Husayn, to symbolism or existentialism skilfully attached to Sūfism, or social realism carrying the day). There are many possibilities to employ a medieval genre or theme for creative purposes (Taha Husayn, al-Hakīm). A social novel by al-Sharqāwī about the Egyptian village—*The Earth*—stirred up the social conscience. A novel by Muhammad Kāmil Husayn—*City of Wrong*—unfolds acute moral problems in a setting of the crucifixion of Christ. It stands out in its stirring humanity.

In a sense, these trends are a substitute for frustrated—because imposed—political conformity. All the same, a group of more independent writers entered the scene, and a few impressive works point to an acute interest focused on the people's well-being. Taha Husayn even saw in this shift of interest to the people, implicit in populism, a danger of dependence on the people's tastes.[18]

The feebleness of the achievements of westernization did not come essentially from any reaction against the values of a foreign culture, but mainly from the heavy pressure of the regime on intellectual life, and the obstinate determination of the ruling caste to maintain the upper hand at all costs. It is probable that if intellectual freedom had been ensured in Egypt, the reaction to Western culture would have produced lasting and creative results. The lesson of India is revealing.[19]

Part Four

BACKGROUND TO
SOCIAL HISTORY

Chapter Ten

Land Tenure in Iraq

After the end of World War I, large landownership in Iraq continued to grow without interruption. It was probably in this period that the greater part of the best and most accessible land passed into the hands of a few. This laid the economic foundation for a community of which over 60 percent is engaged in agriculture. This fundamental fact has powerfully affected the social and political life of the country.

How did this state of affairs come to pass? When the state was founded, it took possession, in theory, of the greatest part of the cultivated and ultimately cultivable land. State lands consisted of the following:

sanniyya (crown lands), acquired mostly in the 1890's by Sultan Abdul Hamid and which comprised nearly a third of the then valuable land of the country. After the upheaval of 1908, it was turned over (*mudawwara*) to the civil administration but retained its separate organization.[1] Subsequently, after 1918, it became merged with *miri* land. In 1913 the area of mudawwara was estimated at 546,200 hectares.

miri (state domain), the "usufructuary possession (tasarruf) of which was granted out on a registered tenure"[2] prescribed by the Ottoman Land Code of 1857. Actually, possession of *miri* land in tribal areas was not always granted. Subsequently, after 1918, *miri* evolved, in theory, to a more definite status: "retained in the full legal ownership [*raqaba*] and possession of the State which may be exploited directly or indirectly at its discretion, subject to due recognition of established occupancy rights."[3] In fact, squatters' rights did not prevent landlords or the authorities from evicting tribes or groups of fellahin.

mawāt, dead or idle land.

matrūka, land reserved for public purposes (roads, rivers, etc.).

tapu, state land, the legal possession of which is granted on a registered tenure as laid down by the Ottoman Land Code. Tapu title deeds conferred no freehold rights, and technically, on any transfer, the government resumed the grant.[4]

Tapu tenure was introduced in Iraq by Midhat Pasha, *wali* of Baghdad, about 1870. Grants of tapu rights amounted to "permanent alienation subject to uninterrupted cultivation."[5] But neglect of the land was hardly ever penalized. As actual rights went, this form of tenure was not very much different from undiluted private property (*mulk*).

The main purposes of tapu tenure were establishment of contact between the cultivator and the government, recognition of customary rights to land as well as tapping fresh sources of income for the treasury. But, as far as it was implemented, it resulted in alienation of by far the greater part of the then cultivated land to noncultivators and helped to perpetuate insecurity of tenure. Grants of tapu areas were often registered over the heads of possessors of, or claimants to, customary rights, in the name of townsmen (by auction or bribery), retired Turkish officials, army officers, and creditors in payment of debts owed by the treasury. The authorities being unprepared for this enormous task, records of ownership became more and more confused. This system was particularly damaging in areas of tribal activity, which often stretched far beyond actual areas of grazing and cultivation.[6] Subsequent regulations, of about 1880 and 1891, banned grant of tapu tenure on payment of valuation fees or by auction in the vilayets of Baghdad and Basra. Nonetheless, grant of tapu land went on.

As regards landownership, the new state seemed in an ideal position. In theory, all the unalienated miri land—that is, land not registered in the names of private persons (mulk, or since 1871, tapu) or the ministry of *waqf*—and echeated rural and urban properties, were state domains and the occupants were tenants-at-will. "Right of occupancy was not contemplated by the existing law."[7]

The British Military Administration found the land registry in a chaotic state. Records had been destroyed or taken away by retreating Turkish officials. Many claimed to have refrained from registration of their land. The wording of title deeds was vague to such extent that boundaries were unidentifiable. Divergent claims of tapu owners holding title deeds, and tribal occupants were a residue of the tapu system.[8]

The policy of the Military Administration has been "to reduce to order the chaos inherited from the Turks by restoring authority to the tribal sheikhs and using them . . . to carry out the behests of the supreme authority."[9] As early as July 1918, the Tribal Criminal and Civil Disputes Regulation empowered certain administrative officials to nominate a sheikh or a body of sheikhs to perform judicial functions, that is, "to settle according to Arab tribal usage any dispute in which a tribesman is involved."[10] At that time, a major part of the population still professed various degrees of tribal attachment. In this way, the authority of the sheikhs among the tribes was enhanced, so much so that disputes over the holding of miri land were settled and "thousands of cases registered for settlement under it."[11] In 1918 the sheikhs of 'Amāra had made their support of the British administration conditional on permission to retain the system of land tenure prevalent in their zone, without any outsiders being associated with them.[12] Naturally, those sheikhs who had not joined the revolt of 1920 also reaped benefits in terms of landholding. Furthermore, sheikhs who had taken part in the outbreak of 1920 were restored to their positions by means of redistribution of the estates leased from the government.[13] The above regulation remained in force after the cessation of the mandate.

The national government, from October 1920 onward, has followed the same line. Even the committee set up by the provisional government under Naqīb for settlement of disputes between tribes and the landowning clan Sa'dūn in Muntafiq was composed entirely of landowners and took a decision favorable to them.[14] The government had to keep a kind of balance between town notables aspiring to a share in state lands and the tribal sheikhs on one side, and between the sheikhs themselves on the other.[15] But not only political aspects had to be taken into account. Long-established occupancy claims, in tribal areas and in villages, and various customary rights in state land could not be disregarded. Disputes had to be settled, especially in the tribal areas: between the paramount sheikh and members of his family, between him and sectional chiefs, between these and the rank and file of the tribe, between tribesmen and their landlords from another tribe, between tribes over traditional boundaries of grazing and cultivation areas.[16] The process of tribal disintegration was so rapid that already in the 1920's there was little tribal land that was communally owned.[17]

The land laws and ordinances passed from 1919 to 1930 were only measures of expediency, but they resulted in rapid promotion of large landownership. They empowered local officers to determine who had the usufructuary rights in tapu land and also to investigate the identity of men who have taken possession of miri land. The Unregistered Sales Confirmation Law of 1921, consolidated by the Unregistered Sales Law of April 1922, dealt with registration of sales and mortgages of land (mulk and tapu) effected during the war and after the occupation, when Tapu offices were closed. Evidently, registration on the basis of documents transmitted to the local authorities for inquiry and without thorough survey of the land, meant preparing the ground for conflicting claims. As orchards and date palm groves had been planted without title deeds to the land, instructions were issued after 1923 and a law passed (Tamlik of Maghrusa Unalienated Land Law for 1927) providing for alienation of this and adjoining unplanted land upon payment of full or half value, or, if fully planted, without it.[18] Since miri land was one of the government's sources of revenue, encroachment on it was often "settled by the payment of the equivalent value."[19]

The Law for the Encouragement of Cultivators for the Use of Pumps, 1926, exempted from government share, for a period of four consecutive harvests—two winter crops and two summer crops—"all enhancement of land produce resulting from the use of pumps in respect of land already under cultivation, and sim-

ilarly the whole land produce resulting from the use of the said
pumps in respect of lands which were previously uncultivated,"
including "land which has been left fallow for four consecutive
years preceding the date of the installation of the pumps."[20] At
the close of 1928 nearly 2,000 grants of land to develop by pump
irrigation had been issued, mostly to wealthy town residents,
deputies, and tribal sheikhs. The total area affected by the
2,000 pumps in 1931 (against about 140 in 1921) was over 10,000
square kilometers. If the land was free from occupancy claims,
the pump owner himself was granted a ten-year lease. Otherwise, the lease of the land was given to the sheikh or sirkal (sectional chief or agent) possessing occupancy rights, and the pump
owner was allowed to make a ten-year cultivation agreement,
in return for a portion of the yearly produce or for payment
of the price of the pumps at a high interest, with the occupants.[21]
Since every kind of nepotism was put to use, grants of areas
free from occupancy right were subsequently made by auction.[22] Owing to the boom in world market prices, the value
of the land increased, especially before the depression in 1929,
and consequently disputes occurred over occupancy rights between sheikhs, or between them and the pump owners over
land and labor. Pump owners even found opportunities to force
landowning cultivators to work on a share basis.

For all this, the *ad hoc* legislation still asserted, to a certain
degree, the legal ownership of the state. The subsequent legislation translated control over land into rights.

It was officially stated in 1932 that "not less than three-fifths
of cultivated, and perhaps nine-tenths of ultimately cultivable
land in Iraq belongs nominally and legally to the State."[23] The
conditions of land tenure were then in "various stages of divorce
from innumerable primitive practices":

Broadly speaking, those who occupy and cultivate miri land
are allowed to do so in the absence of more influential opposition. Possession is ordinarily nine points of the law; but
neither long possession nor any other mode of acquisition
confers security. Personal influence with the most effective

arbiter is commonly the decisive factor at any moment in any particular land dispute; and anyone may find the most convincing claim set aside.[24]

The legislation which began with the Land Settlement Law No. 50, 1932, and the Lazma Law No. 51, 1932, consolidated by the Land Settlement Law No. 29 of 1938 and by the Lazma Law No. 33 of 1938 amending Lazma Law No. 51 of 1932, embodied a deliberate policy. It was a kind of legalization of a continuous process. It inaugurated a period of definite transfer of land to the ruling few. The two land settlement laws laid down a classification of the land into *mulk, waqf, matrūka* and three kinds of *miri*.

1. *miri sirf* (including *mawāt*), undiluted state domain.
2. *miri tapu*, a kind of permanent tenure which conferred rights of transfer, mortgage and inheritance. In its vague wording the law opened up extensive possibilities for accumulation of tapu land. Under it, tapu was made to include all lands which were inscribed in the registry as tapu or if other documents justified their inscription as tapu; land which had been planted for not less than ten years with not less than forty trees (at least twenty fruit-bearing and the rest nonfruit-bearing) per donum; land where the owner or his successor could prove that it has been used productively for a period of ten years prior to the date of settlement. With the abolition of the land tax (Law for extinguishing land tax No. 20 of 1939) against an equivalent of twelve times the tax average to be payed over a period of ten years, tapu is hardly distinguishable from mulk. Law No. 20 of 1941 amending the above law provides for easier conditions of remission in the case of persons who pay the equivalent value over shorter periods.
3. *miri lazma*. A grant of lazma to a person, or his successor, who enjoyed the usufruct of miri land not registered in tapu within the fifteen years prior to the date of settlement. The rights of the lazma owner are the same as those of the tapu owner, only that the government may specify from time to time conditions for transferring and mortgaging it. Lazma areas, when

fully planted (with fruit-bearing or nonfruit-bearing trees), entitle the owner to inscribe them as tapu without payment at any time after ten years subsequent to the date of planting. This form of tenure was meant to anchor in the law traditionally sanctioned lazma (area of residence and work) rights of the tribes who, for a long period, had occupied and cultivated miri land. Actually, it was the rights of the sheikhs which were mainly guaranteed by it, and it helped to convert tribal relations into a feudal pattern. Similarly, lazma rights were granted to pump owners to areas serviced by the pump, unless they were cultivated before its installation. Men of influence in parliament and high offices were given the opportunity, by means of *faits accomplis* and various kinds of evidence, to bring pressure to bear on the authorities. Proof, however tenuous, that a crop was produced in a year sufficed to accord to powerful men tracts of tens of thousands donums without payment. Contrary to a clause in the Lazma law of 1932 (art. 8), neglect of lazma land for four consecutive years without reasonable excuse was not penalized with withdrawal of the grant.[25]

The Law governing the Rights and Duties of Cultivators, 1932, defined the powers and sphere of operations of the landowner, the sirkal, and the fellah. In practice it was calculated, by tying the peasant to the land, to tighten control over labor. Under it, a fellah who owed an agricultural debt to the landowner was not at liberty to leave his place of work. If he left, no government service or municipality or registered company or estate was permitted to employ him, and if it did so, it had to put aside a third of his wages for paying off the debt. This law was one which could not possibly be enforced, and in spite of it tens of thousands of fellahin migrated to the towns.

After the death of Faysal, tribal discontent, fed on long-standing land disputes, was exploited by the struggling factions; the party which came to power helped the partisans among the sheikhs to appropriate estates, or to solve land disputes in their favor.[26] In the polemical literature called forth by the first military *coup d'etat* in 1936, the authorities were reproached with transferring state land to patrons and protégés.[27] As late as 1950 the government still carried out transfers of land. A landowning member of the ruling party had appropriated land arbitrarily, while on the other hand the tenants were evicted with government help.[28]

Vast areas of miri sirf were leased under the Land Tax Law, No. 73, 1936. It provides for leasing vacant lands to persons having no land in their possession, preferably from the same or neighboring district, to exploit it directly or indirectly for a contract period of three, and successively for no more than six years.

Mulk and tapu ownership was also promoted by the Law of selling miri sirf land, No. 11, 1940.[29] The law stipulates to register as mulk: (1) miri sirf land "of which the usufructuary possession has been enjoyed . . . by a person who has erected a building or planted tress not less than 40 per donum on it" against an equivalent to be fixed by the authorities; (2) miri granted in lazma against half the equivalent value; (3) miri granted in tapu against one-fourth of the equivalent value. The miri sirf land may be granted in tapu, by public auction, provided that the area of each plot does not exceed 5,000 donums. Land granted in lazma may be classed as granted in tapu against one-fourth of its equivalent value. Ministers and officials of the liwā as well as their relatives, agents, or servants are barred from participation in this auction. Thus, in order to reduce the inflated volume of currency in circulation, extensive tracts were transferred to town dwellers who had grown rich from the rise in prices and from contracts. Tracts of land thereupon passed from hand to hand at doubled prices, without the transferences being entered in the register.

Even small holders' projects were affected by the current practices. The Dujayla Land Settlement Law, No. 23, 1945, was meant to inaugurate a policy of promoting small ownership. The Dujayla project, to the west of Kūt, covered tracts of irrigated and irrigable land, tribal lazma, partly neglected, and miri sirf. The government, to oblige the sheikhs of five tribes who claimed previous occupancy and use of the land, handed over to them 76,000 acres on a payment of about two dinar per acre over ten years, for perpetual water rights to the Dujayla canal. Fifty thousand fellahin applied for the remaining 88,000 acres.[30]

The Hawīja irrigation project in the Kirkūk liwā, to which 220,000 donums were assigned, including 13,000 miri lazma and 6,000 miri tapu, was based on units of 80 donums. In spite of this, tracts of 500 to 1,000 donums were leased to men with influence, and plots were added to these which had been registered in the name of nonexistent members of their tribe.[31]

The land legislation from 1951, although with no retroactive force, marks a shift in land policy. The Miri Sirf Land Development Law, No. 43, 1951, and the Ordinance No. 4 of 1952 for the amendment of this law were meant to reserve cultivable land for small holders' settlement. They fixed the size of maximum holdings to be granted: 20 donums on mountainous land, 100 on flow irrigated land, 200 on low pumping areas (where water from tributaries is raised to a height not exceeding two meters), 500 on high pumping land (where water is raised from the main rivers to a height of not more than two meters), and 400 on rain-fed land. Areas of development are to be established. Units allotted to the settler are to be gratuitously registered in tapu after ten years from the date of signing the usufruct contract. The settler is not permitted to donate or sell his rights to others during the first ten years. The owners of mulk and lands granted by lazma or tapu that are to benefit from the flow irrigation schemes are given the choice of ceding a quarter of their lands, or paying to the treasury a share in the total expenditure incurred by the government for the scheme. Arable miri sirf land may not be sold, leased, or granted under lazma terms.

Law No. 36 of 1952 amending the Land Settlement Amendment Law No. 29 of 1938 was meant to bar tribal sheikhs from appropriating miri sirf land granted in lazma for the purpose of tribal settlement. The land granted in lazma must be registered in tapu in the names of the tribesmen belonging to the tribe to be settled. Sale, mortgage or lease of this land is prohibited for five years from the date of the grant.

Under these laws six larger and some smaller settlement projects had been initiated. Thus the growth of large landownership had been arrested, but these laws, even if properly applied, did not attack the land problems at their roots.

Some regional features

The area in 'Amāra is miri sirf (previously mudawwara), with the exception of some stretches of tapu. Since Turkish times the government used to lease out the land to about 200 men, sheikhs and some townsmen, for a term of five, later four or three years, by nominally putting it up to auction. At the end of the term the circle started again almost automatically, so that, practically speaking, the lease was permanent. In 1946, it was estimated that 95 percent of the cultivable land was given to 130 men; three-fourths of it to thirteen sheikhs.[32] By contrast, the area put to use in each season did not exceed 400,000 donums. The estates of the sheikhs are sown partly with rice, where flood irrigation is possible, and partly with barley and wheat. The townsmen, whose estates are not large by comparison, own the larger part of the pump-irrigated palm groves on both sides of the Tigris and its tributaries; they also grow wheat, barley, fruit trees and vegetables.

Large holders lease the land to sublessees, for a fixed rent paid in cash or in kind, and these work it with fellahin or rent it to them or to minor sirkals. To give an illustration of the position in 1946: In the zone of Kahla, 90 percent or more of the fertile land was held by two families. A sublessee rented 150 donums of first-class, flow-irrigated land in return for thirty tons of rice. In a good year the area yields sixty tons, which is two tons for each of the thirty fellahin who cultivate it. The sublessee first deducted compulsory taxes: 100 kgs. *ka'āda* for the sheikh; forty kgs. *ma'mūriyya* for the sheik's agent; twenty kgs. *qahwatiyya* for the upkeep of the coffee center; twenty kgs. as tax for the smith and the carpenter for repairing the ploughing implements and the irrigation boats; twenty kgs. threshing tax for the use of the threshing implements. So, too, small optional taxes and a tax for the pump-worker. In some places they had to surrender annually 3 percent of the cattle. If the seeds were provided by the sublessee, the fellah received a quarter of the produce, that is, 450 kgs. From this he had to pay his debts to the sheikh or the moneylender. The share of the sublessee, after deduction of about five tons for seeds, was about 5.5 tons. From the sheikh's share, nine tons were given to the government and about as much to his assistants and servants. From these figures the income of a sheikh from a tract that was divided among a hundred sublessees can easily be calculated.

Owners of 2,000-5,000 donums usually worked the land by means of fellahin. If the seeds were provided by the fellah, the owner received 50, sometimes 40 percent of rice. Otherwise, the fellah received 20 to 25 percent of the rice. Before the division, however, the sheikh separated from the produce, if it was not too scanty, the compulsory taxes, and sometimes also the optional taxes.

In the absence of proper supervision, the terms of the agreement with the government are not carried out, whether in regard to assigning areas for various products, or to repairing dams and clearing out channels. Similarly there is no proper supervision over the additional soil formed by the silting up of marshes. The approximative sharing out of the produce naturally tends to harm the fellah. In this province a kind of feudalism is firmly entrenched. The fellah is commandeered for various services such as work on the dams, road building for cars, and so forth. Scores of retainers and armed guards carry out the orders of the lord. Palaces, peopled by harems and served by slaves, are a feature of the landscape. In contrast, in many villages bilharzia undermines the health of 80 to 95 percent of the population. Steeped in debts as they are, the fellahin have fled to the towns in tens of thousands.[32]

The Law for granting lazma rights in miri sirf land in 'Amāra liwā, No. 42, 1952, was the first attempt to break the feudal hold of the sheikhs. It provided that the lessee shall be granted 200 donums in a rice-growing flow unit or its equivalent (400 donums of flow land growing summer crops, 800 of flow land growing winter crops, 1,600 of lift-irrigated land, and 3,200 of fallow land capable of cultivation). If land growing winter or summer crops other than rice was suitable for rice growing, it must be regarded as such. In addition, he shall be granted half the rest of the unit. The share of the sublessee shall be an area equivalent to one-quarter of flow land leased to the lessee, no more than 150 and no less than thirty donums, and that of the fellah and his family no more than fifteen donums. The fellah may not mortgage land granted to him in lazma for a period of five years. As to the application of the law, "most of the landlords and sheikhs received with their influential pressure more land than they were entitled to, according to the law."[34]

The law was superceded, with no retroactive force, by the Law No. 28 of 1954. It provides that one-half of the holding is to be granted to the lessee and sublessees, and an equal half to the fellahin. A fellah's family is entitled to one unit in the whole of the province. But no mention is made with regard to the lessee or sublessee.[35]

In the *Kut* liwā the land settlement has been completed. Out of 4,750,149 donums of cultivable land 1,595,466 have been inscribed as miri lazma, 618,974 as miri tapu, and practically all the rest is miri sirf. Of the uncultivable area 1,124,000 donums out of 1,458,176 are miri sirf. There are 1,531 holdings in the liwā. Of the lazma and tapu lands 52 percent are estates over 10,000 donums, and of these 70 percent are 100,000-200,000 each; 45 percent 10,001-100,000 each. Actually there are a number of estates over 300,000 donums each.[56]

In the *Hilla* province, with an area of 2,100,000 donums, the cadastral survey by February 1952 covered 94 percent of the cultivable 1,624,834 donums. 758,091 were inscribed as miri lazma, 573,148 as miri tapu, and 262,092 as miri sirf of which the uncultivable area is to the extent of 192,575 donums. 17.5 percent of the lazma and tapu lands were estates of 10,001-100,000 donums, 41 percent of 1,001-10,000 each.[37]

The large estates in *Baghdad* liwā originated mostly after World War I, from the time that pumps came into use. The lazma law confirmed the de facto possession of the land by pump owners. Estates of tens of thousands of donums passed into the possession of one man or one family. Only a small part of the land remained in the hands of Kurdish groups who had cultivated it previously; some of them were banished.

Land speculation had its share in the emergence of a strong moneyed class in Baghdad. After World War I the government distributed some of the waqf and miri sirf land for housing purposes. Land speculators went into partnership with high officials in exploiting the land.[38]

In *Diyāla* liwā, whose irrigated area includes the best fruit gardens of the country—palm and citrus groves—the system of *mughārasa* is in vogue. In this way many villages have sprung up in the liwā. The agreements between the fellah and the landowner give rise to disputes, and many devices are used to settle the disputes to the latter's advantage.

The origin of many estates dates back to the 1880's and 1890's. Influential townsmen in Baghdad came to possess land in Diyāla. About 160,000 donums of tapu land were then inscribed in the name of a certain Greek in liquidation of a debt owed to him by the Ottoman treasury. The tribes of the region had been disputing his ownership for years. In the end the estate was sold to merchants. The tract of Qizil Rubat—about 80,000 donums— was in the possession of one of the heads of the Jāf tribe, and to pay off debts he sold half of it to wealthy men of Baghdad.[39]

Date groves, stretching on the banks of Shatt al-'Arab, are the principal source of livelihood in *Basra* liwā. In the whole liwā there are about eleven million fruit-bearing date trees. Although there are in it about 6,060 holdings, 5,500 smallholders own only about a third of the area; the lion's share is in the hands of "date pashas." All types of ownership are to be found here. The date gardens are worked directly by the owner himself or by fellahin, hired for a short period against payment, or for a season, even a year, against a share in the yield of the palms as well as the fruit trees and vegetables grown between them. In this case, they have no right in the land and the trees. In case of indirect farming, the owner provides the land and the fellah performs all the necessary work. The agreement may be confined to the products of the palms alone, or include fruit trees and vegetables, or the fellah's share in the plants themselves. In any case, the owner's share is 81.25 percent (an ownership's quarter, and three-quarters of the balance). Sometimes the fellah receives, in addition, 18.75 percent of the land and registers it in tapu or its equivalent in cash (tab'a tathminiyya).[40]

In theory, the *ta'ābūn* who plant the trees were reckoned as partners of the landowners, but in fact expulsion from the villages took place in consequence of sales. The interests of smallholders and fellahin were thwarted by wealthy planters, some of whom also own packing houses, and frequently their interests as industrialists took precedence. There were plenty of devices for blinding the eyes of the authorities.

About 55 percent of the date trees are in Kerbelā, Diwāniyya, Diyāla, Hilla, Muntafiq, Baghdad and other provinces. The economic relations between the landlords and the fellahin are, with some modifications, similar to those in Basra.[41] In Diyāla, Kerbelā and Baghdad there are also groves of thirty to forty donums, especially on the outskirts of the towns. The date groves in the country, about 32 million trees, cover an area of 1,500,000 donums.

It is said, by way of generalization, that in *Northern Iraq* the degree of inequality in landownership is similar to that in Syria. In the mountainous districts tribal ties have somewhat mitigated the control of the aghas over miri land, but with the settlement they sought to inscribe it as tapu. Relationships of mere control became legalized in title deeds. In some areas around the towns and in Christian villages, smaller holdings are more common. In the plains areas large tapu ownership is dominant. Its beginning is traceable to the 1870's. The aghas of the villages, who acted as guards and tax-collectors, appropriated land to themselves. Town dwellers gained possession of land by tricks for which the system of registration provided an opportunity, or as a result of mortgages for debt. In Mosul, especially in the south, where pumps have been installed, the land principally belongs to absentee landowners. In the district of Tel'afar, which is a wheat and barley growing area, huge tracts were received by sheikhs of Shammar, under pretext of settling their tribes. Actually, they farmed them on their own or leased to tractor owners in Mosul.[42]

Economic relations

In general, share cropping is in vogue, comprising four or five partners: the sheikh or absentee landowner, the sirkal, the tenant, the government, and at times the laborer. The tenant's share varies greatly according to the local custom, density of population, type of ownership (tapu is better for the owner than miri lazma), system of irrigation (for flow-irrigated products his share is generally lower), fertility of soil, the whims of the sheikh. In the Tigris area, the tenant's share in winter crops is half the produce, the seeds being provided by him; this is meant to encourage him to practice lift irrigation, which is more exacting. In the Euphrates area his share in winter products is two-fifths, and in summer products, of which the most important is rice, a third or less; actually, after deduction of various taxes, only a fourth. The share of the sirkal (*sirkaliyya*) —one-tenth to one-sixth—is nominally collected from the tenant and the sheikh, but in practice the tenant's share predominates. In places where the lazma is still reckoned as tribal, the portion of the sheikh, who is the tribe's representative, is one-tenth; but in places where lazma has become a sort of prerequisite of the sheikh, one-fifth or more.

In the Kurdish zones the absentee landowner collects one-tenth to two-tenths of the rain-fed grain crop, one-third from rice crop, up to one-half from easily irrigated cash crops such as tobacco. If the land is rented to an intermediary, the owner may get a small fee plus one-half of the intermediary's profits. The conditions differ for the inhabitants of the mountains, the foothills and the plains. In the mountainous district of Rowanduz, where the agha is owner and also headman of one or several

villages, his share in summer crops, if working capital is supplied by the fellah and only water by the agha, is half the produce, and if both are his, two-thirds.

Actually, more is deducted from the tenant's share. Most of
his produce is sold at the beginning of the season below the
market price. A considerable part of his share finds its way into
the sheikh's purse or that of the sirkal in the form of various
dues (*nātūriyya*, watchman's dues; *shkāra*, cultivation of a plot
for the benefit of a sheikh or a sirkal, including threshing and
winnowing; *talī'a*, cultivation of a plot for the agent, the plot
itself and the seeds being provided by the landowner; *faz'at*,
emergency help given on behalf of the owner to other owners,
such as closing of a breach in a dam). In addition, there is an
optional tax for the clergy (*sayyid wa-'l-mu'min*). In the zone
of the Jāf tribes in the north, the mukhtar receives one-fifth of
one-fifth from the produce of flow-irrigated land, or in the case
of rain-fed land he is excused from the rent of a certain stretch.
In the Tel'afar district the following taxes are in use: *shay-
khāniyya*, sheikh's tax; *mukhtāriyya*; *mudīf*, guest-house tax;
dhabā'ih, tax from sheep owner; tax levied on every owner of
a machine; tax for feeding the sheikh's horses, etc.[43]

According to the ordinance No. 4 of 1954, the sheikh's share
is not to exceed half the produce, except for dates and fruits.
It prohibits levying special dues from the tenant.[44]

Land settlement

Although the settlement policy was uniform in all the country, the methods by which it was carried out were more complex
in irrigation areas. Here, where irrigation necessitated a group
larger than a village, the tribe was the social unit, with a kind
of living area (*dīra*) at its disposal. There were several forms of
partnership in occupation of land. One was that the area was
parcelled out among the sectional chiefs, the paramount sheikh
receiving a larger share in virtue of his position. Each chief
divided the land among his followers in return for a share in
the produce. In course of time the sheikh would acquire hereditary rights to a portion of the tract through reclaiming a plot,

planting it, or installing a water-wheel for irrigation. In the second form the tribesmen worked the whole area, nominally partners of the sheikh and the minor sheikhs, and set aside for them a portion of the produce. In practice, however, the sheikh's ties with the tribesmen became restricted more and more down to the mere division of the produce. In both ways he gained assured prospects of acquiring the land, or most of it, in miri lazma.[45]

Pump irrigation hastened the break-up of the tribal regime. In the flow irrigation zone, where the method of cultivation compelled the sheikh, the intermediary, and the fellahin to act together more closely, the ties of the tribal lazma lasted longer. In zones where the ties between the sheikh and the members of his tribe were weak (Diyāla, Hilla, Basra) the sheikh appropriated to himself the rights of the tribe even before the settlement. The settlement pronounced the doom of these ties of partnership.

The available statistical data are neither conclusive nor sufficiently revealing. The current classification indicates the size of a holding owned by an individual only within one settlement block (*muqāta'a*), but holdings in various blocks, which are registered in the name of one person, appear statistically as if they belong to different persons. It is, perhaps, for that reason that 200,000 donums have been set as the upper limit to a holding. On the other hand, some holdings are held jointly by more than one person. The larger units in themselves are widely stretched: in 1955, 232 holdings of 4000-5000 donums each, 424 holdings of 5,000-10,000, 168 of 10,000-20,000; the largest unit is termed 20,000 and over—104. Data even differ from one another. More detailed statistics could not but mean a self-indictment.

At the end of 1956 the area covered by the cadastral survey was 78,913,857 donums (mulk 238,975; matrūka 5,135,832; waqf 840,497; miri tapu 12,348,531; miri lazma 11,649,448; miri sirf 48,700,752). This area amounts to about 44.3 percent of the total area (177,776,800 donums) or to about 83.69 percent of the area in the fourteen liwās, namely, excluding the Northern, the Southern and the Jazīra deserts. No doubt, the liwās of 'Amāra and of Muntafiq, not yet covered by survey, and of Kerbelā, where only one district has been covered, are bound to worsen the picture. Together they make up 8.8 percent of the total area. A large part of the unalienated miri sirf land within the fourteen liwās, especially in the Mosul liwā, is submarginal or otherwise uncultivable.

The land policy inaugurated in 1932, which, as Lord Salter mildly put it, was "kept within the bounds of what will not be actively resisted by landowners," contained the seeds of social upheavals. Since in the delimitation of the settlement blocks or the rented areas, as also in sharing out of the produce, mere assessment has played the major part, it is obvious that there are numerous opportunities for circumvention and misuse of law, from connivance of the authorities to overreaching and chicanery. In spite of the provisions of the lazma law, the land is merely cultivated to the extent from a third to a fourth, because, among other things, the income of the owners, not being subjected to income tax or to graduated land tax, was high enough. On the other hand, social rights providing for security of tenure and fair wages were not guaranteed in the legislation.

Development schemes to be financed from the oil revenue are bound to collide with the interests of the large landowners, both on the social and on the economic sides. As early as in 1924, the government was warned that "anything like a permanent alienation of Government land is undesirable in a country where the irrigation system is so incomplete, and where the fullest power of security and proper return on the large capital outlay necessary for irrigation development should be retained in the hand of Government."[46] This warning went unheeded. The various partial irrigation projects benefited mainly the large estates. It has been reckoned that a comprehensive irrigation system based on the two rivers and their tributaries at a cost of 320 million dinar (average of 12 dinar a donum), could supply water for perennial cultivation of 18 million, and for fallow farming of 4 million donums.[47] It will, therefore, enrich, at public expense, the large landowners. Even if proper means were devised to impose improvement levies on privately owned land affected by the irrigation schemes, which is almost inconceivable, the enhanced value of the land is bound to strengthen the economic power of the beneficiaries.

The Agrarian Reform Law No. 30 of 1958 limited the area of agricultural land owned by a person, or alienated to him by tapu or granted to him by lazma, to 1,000 donums irrigated by flow or lift, or 2,000 rain-fed land. The law applies also to family or joint waqf. The owner retains an area of his choice and, until correction, it is to maintain its original character (mulk, miri tapu, miri lazma). The land in excess of the maximum limit is to be seized within five years against compensation in bonds, bearing 3 percent and redeemable within twenty years, to be equal to the price of similar land less the value of government rights in tapu and lazma land. Compenstaion is to be paid also for immovable property, trees and agricultural implements. If the land is owned by one person and the right of usufruct by another, the owner is entitled to two-thirds of the land and the exploiting person to one-third. Seized land, as well as miri sirf land, will be distributed in holdings of 30 to 60 donums of irrigated land, or 60 to 120 donums of rain-fed land. The recipients are to repay the value of the land, plus 3 percent interest and costs of distribution (20 percent of the compensation), over a period of twenty years. The distributed land will be registered as mulk. The beneficiaries are to join agricultural cooperative societies.

The law regulates the distribution of the field crops: land rent and management 10 percent each; water supply 10 percent in land irrigated by flow and 20 percent by lift; labor and seeds 50 percent in flow irrigated or rain-fed land, 40 percent in lift irrigated land. There are special provisions for ploughing, for harvesting and collecting. Minimum wages of agricultural laborers are to be fixed by a government committee every year and in every region. Agricultural laborers may form unions to defend their interests.

Chapter Eleven

Landownership in Syria

The agrarian reform laws of 1958 and 1959 were passed for the purpose of reversing the trend in the evolution of land tenure in Syria, that is, the accumulation of land in the hands of a few. Indirectly, they may also relieve the problem of fragmentation of small and medium holdings.

Large-scale ownership in Syria comprises over 60 percent of the cultivated land.[1] Although its dimensions are less than in Iraq, there are, especially in the provinces of Hamā, Homs, Aleppo, and the Jazīra, estates which include 20 to 40 or more villages, covering a hundred thousand, even several hundred thousand hectares. Medium and small estates are more frequent in the coastal zones and in a number of areas in the interior, especially in the *ghouta's* (oases in Damascus and in the Orontes valley), where irrigated agriculture demands incessant effort, as well as in the mountains, where there are no continuous stretches of land.

In Syria, as in Iraq, landownership continued to grow under the mandate regime and after its termination. Numerous medium and small holdings also belong to residents in towns and villages, and to leading villagers who do not work them personally. A distinctive sign of wealth and high standing, land is considered a safe investment which does not involve great exertion.

The *Code de la propriété* (arrêté No. 3339 of 1930) reduced landownership from the seven types under the Ottoman law to five—one privately-owned land and four types of state or public land:

mulk: freehold, usually found within the boundaries of, or close to cities; also gardens and fields within villages. Some of it was formerly *miri* turned into mulk for a payment to the treasury. Nearly all of it is small or medium property; it makes up 2 to 3 percent of the land under cultivation.

miri: hereditary leasehold registered in tapu. In theory, this is state land, but the right of usufruct, including sale, leasing, and mortgaging, rests with the owner. Unlike mulk, miri, which has been neglected for three years (since 1930 for five years), was forfeited, but this regulation was hardly ever enforced. In practice, miri is hardly distinguishable from mulk.

The greatest part of agricultural land held by individuals, perhaps up to 90 percent, is miri.

matrūka, two kinds:

mahmiyya: land reserved for public use (rivers, banks, roads, cemeteries, etc.).

murāfaqa: land used by one or by several communities (threshing floors, pasture land, etc.).

khāliya mubāha: vacant land, not assigned to a particular community. Anyone authorized to bring it into use acquires miri rights in it.

waqf land is not considered a legal category. Pious waqf (*khayrī*) is land given in trust for religious and charitable purposes. Family waqf (*dhurrī*) was abolished and joint waqf (*mushtarak*) dissolved in May, 1949, under Husnī Za'īm. The latter consisted of land whose produce was set aside for charitable purposes and for the donor's descendants or other persons.

In the 1850's and again in the 1880's, great stretches of land adjoining the frontier of settlement were declared crown lands. Under the Young Turks these lands, nearly all of them in the provinces of Homs, Aleppo, Hamā, the Jazīra, and Euphrates, were converted into state domain (*mudawwara*). The Lausanne Treaty of 1923 recognized it as the property of the state of Syria.

In 1945, the area of registered state domain comprised 1,114 villages or parts of villages: 931 mudawwara and 183 mulk which had become forfeited because there were no legal heirs, and neglected miri land (*mahlūl*).

mawāt (waste, marginal land) is a category of state land not inscribed in the registers. Under decree No. 135 of October 29, 1952, it was included in the state domain. Estimates of its extent varied widely, from one to three million dunams.

Growth of Landownership[2]

The large estates are today in the hands of a few hundred owners, headed by some fifty families. Broadly, these estates came into existence under the following circumstances:

1. The abolition of tax farming by the *wali's* of the provinces in the 1860's did not prevent the accumulation of land. Areas were granted by the sultan or his representatives as reward for military or political services. Tax farming in the villages remained under concession until the end of the Ottoman rule. In theory a tithe, the tax may have exceeded more than 30 percent. The fellahin often lost their lands to the farmer, whose interests were bound up with the local Turkish authorities, or to moneylenders.[3]

2. The land registration, initiated in 1858, opened new avenues of corruption. Fraud and violence were employed to expropriate land. Men in high positions seized the opportunity to extend their boundaries and inscribed in their names land that belonged to fellahin. In the Aleppo region, only 20 to 30 percent of the land remained in the hands of fellahin.[4] Many fellahin did not register their land for fear of conscription or more taxation, or they registered it in the name of local leaders. Moreover, areas set aside by the authorities for sheikhs, on condition that the land should be settled by their tribes, were often inscribed in the sheikhs' own names.

3. In the second half of the last century, especially after 1870, the frontier of settlement of the country, which was then semipopulated, began to shift to the east. The authorities encouraged settlers, including Muslim refugees from the Caucasus and the Balkans, to establish themselves there. Fellahin began to reclaim land, some on their own account and some for townsmen on a basis of share tenancy. On the whole, the land passed into the hands of wealthy persons.[5]

4. In addition to open violence, which was especially ripe in times of unrest, there was much concealed violence. Fellahin seeking protection from the authorities often ceded land to landowners or tribal sheikhs, thus becoming share croppers. In return for land, a notable would settle a dispute between fellahin, or defend them in the law courts; and having obtained a footing in a village, he could encroach further. He might even provoke a quarrel in a village or between two villages, so that the two sides would beg for his good offices; he would be willing to use them in return for some rights in land. The court did not dare decide against a powerful individual.[6] From 1880 to 1915, in the region of Hamā, wealthy families ('Azm, Kīlānī, Barūdī, and Shīshaklī) obtained 21 villages from the tribes for a pittance.[7]

5. During World War I, many title deeds were burned or stolen. Pressure of hunger led fellahin to sell land cheaply in order to buy seed, or else to mortgage it; and when they failed to meet payment, the land was expropriated.

It was a grievous legacy that the mandate authorities received from their predecessors. The greater part of the land held by individuals was not inscribed at all, and the title deeds were in a state of utter confusion.[8] The authorities considered the chaos in the state domain an "economic and social danger." The arrêté No. 275 of 1926 had been designed to regulate the administration of the state domain, estimated to cover 2,000,000 hectares, and to facilitate its alienation, "en vue de constituer la petite propriété rurale, presque inexistante dans le pays sous mandat et dehors des zones montagneuses."[9] Land survey, begun in 1920, had been speeded up in 1927. By December 31, 1938, 2,743, 388 hectares had been surveyed. The Code de la propriété, mentioned earlier, had inaugurated a system of land registration.

Nonetheless, accumulation of land continued under the mandate. It might be said in its defense that the mandate regime was only temporary and that it enjoyed no more than ten years of comparative tranquility. Moreover, the best legislation can be perverted by local authorities. The fact remains, however, that the mandate authorities were not inclined to undertake fundamental reforms; in their struggle with the nationalist opposition, they had to rely on a portion of the ruling classes, especially those representing the minorities and the tribal chieftains; and this dependence proved advantageous in matters of land acquisition.[10] The methods of land accumulation were numerous.

1. Settlement work had some ill-effects. It set a definite seal on ownership. Settlement committees were subject to the influence of powerful individuals. Claims of ownership, whether doubtful, false, or conflicting, were recognized as legitimate and often allowed to cover too large an area for proper supervision. Ignorant fellahin were tricked into waiving their rights of ownership. Tracts occupied by tribes were registered in the names of their sheikhs.

2. The waqf system helped to perpetuate large landownership because division of waqf land was restricted, or in some cases prohibited. Without consent of the authorities, miri land was bequeathed illegally as waqf. Although waqf property could not be transferred or mortgaged, except in cases specified by the sharī'a law and with the consent of a special court, the authorities allowed sale of tracts to private persons.

3. By far the greater part of the state domain was acquired by influential persons either at very low prices, or simply by usurpation. Almost all the state lands in the province of Aleppo, covering about 300,000 hectares in about 600 villages, are controlled by large landowners.[11]

4. Suppliers of motor pumps have become the possessors of tracts turned over to them in payment of debts, or as their quota of the cultivable area gained by irrigation.

5. *mushā'** did not prevent town residents from penetrating into the village, although it made it more difficult for them. Once having obtained a footing, they sometimes converted all of the land into private property, with the former owners working it as share tenants on a mushā' basis.[12] With the abolition

---

* Seemingly collective form of landownership. Originally designed to ensure the protection of crops. Involves narrow strip farming and periodic repartitioning of land.

of mushā' on account of settlement, village notables, in whose names it was often registered, tended to make themselves masters of the best land.

6. Land changed hands, from heavily indebted fellahin to moneylenders and merchants, in payment of loans of money, seeds, and livestock. Two successive droughts are sufficient to force the peasants to sell some of their holdings. In several districts the rate of interest, especially in hard times, amounts to as much as 8 percent per month, or even more. Since taking interest is forbidden by Islam, numerous devices are used to hide it. A fellah will receive cash and sign an undertaking to pay back in livestock or its value, the difference is concealed interest. Or he will sell a part of the coming crop at a low price, and the difference between this and the market price is equivalent to interest. In addition, usurers exploit the ignorance of the fellah in drawing up and interpreting the loan agreements.[13]

7. Large tracts have been acquired for next to nothing from Bedouins in Central Syria.

8. Emergency legislation passed in 1940 and 1941 assigned state lands east of the arbitrarily set "desert line" to tribal chiefs.[14]

These methods of land accumulation have continued under national rule. Syria's parliament has been composed of up to 80-85 percent of large landowners, and the administrators on higher levels come from the same stock.[15]

Some Regional Features

At the end of the nineteenth century the *Jazīra* was a region of Bedouin tribes, with some tribal groups of Kurds and Caucasian Chachans. It is now inhabited by Kurds, nearly all sedentray, Arab tribes, in various stages of sedentarization, Christians or various denominations, and Jews, numbering about 180,000 in all. Inhabitants of small towns form about a fifth of the population, and of these the Christians are a decided majority.

Before 1920, considerable tracts of cultivable land, especially in the region of the railway, belonged to some town dwellers—

Turks, Christians, Kurdish aghas, and Arab sheikhs. Further south, nearer to the steppe, land was considered to be in collective ownership of the Arab tribes, and it was parcelled out every year into units of fixed size. The sheikh's share was a kind of obligatory tax. Minor sheikhs used to lay their hands on stretches adjoining water sources.

In 1926, when Kurdish tribes and swarms of Christians from Turkey, and Yazīdis and Christians from Iraq began to arrive, agriculture became more widespread. Hundreds of new villages sprang up, partly in ethnic blocs—Kurdish or Arab. The tribal framework became looser. Christians settled in Kurdish tribal villages; Armenian villages were founded in the territory of an Arab tribe. There was no uniform trend in the development of landownership. In one area of Kurdish tribes the land was registered in the agha's name, and in other places the tribesmen tilled their own land. In another area of Arab tribes the *mukhtars* (headmen) gradually gained ground at the expense of the minor sheikhs, while the major sheikhs who lived in the nearby town placed themselves and their armed forces at the disposal of Arab, Turksih, and Kurdish landowners. In some cases urban owners worked the land in partnership with tribal sheikhs, or the latter guaranteed protection of the crop in return for a portion of it. In some cases sheikhs let tribal land to towndwellers on a share-cropping basis.

The mandate authorities encouraged the sheikhs to work the tribal grazing areas, which were recognized as their property or were granted to them as a concession. Individual settlers—refugees and displaced persons—generally were not strong enough to withstand the pressure of the sheikhs and the urban owners, and from the status of settlers they sank to that of share tenants. The main factor in this chaotic activity was the competition or collaboration of the new urban élite—tribal notables, Turkish and Christian owners, and civil servants.

In the early 1920's, more than 95 percent of the Jazīra was public domain. By 1940, 8,640 square kilometers were, in the main, in the hands of large landowners, some of whose estates exceeded 100,000 hectares. From 1942, the development of the region was much more rapid. Profits made on wheat and loans in foreign currency for the purchase of machinery stimulated sheikhs to enlarge the area of cultivation. Individuals from Aleppo, Hamā, and Damascus who had made money from contracts and hoarding, obtained concessions, seized extensive tracts of land, or acquired, for a pittance, stretches which had been abandoned by their owners. Groups of peasants who occupied areas within the boundaries of their tribes acquired them from the government in partnership with tractor owners, who paid the entire price of the land. Tracts changed hands, and the distribution of property kept on changing. Irrigation by pump expanded with the rice boom in 1945. Cotton-growing was started and—largely in consequence of the war in Korea—the area under cotton increased considerably.

The economic transformation of the region made no great difference to its social aspect. Side by side with mechanization, primitive methods of tilling are still in use. In the new villages, too, the fellah is beaten down by the sheikh, the moneylender, and the trader who buys the crop while it is still in the soil. The fellah is tied to his field, but when the need arises he is sent off to found a new village. Sometimes the landlord evicts him from good land, which he wants to devote to some new crop, and transfers him to inferior land. And sometimes a fellah resigns his ownership voluntarily or under pressure of the sheikh, and his plot is absorbed into an adjoining estate.

Large holdings are in the hands of some fifty owners, mostly tribal chiefs. A remarkable feature of the Jazīra is the huge estates run by operators or jointly with heads of tribes.[16]

Conditions in the *Euphrates* valley, where the irrigable and cultivable area is estimated at about 1,000,000 hectares, are essentially different from those in the Jazīra in one respect: middle-size holdings (50 to 100 hectares) are far more numerous (11,120 against 1,040). Since about 1880, the 'Aqidāt, a loose confederation of tribal remnants, gradually took to semisedentary life under pressure of the Turkish authorities. At the beginning of the mandate regime, medium and small ownership were still to be found chiefly in the hands of tribal chiefs who controlled the water sources and the adjoining stretches. Crop land that was not irrigable by primitive means was considered communal property, free to be worked at one's own risk. When trading moneylenders began to install motor pumps, the system of crop division changed radically. The owner of the pump would receive half the crop in return for supplying half the seeds; and as the irrigated area was extended, he was entitled to half the extension. Men from the towns began to install water mills the motors of which also worked the pumps. Sometimes they received concessions for first-grade land by the river bank, and in the course of time, they would obtain control of the land. Sometimes a townsman would squeeze his way in as an overseer; in time he became a partner, and finally owner of the land. This process was accelerated since the last war, when the cultivation of cotton was started on the banks of the Euphrates and the Khabur. Mechanized dry farming enabled townsmen and sheikhs to enlarge their holdings. With the increase in sedentarization, many tribesmen became share-croppers.[17]

In the provinces of *Hamā* and *Homs,* land settlement has been almost completed. Here the proportion of state domain is larger than in other provinces (69 percent of the cultivated land in Homs, 44 percent in Hamā). In the first half of the nineteenth century, these provinces were almost desolate. From about 1870 up to the present, there has been a ceaseless occupation of the land by Ismā'īli emirs in the district of Salamiya. In the 1890's, Circassians founded four villages north of Salamiya. Before and after World War I a large part of the land passed from the hands of the Bedouin to notables from Hamā who used the labor of 'Alawis brought from the mountains. Most of the villages are inhabited by Sunni Arabs; there are also some Christian and Turkoman villages.

After World War I, lands were granted to anyone who wanted to work them, or they were appropriated practically without government interference. Although the authorities decided in 1926 to limit the maximum area which an applicant might hold, the growth of large estates continued. Because of the occupation of state land, large ownership amounts to at least 50 percent in the district of Hamā, 72 percent in the district of Salamiya, and 47 percent in the province of Homs. Medium estates (47, 28, and 42 percent respectively) belong also, to a great extent, to townspeople.

In the province of Hamā, large landownership takes the form of latifundia. In the 1930's, eighty-six villages belonged to four families—al-'Azm, al-Barāzī, al-Kīlānī, and Tayfūr. By contrast, in the province of Homs there are by far more small holders. Unlike Hamā, where the new areas under irrigation are the property of city notables, the new irrigation works on the Orontes have also benefited fellahin.

Since 1938, corn crops have been replaced by irrigated products (vegetables, fruit, vines, and in particular, cotton and rice). In the district of Salamiya alone, hundreds of motor pumps have been installed since World War II. Because of overspending and indebtedness, land in Salamiya is often ceded by landowners to tradesmen.

Practically all the cultivated area in the plain south of Homs was mushā', both in private property of the peasant and in leased land. The settlement confirmed the rights of the urban landowner without eliminating the practices of mushā'. On the other hand, mushā' is being abolished through land settlement in the sphere of small ownership, and permanent allotment of land is greatly benefiting the fellahin. The abolition of mushā' has its drawback in the fact that it facilitates the penetration of outsiders for the purpose of acquiring land in the villages.[18]

In the 'Alawi mountains, medium and small properties are more common than in the lowlands. The large estates are in the hands of sheikhs, who are linked with their tenants by a kind of religious-tribal bond—weak or fanatical, as the case may be. The large estates in the coastal plain which belong to families in the towns are parcelled out, though estates of hundreds of hectares are still to be found. But small and medium properties, up to 10 and from 10 to 50 hectares, are also owned by townspeople—Sunnis and Christians—and leading villagers. The land is worked almost exclusively by 'Alawi sharecroppers. The soil is fertile; and tobacco, which makes up about 70 percent of the entire crop of the country, is grown on it. As a rule, tenants or smallholders in the valley sell the tobacco to a townsman, who then transmits it for fumigation. Tobacco is also grown by large landowners.

Toward the east, the mountain loses height, thus providing more suitable conditions for large holdings. In the lowlands there are estates of one, two, or several villages, the owners of which are mostly Sunni families. The Dendashli family owns sixty villages.[19]

In the *Hawrān* and *Jabal al-Durūz*, medium and small holdings are prevalent. Before World War II, large estates in the latter accounted for about a third of the cultivated area, but in the meantime, they had diminished considerably. Owing to extreme poverty and backwardness in the Hawrān province, the large landowners have been able to assume a dominant position, both politically and economically.

Types of Settlement

1. Small subsistence farms in irrigated areas around villages or towns or in the mountains. The farmer sometimes employs laborers at harvest time.

2. Capitalist cultivation by individuals and societies. One might point to large-scale exploitation with paid labor in the newly developed areas of the Jazīra, the Euphrates province, and the eastern part of Aleppo province, as well as some estates in the regions of Hamā and Homs.

Laborers' wages vary greatly. Sometimes the worker receives food, dwelling, and shoes, or an annual payment in foodstuffs, such as flour, oil, and maize. Some of the harvest workers are hired by the day and are paid in cash, and some receive part of the crop. In a few estates in the Jazīra, where labor is mechanized, they receive a monthly wage and a share in the net profit.

3. Cash tenancy is very rare, as is tenancy in return for a fixed quantity of grain.

4. Share tenancy (*murāba'a*), almost universal in large landownership, and largely in vogue in medium estates, embraces at

least 70 percent of the land under cultivation. The proportion of tenants among the fellahin is even greater than this, because some owners of small plots lease land for tilling.

Conditions of tenancy are determined by the amount of rainfall and the fertility of soil, the availability of labor, the type of agriculture, the crop produced, and so forth. The share of tenant's labor may amount to 25-30 percent or less of the yield in rain-fed areas. Or the tenant may supply all the working capital, including taxes, and receive up to 70 percent, or more. Sometimes the lessee engages fellow tribesmen of the landlord or laborers. He sets aside a portion of the crop for the landlord and pays the wages of the workmen. The rest of the crop is his, including what he can get by cheating or extortion. In some cases the tenant supplies an additional small sum representing a specified weight of butter and of wool for each sheep, or a part of the offspring of the flock.

A number of variations are bound up with local practices. In some zones the relations between the landlord and the tenant are on a business footing; in others, as for instance in Hamā and Homs, they are those of master and vassal.

In some zones servitudes are customary, among others *shkāra*, that is, ploughing of a field by tenants for the benefit of the landlord or the agent, without payment. Similarly, the landlord receives so-called voluntary gifts.

On irrigated land, the share of the tenant's labor is 20 to 30 percent, and about half if he also provides the working capital. In plantations *mughārasa* is in vogue; this entitles the tenant to a portion of the shoots also.[20]

In these and similar ways the upper class in Syria has gained possession of the greater part of the land. The available statistical data are not sufficient to substantiate this fully. By the end of 1952 only 45 percent of the cultivable land was covered by the cadastral survey (3.54 out of about 7.82 million hectares), and of this area 49 percent were holdings of over 100 and 16 percent of more than 1,000 hectares.[21] At the end of 1955, the area surveyed was 4,406,498 hectares. Land cultivation has increased from 1.76 million hectares before World War II to 3.67 million in 1953, and to 4.59 million in 1956.[22] The frontier of settlement has already reached the submarginal land.

Irrigation works, mainly in the Euphrates and Khabur valleys and in the Orontes area (Ghāb project), are estimated to increase the area under irrigation from 500,000 up to 1,000,000 hectares and to assure sustenance to a larger agricultural population. As in Iraq, government irrigation projects are to improve the value of a great deal of private land. The Ghāb project covers 65,000 hectares, more than half of it privately owned land.

The Legislative Decree No. 135 of October 29, 1952, stipulated that occupation of state land, including dead land not already registered, confers the right of usage only up to 200 hectares for each person and for each of the immediate members of his family (wives and children). Lands that had already been registered in the name of the occupant were exempted from this provision. Under existing political conditions this provision could hardly have been applied. On the other hand, even in recent years, large stretches of state domain have been leased to operators temporarily.

A grave social issue was at stake: the main resource of the country had been wasted without responsibility to the nation. Large-estate agriculture is by no means a proper vehicle for relieving population pressure in the southern regions (Hawrān, Jabal al-Durūz, and especially Latakiya). The state would have to cope, mostly for the benefit of large landowners, with problems of salinity, dropping of water levels, and erosion. Economic and social renovation of the country was hardly conceivable without a fundamental land reform, coupled with bold social legislation to ensure its implementation.

Law No. 134 of September 4, 1958, regulates the relations between landlord and share-cropping tenant. It provides for a minimum share of tenant's labor (25 percent in irrigated land under cotton and land planted with trees, 33 percent in irrigated land under vegetables, and 60 percent in rain-fed land planted with tobacco). The maximum share of the landlord shall be 20 percent in rain-fed land, 33 percent in gravity-irrigated land, and 20 percent in pump-irrigated land. The law limits the working day of an agricultural worker to nine hours and the working year to 300 days. The law also makes provisions for fixing the laborer's wages.

Law No. 161 of September 27, 1958, limits the maximum size of a holding irrigated by river water or wells or planted with trees to 80 hectares, and of a dry-farmed holding to 300 hectares, plus 40 or 160 hectares, respectively (a maximum of 4 shares for the landlord's wife and children). The land above these limits will be seized within five years, but from January, 1959, the landlord will have to pay the state three-quarters of the rent on excess land. Compensation at ten times the average rental value over three years will be paid in bonds bearing 1.5 percent interest, redeemable over a period of forty years. The excess land is to be distributed in such a way that the lots of the beneficiaries should not exceed 8 hectares of irrigated land or 30 hectares of rain-fed land. The beneficiaries will have to repay the compensation, plus 10 percent for expenses, at the same interest and over the same period. They must join agricultural cooperatives.[23]

Chapter Twelve

Conclusion

During the past forty years the Near Eastern panorama has changed miraculously. When all is said about grievances, real and imaginary, the short-lived mandate regime did benefit the region. It provided an administrative and legal framework for future emancipation. The two world wars resulted in ten Arab states (six were carved out of the Ottoman empire, while four emerged from the second). It may be argued that the tenet of self-determination was not strictly upheld in the area. It was not applied with regard to other ethnic entities nor within the Arab community itself. By sheer force the ruler of Najd ousted the Hāshimis from Hijāz, eliminated another ruling family—the Rashīds—from Northern Arabia, and set up Saʻudi Arabia. Likewise the Kurdish area was joined to Iraq despite violent opposition. When the Sudan became independent, the non-Muslim Negro south—about a third of the population—was not permitted to assert its will. The legacy of colonialism was kept intact. In a way, the same holds true for the Berber half of Morocco.

Broadly, four stages are to be observed in this period. In the first, hopes were pinned to the West, despite violent argument. The mandate system, embattled though it was, was considered a temporary device of patronizing until those it was to guide came of age. Western techniques, both in politics and economics, were regarded as the motive power for a speedy march into modern life. At the time, chroniclers tended to identify, or at least to confuse, liberalism with what Benedetto Croce termed "liberism," an economic laissez-faire not anchored to a social and moral purpose. Some of them delighted in the replacement of camels by motor cars, in the search for oil, in the improvement of communications, in the rise of the press, in the trappings of parliamentarism—all signs of the awakening of a new *homo politicus* and *economicus*. The impact of European contacts on the East was even likened to that of the French Revolution on Europe.

The second stage, in the 1930's, was marked by the impact of fascist dynamism. The vacillations of the Western powers lowered their standing in the area. Hopes for resurgence, linked to past glory, were fanned by the new tide from Europe and its means adapted, or native practices revived. World War II vindicated the desire of Great Britain and France to retain a foothold in this area. The failure of Rashid 'Ali's revolt in 1941 and the victory at 'Alameyn in the following year swung the pendulum back once again towards Western concepts. Watchwords of planned constructivism gained currency. An awakening social conscience stirred the area, and socialism was injected even into programs of right-wing and religious extremists. The United Nations Charter was deemed a panacea for independence.

After the war the tension over unresolved issues between the Western powers and some Arab states rose to a peak, no doubt heightened by the cold war and the Palestine issue. At first a policy of neutralism was adopted by the opposition, both right and left. The argument over neutralism separated Arab governments and caused dissension within them. Later, spurred by the Bandung Conference in 1955, a version of "positive neutralism" gained ascendancy. In terms of outside aid it is seemingly more rewarding, but its social impact, the way it is given and obtained, may be questioned. Under its shelter one-party, in fact personal dictatorships hold sway. Having despaired of winning the uncommitted over, the "have" nations make efforts to keep them "uncommitted."

The 1948 war in Palestine inaugurated a period of military *coups d'état* (Syria, 1949; Egypt, 1952; Iraq, 1958). To be sure, a *coup d'état* had been staged in Iraq as far back as 1936, and royal coups against the constitution had been frequent in Egypt. The utter ineptitude and greed of the ruling classes reduced their regime to absurdity, and it was not difficult to overthrow them. They evinced no loyalty whatsoever. After the merger of Syria and Egypt, when the way seemed open to further fusion, the events in Iraq occurred. In his drive to impose a one-way nationalism, 'Abd al-Nāsir overreached himself, and his claim to monopoly has vigorously been challenged.

The initial cooperation of the diverse factions in Iraq was not to be taken for granted, and its leader's course is far from being definite. But there are some compelling elements there, among others the attitude of the Kurdish community and the relationship of the dominant faction in it with the Communist party.[1] In the long run, the army cannot be the sole arbiter. In this respect, it is all but a myth, and the attitude of the top commanders is not to be taken for granted. It cannot but reflect the divisions in the country, and it seems to be kept together by the leader's equivocal policies. Furthermore, the impact of the Kurdish element in it is not to be discounted.

Both regimes, in Iraq and in the U.A.R., are authoritarian and paternalistic, but in Iraq the movement touched off diverse social spontaneity. The Egyptian regime embodied a protest against party corruption; consequently mass associations have been suppressed or regimented (trade-unions). The National Union that aims at "pyramid democracy" is all but artificial and imposed. In Iraq, however, some parties have immediately resumed their activity, and mass organizations, with the Communists riding the tide, have cropped up. Of course, social spontaniety can be curbed or perverted by the men in power, and expressions of the will of the "masses" turned on and off. At first, the ideological framework in Iraq seemed borrowed from both West and East, and the first framers of economic policies were men of some Marxist schooling. By contrast, in Egypt a deliberate if crude attempt at originality can be discerned.

In both countries political power, as far as it can be exercised under a ruling clique, shifted markedly to descendants of the middle classes, professionals and intellectuals, the same spokesmen who under the former regime insisted on "genuine democratic freedoms." Both regimes hold out a promise of "true democracy" as soon as the elements of the old regime are silenced "forever." But whereas the regime in Egypt is practically under one-man control, extremely opportunist in matters of ideology, in Iraq, the sole leadership notwithstanding, the above-mentioned human factors must be reckoned with. Barring unpredictable elements of plot and violence, Iraq's policy has to be conditioned also by considerations of its neighbors and dependence on oil markets; on the other hand, its resources allow for a more independent policy. The unfavorable balance between population and resources here and there are opposite extremes. Iraq has no strong capitalist class firmly entrenched in industry and banking to contend with, or, as in Egypt's case, to make it cooperative. For both, étatism, at least with regard to major development projects, seems inevitable.

There is, no doubt, in both regimes a wider response to the needs of the common man. But for how long will the awakened middle and working classes be content with a passive role as an object of care and regimentation amidst fear and tension of uncertainty, and no tangible improvement of their lot? Will the test come only when the leader gives way of his own accord, and staged mass approvals of policies are supplanted by less dictated expressions of the people's will? In October 1954, when for a time the reins were slackened and freedoms were on the point of being granted, the "masses" in Egypt rallied around the leaders who were claiming those freedoms. Convulsions in the area are often signals of a repressed quest for a increased measure of assent in public life. The present targets of an aggressive nationalism carry less and less weight. Seeking a scapegoat (imperialism, communism, Zionism, Tunisia, Jordan, Lebanon, Iraq) is no substitute for positive values. A creative nationalism will have to assert itself more and more through the medium of the individual, his inherent needs and right of participation.

The revolt in Mosul, in March 1959, had some sobering effects. Baghdad charged 'Abd al-Nāsir with complicity, one of the proofs being the arms sent to Mosul from the U.A.R.[2] From

Egypt are voiced complaints about the behavior of "Communists, populists and agents of imperialism," robbery and "slaughtering of thousands" during the revolt.[3]

Since the issue of communism in Iraq versus anticommunism in Egypt has lost momentum, and Iraq's leader steers an equivocal middle course, taking swings to left and right, the real bone of contention is Egypt's drive to lead, and (inasmuch as 'Abd al-Nāsir is averse to the freedom to discuss and dissent) to rule. Paradoxically, both regimes eliminated the Ba'th party. The self-admitted overbearance of the Communists in Iraq is now undergoing self-criticism. Violent outbreaks, especially within the now outlawed peasant associations, helped undermine their standing.

The era of forging the destinies of a nation through a net of conspiracy and intrigue cast over all Arab lands is not yet over. In September 1960, radio 'Ammān charged Egypt with responsibility for the death of Majālī, Jordan's premier, by a bomb explosion, and radio Cairo called Jordanians to "finish the job," for, as some oratory recalling that of al-Hajjāj, the seventh-century Muslim commander, declares: "Between you and freedom there is a group of treacherous heads." At the same time, this case is construed as a Hashimite plot to create a pretext for bringing in British soldiers.

Oil has become a factor making either for unity or dissension in Arab nationalism. A million tons of oil have been produced in: Iraq (1934), Bahrayn (1937), Sa'udi Arabia (1944), Kuwayt (1947), Qatar (1950). Estimates of oil production in 1958 were, respectively (in millions of tons): 35.7; 2; 50.2; 70.2; 8.2, and oil revenues (in millions of U.S. dollars) were: 224.4; 6; 304; 415; 57.[4]

The ratio of oil wealth to population in the Arab countries is so disparate that it is bound to upset any equilibrium between them. Kuwayt with its huge oil reserves and cheapest crude oil has a population of 200,000. Revenues from oil transport for 1958 of the "have nots" were (in million dollars): 15 (Syria): 71.6 (Egypt); 1.3 (Lebanon); 1 (Jordan). Such a situation seems nonsensical when viewed from the angle of integral Arab nationalism.

In some respects the effects of oil have already been far-reaching. To begin with, the encounter of puritanical Wahhabism with a steady flow of gold has proved fatal. Gone is the impetus of the movement. Simplicity and austerity, the mainspring of Wahhabism, have given way to lust for luxury and modern license. The Wahhabi impact on Islam, once keenly felt in North Africa and India, has nearly vanished. As far as government policy goes, the tribal structure of the state is kept intact, and the bulk of Bedouins have hardly been touched by the blessings of the new era.

It had been assumed that technical amenities, if assimilated, might pave the way for democratic processes in the society. For the present, this hope seems faint. Modern welfare institutions may go hand in hand with old social practices. And yet the inevitable is not to be avoided. Improved educational facilities germinate social consciousness. Indignation is fed on the waste of oil royalties and on misrule. The new middle class, even in Sa'udi Arabia, is growing restive; it is demanding a voice in public affairs and up-to-date methods of governing.[5] With all its shortcomings, Iraq has taken a long-term view in the handling of oil revenue. Kuwayt and Qatar are not likely to be able to absorb their revenue. A rational measure would be the pooling of at least a fraction of it for the benefit of the less fortunate sister countries. Oil revenue may well prove a passing, at any rate a diminishing chance. But the salvation of these countries is to come not from outside; it shall neither be imposed nor extended on a brother's tray.

Iraq's claims to Kuwayt and Arab reactions elsewhere indicate future explosions. Kuwayt is the main link in a chain of problem principalities, notably Bahrayn, Qatar, Abu Dhabi. There criteria like independence and self-determination ring hollow, and neighbors' claims smack of indigenous imperialism. There an approach of a higher order is needed. But the Arab League, a national edition of the United Nations, is a dubious instrument even as a fire brigade.

The 1948 war, with the ensuing demographic upheaval, has had a revolutionary impact on Arab life, too. In terms of awareness of the people's needs and stimulation, it has even been a salutary one. It hastened the end of a nationalism which, for a generation, had mainly benefited a small propertied class and its retainers.

How can justice be done in posing the Jewish-Arab problem? It cannot be argued out, and the pros and cons are not convincing to either side. Furthermore, the Arabs are in the unfortunate position of not being able to dissent, on this plane, from each other. One wonders where reflection should begin: with the giving of the law on Mount Sinai, with the conquest of Jerusalem by Caliph 'Umar in 638, or with the abolition of the four-centuries-old Ottoman rule? With the unique place of Palestine in Jewish history, or with the fact of the Arab majority becoming a minority in the greater part of the country? The Arabs have known expansion through conquest and migration, but for centuries they have not experienced a mass exodus. Is the argument compelling that the culture of a nation grew out of its roots in this country? How far does a claim of self-determination constitute a right? Should justice to a fraction of a people prevail over justice to a people as a whole? In fairness, one must admit a facet of relativity in this question. In view of the adjoining countries, would any other compromise have been possible without reducing one people to a minority status in a part of the country and without denying the very essence of a national home? Was the 1948 war a life-and-death matter to the Arab states? These questions may have some bearing on our attitude to the present. As an ancient Arab sage said: "Half of knowledge is the question; the other half is the answer."

When all is said about cause and effect, and all arguments over the Arab refugees from Palestine and the Jewish refugees from Arab lands are exhausted, it is incumbent upon the nation which has attained statehood—with all that that means to a stateless people—to prepare for a future dialogue.

Meanwhile, there seems no way in sight to solve the Arab-Jewish differences. As long as conspiratorial policies prevail in inter-Arab relations, and the era of coups and trials continues, there is no Arab leader in the Near East willing to break the vicious circle. However, the Arab peoples, having experienced a succession of saviours, seem on the point of realizing that there is no miraculous path to any kind of union. The ways to it are subtler, leading through a process of adjustment based on genuine cooperation. Violence as an instrument of policy has bred dissension, and a unity emerging from it has little chance of surviving.

In spite of drawbacks, East-West relations are undergoing a profound change. The race for political and moral prevalence in the world is conceived more and more in terms of creative ingenuity and also concern for the welfare of the emergent one humanity. In this decade of scientific revolution, making for an acute sense of human destiny that transcends opposing ideologies, a nationalism thinking to draw much of its strength from strategic location and oil wealth is to be re-evaluated; especially since this oil will soon be rivalled by sources beyond the Suez Canal, and for the foreseeable future, oil production, including that of the Soviet Union, is in excess of demand. Neutralism is no longer a cause of contention. The policy of "aid without strings" seems to have won the day. Unfortunately, a kind of quietism is now descending; it is bound to foster helpless and senseless self-negation in the donor and adventurous self-indulgence in the recipient. But after eleven convulsive years, it may dawn upon thinking men in the Arab world that an increasing measure of internal freedom for a people that never had freedom, is the shortest way to freedom and, consequently, one has to have more patience with humanity and come to reciprocal terms with it. The acute crisis of mind of the new generation, confused though it is because of the exertions of violent changes, may augur a remedy. The possibility of Jewish-Arab cooperation should not be excluded. The new generation, Arab and Jewish alike, will have to give an affirmative answer.

From the above it should not be inferred that the Jewish-Arab tension is the main cause of the ferment in Arab lands. One has only to look around to ponder whether the thousands of casualties of word and sword (in Lebanon, in Mosul, in Kirkuk, where an apocalyptic *mêlée* involved non-Communists, pro-Communists, and non-labelled human beings—Turkomans, Kurds, Arabs, Kurdish soldiers and pacifying military units) were concomitants of nationalism. Are distances of deserts and centuries and ways of life to be bridged by violent unification? Are torrents of hate for the sake of an eschatological mission to release creative energies in a nation?[6]

Notes

NOTES TO CHAPTER ONE

1. Even the reports of the mandatory government in Syria did not mention Kurds, Turkomans, and Circassians. Presumably they were included among the Sunnis, that is, Arabs.

A. Hourani (*Minorities in the Arab World*, 1947, pp. 1-2) classifies them according to religion and spoken language. J. Weulersse ("La Question de minorités en Syrie," *Politique Étrangère*, Feb. 1936, pp. 28-39) puts a few of them into a category of *minorités mourantes* (linguistic: Circassians; religious: Ismā-'īlis).

Attachment to a language does not always imply identity of ethnic origin. Some Turkoman tribes in Iraq, particularly in the Diyāla province (Qara Ulus, Bajlan) are Kurdish-speaking; al-Kird in the Diwāniyya province speak Arabic. See al-'Azzāwī, *'Ashā'ir 'Irāq* (Baghdad, 1947), II, 182, 183-84, 187-88.

2. B. Lewis, *The Origins of Ismā'ilism* (Cambridge, 1940), pp. 91-92.

3. See Steven Runciman, *The Medieval Manichee* (Cambridge, 1947), pp. 5-25.

4. On the composition of the population in the southeast area of Asia Minor, see Arnold J. Toynbee, "A Summary of Armenian History Up To and Including the Year 1915," in *The Treatment of Armenians in the Ottoman Empire, 1915-16 (Documents presented to Viscount Grey . . .)* by Viscount Bryce (London, 1916), pp. 611-16.

5. Of the two main dialects, *soreni*, spoken in Sulaymāni region, is close to the major dialect of Iranian Kurdistan; *kurmanci* is spoken in Mosul region, in Turkish Kurdistan and by Syrian and Soviet Kurds. Most of the publications in Iraqi Kurdistan have been written in *soreni*. At present the question of fusing the two dialects is being discussed. See Nêveran, "Notes sur la presse kurde d'Irak," *Orient*, No. 10, 1959, pp. 139-48. Cf. C. J. Edmonds, *Kurds, Turks and Arabs* (London, 1957), pp. 10-11; Kamuran Ali Bedr Khan, "The Kurdish Prob-

lem," *JRCAS*, XXXVI (1949), 240; C. J. Edmonds, "A Bibliography of Southern Kurdish, 1920-36," *JRCAS*, XXIV (1937), 487-89; *ibid.*, "A Bibliography of Southern Kurdish," 1937-1944, *JRCAS*, XXXII (1945), 187.

6. For a survey of Kurdish literature, especially in 1920-1955, see Thomas Bois, "Coup d'oeil sur la littérature kurde," *al-Mashriq*, XLIX (1955), 201-39. On recent literary activity and folklore in Iraq, Syria, and U.S.S.R., see Thomas Bois, "Les Kurdes," *ibid.*, LIII (1959), 128-41, 266-99.

7. B. Nikitine, *Les Kurdes* (Paris, 1956), pp. 210-19; Edmonds, *Kurds, Turks and Arabs*, p. 63.

8. Edmonds, pp. 141-42; al-'Azzāwī, *op. cit.*, II, 28-29, 101, 134, 197-98, 207.

9. Nikitine, *op. cit.*, pp. 191-97; also Edmonds, p. 143.

10. Cf. H. M. Burton, "The Kurds," *JRCAS*, XXXI (1944), 70-72; W. G. Elphingston, "Kurds and the Kurdish Question," *ibid.*, XXXV (1948), 48-49; Malcolm Burr, "A Note on the Kurds," *ibid.*, XXXIII (1946), 289-92.

11. W. L. Westermann, "Kurdish Independence and Russian Expansion," *Foreign Affairs*, XXIV (1946), 681-82; *New Statesman and Nation*, Jan. 26, 1946; Philips Price, "Soviet Azerbaijan," *JRCAS*, XXXIII (1946), 194.

12. Archie Roosevelt Jr., "The Kurdish Republic of Mahabad," *MEJ*, I (1947), 247-69.

13. P. Rondot, "L'Expérience de Mahabad et le problème sociale Kurde," *En Terre d'Islam*, May-June 1948, pp. 179, 182-83; P. R., "Où va la question kurde?" *L'Afrique et L'Asie*, 1949, 2 trim., pp. 51-55; P. Price, "The Present Situation in Persia," *JRCAS*, XXXVIII (1951), p. 109.

14. Price, *op. cit.*, pp. 193-94; Kurdoyev, "The Kurdish Literature Across the Border" (in Russian), *Učënye Zapiski*, No. 128, (University of Leningrad, 1952), pp. 136-39.

15. According to the census of 1947, 17 percent of 4,799, 500. Kurdish circles contend that nomadic tribes are not included in these numbers.

According to Shākir Khozbak, *Al-Kurd wa-'l-mas'ala al-kurdiyya*, 1959, p. 41, they make up in the liwās Sulaymāni, Arbil, Kirkuk, and Mosul, respectively, 100, 91, 52.5, and 35 percent of the population.

16. See F. Barth, *Principles of Social Organization in Southern Kurdistan*, Universitetets Etnografiske Museum Bulletin, No. 7,

Oslo, 1953; E. R. Leach, *Social and Economic Organization of the Rowanduz Kurds*, London, 1940.

17. See Gertrude Bell, *Revue of the Civil Administration of Mesopotamia* (London, 1920), pp. 57-74.

18. ". . . it is no exaggeration to say that but for the British air cooperation Kurdistan today would not be administered by an Arab government in Baghdad." See Ernst Main, *Iraq from Mandate to Independence* (London, 1935), pp. 117, 136-38.

"The British desire to control the sources of oil in the Vilayet of Mosul resulted not only in the incorporation, thanks entirely to British diplomacy, of that province into the Arab State, but also in effective Anglo-Iraqi cooperation towards the solution of the Kurdish problem." G. Antonius, *The Arab Awakening* (New York, 1946), p. 367. See also W. L. E., "Iraqi Kurdistan," *The World Today*, XII (1956), 419.

19. Special Report . . . on the progress of Iraq during the period 1920-31 (London, 1931), pp. 252-64; *Survey of International Affairs: 1925*, I, 471-528; 1934, pp. 122-34.

20. Dr. 'Abd al-Karīm, *al-Siyāsa*, July 12, 1946.

21. Majid Mustafa in the Chamber of Deputies, *al-Zamān*, Jan. 23, 25, 28, 29, 1946; Sawt al-Ahālī, Jan. 30, 1946.

22. See *Memorandum sur la situation des kurds et leur revendications*, presented to Mr. Trigve Lie, Paris, 1948, pp. 28-30; see also Rambout, *Les Kurds et le droit* (Paris, 1947), pp. 71, 77.

23. Majid Mustafa in the Chamber of Deputies, *Sawt al-Ahālī*, Jan. 2, 1945; Amin Zaki in the Senate, *ibid.*, April 22, 1946.

24. Majid Mustafa, *op. cit.*, April 22, 1946; see also his statement in *al-Balad* (Damascus), March 21, 1946.

25. See *al-Zamān*, Jan. 11, 1946; *al-Bilād*, Jan. 13, 1946; *al-Sāʿa*, Jan. 10, 11, 1946. See also *Sawt al-Ahālī*, April 12, 22, 1945.

26. *Siria, Palestina pod tureckim pravitelʼstvom* (Odessa, 1875), II, 128-29.

27. Oppenheim, *Die Beduinen* (Leipzig, 1939), I, 25-26, 54, 233-34.

28. Rondot, "Les Kurds de Syrie," *La France Méditerranéenne*, 1939, pp. 81-126; Oppenheim, pp. 233-34.

29. For the historical background of the problem, see Nikitine, "Problème Kurde," *Politique Étrangère*, XI (1946), 250-60.

Other sources: Arshak Safrastian, *Kurds and Kurdistan* (London, 1948); Edmonds, "The Kurds of Iraq," *MEJ*, XI (1957), 52-62; *ibid.*, "The Place of the Kurds in the Middle Eastern

Scene," *JRCAS*, XLV (1958), 141-53; *Bulletin du Centre d'Études Kurdes*, Paris, 1948-50, Nos. 1-13; W.L.E., "Iraqi Kurdistan," *op. cit.*; Elphingston, "The Kurdish Question," *International Affairs*, XXII (1946), 91-103.

30. Homer Bigart, *New York Times*, May 26, 1957.

31. See "Chronique de sociologie kurde," *L'Afrique et L'Asie*, No. 40, 1957; Nos. 43, 44, 1958.

32. J. Weulersse, *Les Pays des Alaouites* (Tours, 1940), pp. 47, 64, 66, 126; R. Strothman, "Festkalender der Nusairier," *Der Islam*, XXVII (1946), 1-14; *ibid.*, "Die Nusairi im heutigen Syrien," *Nachrichten der Akademie der Wissenschaften in Göttingen* I, 1950, No. 4; E. J. Jurji, "The 'Alids of North Syria," *The Moslem World*, XXIX (1939), 329-41; É. de Vaumas, "Le Djebel Ansarieh," *Revue de Géographie Alpine*, XLVIII (1960), 266-311.

33. J. Wortabet, *Research into the Religions of Syria* (London, 1860), p. 289.

34. See Bouron, *Les Druzes* (Paris, 1930) pp. 411-13; F. Désidéri, "Au Djebel Druze," *L'Asie Française*, April 1932, pp. 133-35; Kurd 'Alī, al-Rifā'ī, *Jaghrafiyyat al-bilād al-'arabiyya* (Damascus, 1950), p. 121; Haim Blank, "Druze Particularism," *Middle Eastern Affairs*, III (1952), 320.

For their origin, see N. M. Izzedin, *The Racial Origins of the Druzes* (The University of Chicago Press, 1944).

35. The government newspapers did not conceal their affection for the adversaries of Atrash (*al-Qabs*, July 7, 1947). The opposition papers, however, accused the government of stirring up trouble (*al-Ahrār*, June 27, 1947; *al-Nidāl*, Nov. 12, 1947). According to *Alif Bā'* (Sept. 25, 1947) and *al-Ittihād al-Lubnānī* (Sept. 19, 1947), the great majority of the Jabal favored Sultān Atrash, but the government was seeking to overthrow his rule, so as to undermine the autonomy of the Jabal.

36. *al-Balad*, July 2, 1947; *al-Inshā'*, August 17, 1947. In respect to landed property, the accusation of feudalism levelled at one side does not correspond to facts, since both sides contained wealthy proprietors, followed by small owners.

37. *al-Hadaf*, April 23, 1946.

38. *al-Baradā*, April 27, 1946.

39. *al-Nasr*, Dec. 9, 1946.

40. Cf. the conflicting views of Menzel in EI and of F. Maier, "Der Name der Yazīdi's" in *Westöstliche Abhandlungen* (Wies-

baden, 1954), pp. 244-57. Maier holds to the probability of the derivation from Yazīd and of devil worship.

41. See the list of their villages in al-'Azzāwī, *Ta'rīkh al-ya-zīdiyya* (Baghdad, 1935), pp. 99-109.

42. Other sources: Lescot, *Enquête sur les Yezidis de Syrie et du Djebel Sindjar* (Beyrouth, 1938); Empson, *The Cult of the Peacock Angel* (London, 1928); Nikitine, *op. cit.*, pp. 226-29. A few different data are given in Sebri, Osman & Wikander, Stig: "Un témoignage sur les Yézidis du Djebel Sindjar," *Orientalia Suecana*, II (Uppsala, 1953), 112-18; *Report on the Administration of Iraq . . . For the Period January to October*, 1932, (London), pp. 5-6.

For somewhat different views see the exhaustive study by Thomas Bois, *al-Mashriq*, LV (1961), 109-20, 190-244. To him, "it is not easy to deny the Islamic origin of Yazīdism, although nothing of the Islamic religion is preserved in it" (p. 244).

43. *al-Kakā'iyya fī 'l-ta'rīkh* (Baghdad, 1949), pp. 30, 35, 95-98.

44. According to Edmonds, *Kurds, Turks, Arabs*, pp. 182, 190, 194-96, Kakai are known in western Persia as 'Ali-Ilāhi (*ahl i-haqq*, people of truth), although their latter name may denote other sects. In Iraq they "remain on the Sunni rather than on the Shi'a side of the border." They feel themselves Kurds.

45. Ahmad Hāmid al-Sarrāf, *al-Shabak, min firaq al-ghulāt fi 'l-'Irāq* (Baghdad, 1954), pp. 2, 92, 99, 121.

Sarli, a sect to be found in some villages, claim to belong to Kakai. See Minorsky, EI, Shabak.

Bajorān, who live in several villages, reverence the prophet Ishmael.

Minorsky stresses the attachment of these sects to Shī'i imāms and the syncretic tendencies of their faiths.

46. For the position of the Armenian Church in the Middle East and the hold of the pro-Soviet faction of the community on it, see S. Atamian, *The Armenian Community* (New York, 1955), pp. 440-70.

47. Louise Nalbandian, "Armenians in the Middle East," *The Armenian Review*, VIII (1955), 76-79; Vahe A. Sarafian "Armenian Population Statistics . . . ," *ibid.*, XI (1958), 83.

48. Oppenheim, *Vom Mittelmeer zum Persischen Golf* (Berlin, 1900), II, 69, 70.

49. Weulersse, *op. cit.*, pp. 47, 64, 66, 126.

50. *Ibid.*, p. 221, n. 1.

51. Oppenheim, *Die Beduinen,* I, 52.

52. Here they take an active part in political life. They are represented in the government and in the parliament and are a reliable element in the army.

53. The above is based mainly on a paper by Mlle. Proux, "Les Tcherkesses," *La France Méditerranéenne et Africaine,* 1938. See also: "La situation actuelle des Tcherkesses en Syrie," *L'Asie Française,* Mars 1933, pp. 94-95.

54. Edmonds, *op. cit.,* pp. 267-69, 275.

55. See Enzo Sireni, "Ba'ayat Yehudei Iraq," *Yalqut Hamizrah Hatikhon,* Jan. 1949, pp. 10-17; W. J. Fischel, "The Jews of Kurdistan," *Commentary,* VIII (1949), 554-59; Dr. Hayim Shushkes, *Hadoar,* March 3, 1961.

56. *Hapoel Hatza'ir,* June 25, 1957.

57. For the Nizāri Ismāʿīlis and their predecessors, see M. G. S. Hodgson, *The Order of the Assassins* (Hague, 1956).

58. Sources: W. Ivanov, *Studies in Early Persian Ismailism* (Leiden, 1948), pp. 1-31; *ibid., Ismāʿīlīya,* EI; Weulersse, *op. cit.,* pp. 61-64, 341; N.N. Lewis: "Malaria, Irrigation and Soil Erosion in Central Syria," *The Geographical Review,* XXXIX (1949), 284-86; "The Isma'ilis of Syria Today," *JRCAS,* XXXIX (1952), 69-77; "The Frontier of Settlement in Syria, 1800-1950," *International Affairs,* XXXI (1955), 57-58.

59. Widengren, *Mesopotamian Elements in Manichaeism,* Uppsala Universitets Årsscrift, 1946: 3, pp. 175-79.

60. Sources: E. S. Drower, *The Mandaens of Iraq and Iran* (Oxford, 1937), pp. xv-xxi, 1-16; Lady Drower, "Marsh People of South 'Iraq," *JRCAS,* XXXIV (1947), pp. 88-89; Oppenheim, *Vom Mittelmeer zum Persischen Golf,* II, 290; Alfred Loisy, *Le Mandéisme et les origines chrétiennes* (Paris, 1934); *Divan Abatur or Progress through the Purgatories* (text with translations by E. S. Drower), *Biblioteca Apostolica Vaticana,* 1950, p. iv.

61. S. Reich, *Études sur les villages araméens du L'Anti-Liban,* (Institut Français de Damas, 1937).

A. J. Maclean, *Grammar of the Dialects of Vernacular Syriac* . . . (Cambridge, 1895), pp. ix-xv; *ibid., A Dictionary of the Dialects of Vernacular Syriac* (Oxford, 1901), pp. ix-xii.

According to A. v. Kremer, *Mittelsyrien und Damascus* (Wien, 1853), p. 196, the inhabitants of the village Qaryaten on the way to Tadmor, Christians and Muslims alike, belonged to the tribe Qarāwina—"a collective name given to a certain sector of the rural population, perhaps originating from the ancient Syrian community." Many of the fellahin in Qaryaten spoke Aramaic along with Arabic.

In the 1870's Aramaic was said to have been spoken in Syria in 30 to 40 villages. See Prym, Socin, *Der Neu-Aramäische Dialect des Tûr 'Abdîn,* (Göttingen, 1881), I, vii.

62. For the vicissitudes of this church, see P. Kawerau, "Die nestorianischen Patriarchate in der neueren Zeit," *Zeitschrift für Kirchengeschichte,* LXVII (1955/6), 119-31; Wigram, *The Assyrians and Their Neighbours* (London, 1929).

63. *Report on 'Iraq Administration,* October 1920 to March 1922, pp. 102-10; *Special Report on the Progress of 'Iraq: 1920-1931,* pp. 267-74; *Report . . .* for January to October 1932, pp. 6-10; S. A. Morrison, "Religious Liberty in Iraq," *The Moslem World,* XXV (1935), 118-22. See also *Survey of International Affairs,* 1934, pp. 134-74; R. S. Stafford, *The Tragedy of the Assyrians* (London, 1935).

64. J. Rowlands, "The Khabur Valley," *JRCAS,* XXXIV (1947), 147, 144-49; H. B. Mar Eshai Shimun, "Assyrians in the Middle East," *JRCAS,* XL (1953), 151-56.

65. For the early patriarchates, see R. Strothmann, "Heutiges Orientchristentum und Schicksal der Assyrer," *Zeitschrift für Kirchengeschichte,* LV (1936), 36-39. For some statistical data I am indebted to Raymond Etteldorf, *The Catholic Church in the Middle East* (New York, 1959). See also G. Khouri-Sarkis, "Les églises de langue syriaque," *L'Orient Syrien,* I (1956), 9-22.

66. Kawerau, *"Die Jakobitische Kirche im Zeitalter der Syrischen Renaissance* (Berlin, 1950), pp. 97-100; R. Strothmann, "Ein orientalischer Patriarch der Gegenwart. Mar Ignatius Aphrem I Barsaum," *Zeitschrift für Kirchengeschichte,* LXIV (1952/3), 292-98.

67. L. Yaure, "A Poem in the Neo-Aramaic Dialect of Urmia," *JNES,* XVI (1957), 73.

68. Sources: F. Rosenthal, *Die aramäistische Forschung seit Nöldeke's Veröffentlichungen* (Leiden, 1939), pp. 254-69; A. Socin, *Die Neuaramäischen Dialecte von Urmia bis Mosul* (Tübingen, 1882), pp. v-viii; Nöldeke, *Grammatik der Neusyrischen Sprache am Urmia See und in Kurdistan* (Leipzig, 1868), pp. xxiv-xxvii; Ed. Sachau, *Skizze des Fellihi-Dialects von Mosul* (Berlin, 1895), pp. 3-4; Guidi, *Beiträge zur Kenntniss des*

neu-aramäischen fellîhî-dialectes, ZDMG, XXXVII (1883), 294-95; L. Yaure, *op. cit.,* pp. 76-79.

69. As far back as the 1830's, the Kurds served as a tool of the Ottoman government in assisting to eliminate the Aramaic-speaking Christians, and in massacres of Armenians in 1875 and 1915, a policy initiated by Abdul Hamid and continued by the Young Turks. The fate of the Kurds during 1914-17 at the hands of the government was not different from that of the Christians. In addition the Armenians retaliated under the cover of the Russians. See E. W. C. Noel, *On Special Duty in Kurdistan, July 1919* (Baghdad: Office of Civil Commissioner of Mesopotamia, 1919), pp. 4-15; Strothmann, "Heutiges Orientchristentum und Schicksal der Assyrer," *op. cit.,* pp. 41-42.

70. Weulersse, *op. cit.,* pp. 67, 70-71, 368-69.

71. In Palestine, with its larger Greek colony, the struggle between the high Greek hierarchy and the lower Arab clergy continued during all the period of the mandate. Prior to the 1948 war, the Orthodox community numbered 40,000, and in Transjordan, 10,000.

72. For the Christians in Central Syria, see R. Thoumin, *Géographie humaine de la Syrie Centrale* (Paris, 1936), pp. 213-14, 261-67, 332-33.

73. Weulersse, "Influences confessionnelles sur la démographie du Proche-Orient," *Cong. int. de la population* (Paris, 1937), VI, 23-26.

74. See N. Edelby, "Notre vocation de Chrétiens d'Orient," *Proche-Orient Chrétien,* III, (1953), pp. 201-17.

75. See Lootfy Levonia, "The Millet system in the Middle East," *The Muslim World,* XLII (1952), 90-96; Sir Harry Luke, *The Old Turkey and the New* (London, 1955), pp. 66-101.

I am much indebted to the following sources: R. Janin, *Églises orientales et rites orientaux* (Paris, 1955); P. Rondot, *Les Chrétiens d'Orient* (Paris, 1955); P. H. Musset, *Christianisme, spécialement en Orient* (Harissa-Liban, 1949), Vol. III.

NOTES TO CHAPTER TWO

1. Cf. estimates in Ziyadeh, *Syria and Lebanon* (New York, 1958), p. 25.

2. R. Thoumin, *Géographie humaine de la Syrie Centrale*

(Paris, 1936), pp. 332-37; Eliahu Epstein, "Demographic Problems of the Lebanon," *JRCAS*, XXXII (1946), 150-54; W. B. Fisher, "Some Problems of Population of the Lebanon" (in Arabic), *al-Abhāth*, IV (1951), 438-47; É. de Vaumas, "La répartition confessionnelle au Liban et l'équilibre de l'État libanais," *Revue de Géographie Alpine*, XLII (1955), 588-89; Salim Hass, "Emigration from Lebanon, Its History and Its Causes," *al-Abhāth*, XII (1959), 59-72.

3. This is their line of reasoning: The caliphs who conquered Syria left them their independence. In the tenth century the Druzes joined them. For about a thousand years the communities lived in harmony, and only in the nineteenth century, through foreign intrigues, the relations between them deteriorated. In the thirteenth and fourteenth centuries Sunnis and Shī'is reached Lebanon, in the seventeenth and eighteenth, groups of Orthodox and Catholics, and in our own days Armenians, Chaldeans, and Assyrians. Thus Lebanon became a refuge for Christian and Islamic communities who sought freedom at a time when it was not known in the Ottoman empire (Archbishop Mubārak, *al-Hadīth*, February 10, 13, 1943).

For an analysis of this concept see Nabih Amin Faris, Lebanon, "Land of Light," *The World of Islam*, Studies in honour of Philip K. Hitti, ed. by James Kritzek and R. Bayly Winder (London, 1959), pp. 335-50.

4. Y. Mārūn, *al-Makshūf*, March 30, 1942.

5. "If a generation shall arise which does not know what is national egotism, a ban on thought, and fanaticism of all kinds, the culture of Lebanon and its vocation can be an example to it —an example of synthesis and a vocation of mutual attachment." See 'Umar Fākhūrī, *al-Adīb*, March 1942.

"Lebanon is not just a geographical expression, but a historical reality, which has taken hundreds of years to be established so as to make it a refuge for oppressed peoples and a gathering place for courageous men burning for freedom and independence.

"Lebanon is not merely a conventional term, but a social and cultural necessity which the East cannot dispense with." See *al-Anbā'*, quoted in *La Syrie et l'Orient*, July 24, 1943.

To Faris (*op. cit.*, p. 349), "the Arab awakening of the nineteenth century was to a large extent the result of this rivalry between the foreign missionaries and their schools."

6. For an exposition of this concept see Michel Chiha, *Liban d'aujourd'hui* (1942), Beirut, 1949.

Undiluted nationalism was also advocated by Dr. Ayyūb Thābit, the late Protestant leader.

7. The pan-Arabs in Lebanon saw in the concept "Mediterranean culture" a thin veil for the extension of French Catholic influence in Lebanon.

8. "The Near East: The Search for Truth," *Foreign Affairs*, XXX (1952), 239. See also "The Meaning of the Near East," *Journal of International Affairs*, VI (1952), 32:

"For the significance of the Near East today is reduced into a function of its economic resources (mainly oil), strategic importance, and political relations. . . . But it is precisely in this habit of dissolving everything into oil and strategy and politics that the deepest crisis of Western culture at present consists."

9. A. I. Tannous, "The Village in the National Life of Lebanon," MEJ, III (1949), 157-63.

10. J. Gulick, "Conservatism and Change in a Lebanese Village," *MEJ*, VIII (1954), 283-307; M. Févret, "Un village du Liban: El Mtaïne," *Revue de Géographie de Lyon.*, XXV (1950), 267-87; R. E. Crist, "The Mountain Village of Dahr, Lebanon," *General Appendix to the Smithsonian Report for 1953* (Washington, 1954), pp. 407-18.

11. Najib Alamuddin, "Practical Proposals for the Solution of Land Tenure Problems in Lebanon," *Proceedings of the International Conference on Land Tenure* (Wisconsin, 1956), pp. 104-5.

12. 'Isām 'Ashūr, "Métayage in Syria, Lebanon and Palestine" (in Arabic), *al-Abhāth*, I (1948), 32-48, 47-69; *ibid.*, II (1949), 61-72. See also: P. A. Le Génissel S. L., "Le Liban a la croisée des chemins" (in Arabic), *al-Mashriq*, April-June 1951, pp. 276-91; *ibid.*, September-October 1951, pp. 185-202.

13. R. Pearse, *Three Years in the Levant* (London, 1949), pp. 234-36. For their origin, see P. H. Lammens, *Les "Perses" du Liban et l'origine des Métoualis* (Beirut, 1929).

14. M. Salamé, 'Un tribu chiite des montagnes de Hermel (Liban)," *Revue de Géographie de Lyon*, XXXII, No. 2 (1957), 9-26.

15. R. D. Matthews, M. Akrawi, *Education in Arab Countries of the Near East* (Washington, 1949), pp. 421-22, 504; Lucie Vidal, *l'Orient*, quoted in *l'Afrique et l'Asie*, 1950, 1er trim., p. 77.

16. "Ce qui s'impose, c'est dans l'infinie suplesse, dans l'adaptation indéfinie de la vie libanaise, un durcissement de la personnalité et du caractère." (M. Chiha, quoted in *L'Afrique et l'Asie*, 1949, 4e trim., p. 57).

17. C. G. Hess, Jr. and H. L. Bodman, Jr., "Confessionalism and Feudality in Lebanese Politics," *MEJ*, VIII (1954), 24.

18. The two sections of the community often help one another, especially in settlement of disputes. On his visit to Jabal al-Durūz, Kamāl Janbalāt recalled the memory of the time when "the hearts of the conquerors from the banks of the Bosporus to 'Arīsh in Egypt trembled before the Druzes." By their union and mutual help the two sections of the community created "the greatest social, political and military force in the Arab East" (*al-Jabal*, April 26, 1946).

19. The attitude of various factions on this matter found expression in the Chamber of Deputies on April 7, 1945. The Arab League Covenant was opposed by nine deputies, the remnant of the National Bloc, because they saw in it a curtailment of independence. They remembered the declarations of Nūrī al-Sa'īd, Sa'dallah al-Jābirī, and Fāris al-Khūri. But even those deputies who supported the Covenant differed as to its value. Joseph Karam, a Maronite, regarded fear as a source of discrepancy in Lebanon. "One party clings to the West for fear of the East, and the other turns towards the East." There was, however, an "intermediate view," which was that Lebanon should be completely independent. Syria recognised Lebanon conditionally, and these obscure conditions were sufficient to restrict the country's independence. Karāmeh, the Sunni premier, saw in the Covenant only a first step toward the goal. He himself had been one of the extreme advocates of "comprehensive Arab unity without condition or limitation," but he had crossed over to the camp of those "who wanted an independent and Arab Lebanon which would not be afraid of the Arab East," on condition that it "would act in concert with the Arab countries to the utmost limit."

Referring to the relations of Syria and Lebanon in the Syrian Chamber of Deputies, Fāris al-Khūri, who was then premier, stated that "the government of Syria had never recognised Lebanon, and had never abandoned its territorial demands in regard to it save in the Protocol of Alexandria, and then only on condition that Lebanon should be Arab and independent." It was better, in his opinion, that it should be independent and with a larger territory than small and under foreign domination, so as to become a center of propaganda and colonialist methods in the neighboring regions (*Alif Bā'*, April 5, 1945).

20. "Au Liban comme dans tous les pays d'Orient, le Parlementarisme, depuis 30 ans, est un instrument de corruption administrative et de régression sociale. . . . Et le premier problème pour un véritable 'progressisme libanais,' c'est de libérer le pouvoir exécutif des servitudes d'un électorat qui demeure soumis à l'Argent et aux vieux prestiges des forces féodales et des totems confessionnels." (G. Naccache, *L'Orient*, quoted in *L'Afrique et L'Asie*, 1952, No. 20, pp. 68-69.)

21. J. Donato, "Lebanon and its Labour Legislation," *International Labour Revue*, LXV (1952), 64-92; G. E. K., "Some Aspects of Lebanese Trade Unionism," *The World Today*, IX (1953), 409-13.

Other sources: N. N. Lewis, "Lebanon—The Mountain and its Terraces," *The Geographical Review*, XLIII (1953), 1-14; É. de Vaumas, "Les conditions naturelles de l'occupation humaine au Liban," *Annales de Géographie*, LVII (1948), 40-49; *ibid.*, "La répartition de la population au Liban," *Bulletin de la Société de Géographie d'Égypte*, XXVI (1953), 5-76; Arthur Edward Mills, "Economic Change in Lebanon," *Middle East Economic Papers* (Beirut, 1956), pp. 75-97; *ibid.*, "Private Enterprise in Lebanon," 1959; Charles Badly, "Contribution a l'étude climatique du Liban, *Revue de Géographie de Lyon*, XXXIV (1959), 57-73; M. Févret, "La sériculture au Liban," *ibid.*, XXIV (1949), 247-60, 341-62.

Also see P. Rondot, *Les Chrétiens d'Orient* (Paris, 1955); *ibid.*, "Les structures socio-politiques de la nation libanaise," *Revue Française de Science Politique*, IV (1954), 80-104; "Les nouveaux problèmes de l'État libanais," *ibid.*, pp. 326-56; G. Ménassa, *Plan de reconstruction de l'économie libanaise et de réforme de l'État* (Beirut, 1948); P. K. Hitti, *Lebanon in History* (London, 1957), pp. 482-507.

On the confessional and social composition of the Parliament see Ahmad Mustafā Haydar, *al-Dawla al-Lubnāniyya*, 1920-1953, Beirut; Lucien George, Toufic Mokdessi, *Les Partis Libanais en 1959* (in Arabic), ed. L'Orient-al-Jaryde.

NOTES TO CHAPTER THREE

1. *al-Misrī*, April 18, 1945.

2. Here are a few examples of the way in which these interests were intertwined.

Hāfiz 'Afīfī Pasha, former minister and king's chamberlain, was a partner in 31 companies, some of them owned by Bank Misr (banks, transport services, insurance, real estate, factories, film production, cotton ginning, export, etc.). He was chairman of 21 of them. The capital of the companies was £E 22 million.

Ismā'īl Sidqī, a partner in 14 companies with capital of more than £E 25 million. He was prime minister and head of the Federation of Manufacturers.

Sādiq Wahba Pasha, a partner in 12 companies with capital of more than £E 15 million. He owned large estates. Much capital of his own was invested in buildings. He had been minister of agriculture and a member of the Senate.

Husayn Sirrī Pasha, a partner in 27 companies and chairman of ten of them. Their capital was more than £E 27 million. He had been prime minister and a member of the Senate.

Similar positions were occupied by other ex-ministers—'Alī al-Shamsī, Muhammad Mahmūd Khalīl, Ahmad Ziwar, Ahmad Māhir, Hilmī 'Isā, and others. See *al-Wafd al-Misrī*, June 3, 9, 10, 12, 16, 1946; *al-Musawwar*, March 26, 1943.

3. Taha Husayn said to a Reuter's correspondent in Florence, in May 1951: "In special training we do not meet any difficulties, since Egyptian industry is interested in experts. On the other hand, in the sphere of general education there are those among us who are opposed to raising the intellectual level of the masses and to bringing up a free generation."

4. *al-Balāgh*, December 7, 1941.

5. Dr. Ahmad Husayn, *al-Misrī*, *op. cit.*

6. al-Ithnayn wa-'l-Dunyā, March 22, 1948.

7. *al-Ahrām*, April 11, 1945.

8. *Musāmarāt al-Jayb*, June 8, 1947; March 7, 1948; *al-Muqattam*, April 2, 1945.

9. *al-Ithnayn wa-'l-Dunyā*, *op. cit.*

10. *al-Wafd al-Misrī*, May 5, 1946; *al-Ahrām*, July 15, 16, 23, 1946. In 1946, the trade unions numbered about 130,000 members, constituting about a fifth of the industrial workers. See

Thomas B. Stauffer, "Labor Unions in the Arab World," *MEJ*, VI (1952), 86.

11. *L'Égypte Indépendante* (Paris, 1938), pp. 31-33.

12. Fu'ād Sirāj al-Dīn, whose family possessed estates estimated at 8,000 feddan. He also had money invested in the papers of the Wafd. See *al-Ahrām*, April 2, 1942; *al-Musawwar*, April 10, 1942.

13. *L'Égypte Indépendante*, pp. 390-91.

14. *Oriente Moderno*, II (1922/23), 388-89, also: Haykal, *mudhakkirāt fī 'l-siyāsa al-misriyya* (Cairo, 1951), I, 231-40.

15. See Haykal's address, *al-Siyāsa*, October 31, 1945.

16. *Oriente Moderno*, XVII (1937), 580.

17. *Ibid.*, XVIII (1938), 93.

18. *Ibid.*, p. 94.

19. *al-Ahrām*, July 7, 1942.

20. *Ibid.*, May 24, 1942.

21. *Ibid.*, August 19, 20, 1942.

22. "We are a non-belligerent nation, we have taken no part in the war, and our general policy is to keep free from the accidents of war." (*Ibid.*)

23. *al-Misri, Egyptian Gazette*, April 13, 15, 20, 22, 24, 29, 1943.

24. 'Ubayd drew a different conclusion: From 1919 to May 24, 1942, he was a "great fighter," but on the day on which he was expelled from the government, he became a "great liar," and only because he sought to give advice to his leader and colleague. "By Allah, I weep no tears but blood to see my companion in exile driving men into exile from their houses, throttling the press, and suppressing public opinion." See *al-Misri*, July 13, 17, 1943.

In this Wafdist paper 'Ubayd was pictured as follows: "A man who belittled everything great and mocked at everything precious and showed no respect for any heritage, and shot his arrows at every breast and dug his teeth into every heart and whose attacks spared neither the ministerial council nor the parliament . . . nor the parliamentary regime in general nor the honour of the nation either in the present or for the future." (*Ibid.*)

25. Oriente Moderno, *op. cit.*, pp. 450-51, 491-94. He is not identical with the above mentioned Ahmad Husayn.

26. The objects of the party were to make Egypt a great

state, the leader of Islam, united with the Sudan and allied with the Arab countries, and the liberation of the people from domination of the capitalist class.

Some of its "ten commandments" were: speak Arabic and only Arabic; buy Egyptian products, and if not available, Arab ones; purify yourself and pray to Allah; your nation is an Islamic nation and your land—Egypt and the Sudan—must not be divided; your fatherland is the whole of the Arab countries; your aim is to relieve your country from poverty and ignorance in order that Egypt may be a shining light to East and West in knowledge and faith and restore the greatness of Arabia and Islam.

Youth was called upon to "die the death of martyrs for the freedom of the fatherland." (*Misr al-Fatāh*, October 10, 17, 1945; *Egyptian Gazette*, September 17, 1945.)

27. *al-Ahrām*, August 15, 1949.

28. *Nahw Daw'* (Toward Light), Cairo, 1945, a letter sent by al-Bannā' to Fārūq and to al-Nahhās and the Arab kings. See also F. Rosenthal, "The Muslim Brethren in Egypt," *The Muslim World*, XXXVII (1947), 278-91.

29. *Da'watunā*, Cairo, 1945.

30. *Ibid.*, p. 8.

31. *Ibid.*, p. 15.

32. *al-Ahrām*, January 18, 1951.

33. In reference to its alleged connection with the murderers of the king of Yemen, see *al-Misrī*, March 27, 1948.

34. *al-Wafd al-Misrī*, May 5, 1946.

35. *al-Kutla*, October 5, 1946.

36. *al-Ahrām*, December 1, 1946.

37. In his letter to al-Nahhās, al-Bannā' sought to put a stop to this attack on the Brotherhood. The Wafd was still identifying itself with the people, but it was already decrepit. Communist elements had found their way into it. See *Akhbār al-Yawm*, May 10, 1947.

The Wafdist *Sawt al-Umma* of May 9, 1947, retorted with bitter attacks on al-Bannā', "the enemy of Allah and the Muslims, a tool of the existing regime and of imperialism."

Al-Bannā thereupon discarded al-Sukkarī, his assistant, who was accused of taking bribes from the Wafd. Al-Sukkarī then made public some of the "corrupt transactions" of al-Bannā' in the opposition papers. Sukkarī's supporters brought to light financial connections between al-Bannā' and the government of Sidqī and al-Nuqrāshī, and even with foreigners. See *Egyptian Gazette*, October 16, 1947; *Sawt al-Umma*, October 14, November 5, 19, 1947.

38. *Sawt al-Umma*, 1950, quoted in *Hamisrah Hehadash*, January 1950, p. 150.

39. *Le Monde*, December 1, 1952.

40. Cf. Ishak Musa Husaini, *The Moslem Brethren* (Beirut, 1956), pp. 136-37. For greatly differing views on the last period see Lacouture, *Egypt in Transition* (New York, 1958), especially, pp. 179-91, 244-56.

41. *al-Musawwar*, October 11, 1946.

42. *Bilādī*, July 16, 1946.

43. *Musāmarāt al-Jayb*, October 6, 1946.

44. *Sawt al-Umma*, October 26, 1946.

45. *Mabādī fī 'l-siyāsa al-misriyya* (Cairo, 1942), p. 113. Hence change of party attachment became unusually frequent, especially in the first half of the period under review.

46. See Thomas Russell, *Egyptian Service*, 1902-1946 (London, 1949), pp. 214-15.

47. al-Nahhās accused, as organizers of the attempts, the office managers of Ibrāhīm 'Abd al-Hādī, king's chamberlain, and of al-Nuqrāshī, both of them Sa'dists. See *al-Misrī*, January 12, 1951.

The assassin of Amīn 'Uthmān confessed that he had also made an attempt on the life of al-Nahhās. The murderer of Ahmad Māhir was also a member of his society. See Akhbār al-Yawm, January 12, 1946.

To Anwar El Sadat (*Revolt on the Nile* [London, 1957], p. 110), the "Muslim Brothers had to their credit the assassination of Ahmed Maher, Amin Osman, and Selim Zaki, the Cairo Chief-of-Police, as well as several attempts against Nahhās Pasha's life."

48. See Dr. Haykal's address on the aniversary of the death of Mahmūd Pasha (*al-Ahrām*, February 1, 1943). Also the address of al-Nahhās on Constitution Day. (*Ibid.*, March 16, 1943).

49. *al-Ithnayn wa-'l-Dunya*, March 15, 1943. Other sources: Jacob M. Landau, *Parliaments and Parties in Egypt* (New York, 1954); J. Heyworth-Dunne, *Religious and Political Trends in Modern Egypt* (Washington, 1950).

NOTES TO CHAPTER FOUR

1. See *Majallat al-Sharq* (San Paolo), special issue on Syria, 1951, p. 58.

2. *Ibid.*, pp. 58-63; *al-Ahzāb al-siyāsiyya fī sūriya* (Damascus, 1951), pp. 11-16.

3. King 'Abdallah thought that "the blood of al-Shahbandar removed [in 1948] al-Quwwatlī from his seat and exiled Jamīl Mardam from his country." See also his *My Memories Completed* (al-Takmilah), Washington, 1954, pp. 28-29.

4. See *al-Ahzāb, op. cit.*, p. 134.

5. *Ibid.*, p. 138.

6. *Ibid.*, p. 143; see also *Entretiens sur l'évolution des pays de civilisation arabe* (Paris, 1938), p. 100.

7. *al-Ahzāb*, p. 215.

8. *Ibid.*, pp. 218-19.

9. *Ibid.*, p. 92.

10. *Ibid.*, p. 117.

11. *Ibid.*, p. 97.

12. *Ibid.*, p. 116.

13. *Majallat al-Sharq*, p. 74. Another version: it includes, too, the Sinai peninsula, the 'Aqaba gulf, the Sahara and Cyprus, the latter being a "star in the Syrian Fertile Crescent." See *al-Ahzāb*, p. 115.

14. *al-Ahzāb*, p. 120.

15. *Ibid.*, p. 121.

16. *Ibid.*, p. 126.

17. *Ibid.* See also a partisan publication *Sa'āda wa-'l-hizb al-qawmī*, 1933-1951 (Damascus, 1950), pp. 17, 20, 23-24, 100; a pamphlet of the Ministry of Information in Lebanon: *Qadiyyat al-hizb al-qawmī*, Beirut, 1949.

18. *al-Ahzāb*, p. 51.

19. *Ibid.*, p. 60.

20. *Ibid.*, p. 51.

21. *Ibid.*, p. 60.

22. *Ibid.*, p. 51.

23. *Ibid.*, p. 12.

24. *Ibid.*, p. 16.

25. *Ibid.*, p. 27.

26. *Ibid.*, p. 16.

27. *Majallat al-Sharq*, p. 67.

28. *Ibid.*

29. *al-Ahzāb*, p. 242.

30. *Ibid.*, p. 241.

31. Michel Aflaq, *Middle East Forum*, February 1958, p. 10.

32. *Ibid.*

33. Salāh Bītar, *ibid.*, p. 8.

34. *al-Ahzāb*, p. 251.

35. Aflaq, *op. cit.*, p. 10.

36. *al-Ahzāb*, p. 244.

37. *Ibid.*, p. 245.

38. *Ibid.*, p. 251.

39. *Aflaq, op. cit.* For data on the parties see also *Oriente Moderno*, XXX (1950), 136-38.

NOTES TO CHAPTER FIVE

1. V. H. Dowson, "Iraq in 1946," *JRCAS*, XXXIII (1946), 254.

2. In 1930 the moderate Covenant (*'ahd*) Party of Nūrī al-Sa'īd faced the National (*watanī*) Party which declined co-operation with the British. The National Brotherhood (*al-ikhā al-watanī*) Party, a merger of members of two parties—*al-watanī* and *al-sha'b* (people)—emerged out of opposition to some stipulations of the Anglo-Iraqi Treaty of 1930. See Majid Khadduri, *Independent Iraq*, London 1960, p. 29.

The citizens' (*ahālī*) group in the thirties was the first attempt to form an association professing social reformism. It comprised some young intellectuals schooled in the West (Kāmil al-Jādirjī), and some of the old-school nationalist leaders. In spite of this it took part, if temporarily, in the *coup d'état* government of Hikmat Sulaymān (October 1936–June 1937).

3. The main criticisms directed against the government were that it ruled as a dictatorship, that anyone who demanded reforms was regarded as a dissenter and that young intellectuals were thrown into prison and beaten for adopting "subversive principles" which were only the principles of social justice. The press was fettered by emergency laws, and it was forbidden to publish a debate in the parliament which was not approved of. The economic system was rotten; the plague of bribery and peculation had spread to offices of the government. Powerful men

received thousands and tens of thousands of donums of state land, and it was they who mainly benefited from the twenty million dinar which in the course of twenty years had been spent on irrigation. Tens of thousands of fellahin had migrated to the towns, where they were living on dung heaps and in reed huts. Only seventeen children out of a hundred had attended primary schools of four classes only. See *al-Zamān*, Feb. 18, 20, 26, 27, 1946.

4. Social criticism in the periodicals, mainly edited by left-wing or pro-Communist intellectuals (*al-Majalla, al-Rābita, Muthul 'Ulyā*) tackled largely the agrarian conditions.

5. See Jādirdjī's speech outlining the party's program, *Sadā al-Ahālī*, October 30, 1950.

6. To him, the coup was justified because the governments that preceded it were tyrannical. See *Sawt al-Ahālī*, January 21, 1946.

7. Among its founders was Muhammad Mahdī Kubba, leader of this party. In July 1958 he became a member of the Council of Sovereignty established to carry out presidential duties until a referendum had been held.

8. See Kubba's speech at a party conference. To him, the country has to adopt principles of "democratic national socialism." Other leaders: Fā'iq al-Sāmarrā'i, Siddīq Shanshal. See *Liwā al-Istiqlāl*, November 5, 1950.

9. See *al-Qā'ida*, organ of the Iraqi Communist Party, January 18, February 15, 1946; *Shursh*, February 1946.

10. Judging from a declaration of the Communist Party in Iraq, in 1956, it contains a "section of Kurdistan." Through participation in the Arab liberation movement, Iraqi Kurdistan aims at preserving its national identity within Iraq. Likewise, the common struggle is to enable the Kurdish nation to prepare the conditions needed to exercise the right of self-determination, including the right to form an independent state comprising the whole of Kurdistan. See *Ittihād al-Sha'b*, January 30, 1959, quoted in *Orient*, No 10, 1959, pp. 151-54.

11. When Tawfīq al-Suwaydī said, while in London in 1938, that in case of war Iraq would have to observe the clauses of her treaty with Great Britain, the German ambassador appealed to the Rashīd army camp. This was one of the reasons of the "movement" within the army. See Nūrī al-Sa'īd's speech in the House of Deputies, *al-Thaghr*, November 13, 1941.

A curious means of preventing a drift into chaos in the thirties was *isdāl al-sitār* (drawing the curtain), that is, to ignore or condone various illegal actions, including coups, of the elements in opposition.

12. See E. A. Kinch, Social Effects of the Oil Industry, *International Labour Revue*, LXXV (1957), No. 3, pp. 192-206.

13. The United Democratic Party seems to be closely allied with the Communist Party, at least in matters of terminology. It stands for "struggle against imperialism, reaction and feudalism," for protection of the "anti-imperialist, anti-feudal social classes" and the ethnic minorities, and for solidarity of the two ethnic groups. "The problem of the Kurdish people in Iraq is an integral part of the problem of Iraq itself." See *Ittihād al-Shaʿb*, May 7, 1959, quoted in *Orient*, No. 10, 1959, pp. 159-60.

NOTES TO CHAPTER SIX

1. In September 1952, a period of self-purge was set up for the parties, but the government considered it a failure. In January 1953, all of them, except the Muslim Brotherhood, were disbanded.

2. "It was to prepare the people to participate . . . in the new political parties that we hoped to create before the third anniversary of the revolution." See Neguib, *Egypt's Destiny* (London, 1955), p. 181.

3. *Ibid.*, p. 184; *al-Ahrām*, December 15, 1952.

4. The old constitution, abrogated on December 10, 1952, safeguarded these rights, too, within the limits of the law.

5. *al-Ahrām*, July 27, 1953.

6. Neguib, *op. cit.*, p. 186.

7. *Ibid.*, p. 187.

8. See Jean Vigneau, "L'Idéologie de la révolution égyptienne," *Politique Étrangère*, XXII (1957), 448.

9. Neguib, p. 199.

10. *Ibid.*, p. 214.

11. *Ibid.*, p. 216.

12. *Ibid.*, p. 222.

13. *Ibid.*, p. 226.

14. *Ibid.*, p. 232-35. For other versions, see "The Middle East

and North Africa," *Survey of International Affairs,* 1954 (London, 1957), pp. 185-89.

15. *al-Ahrām,* March 30, 1955.

16. *Egyptian Gazette,* May 20, 1955.

17. *al-Ahrām,* July 5, 1955.

18. "How Should an Arab Unity Be?" *al-Hilāl* (December 1940), p. 2; also "Egypt after 25 years," *al-Balāgh,* March 3, 1942.

19. *al-Muqattam,* September 16, 1941.

20. Ahmad Amīn, a broadminded Muslim thinker, saw Arab unity as a kind of confederation of four states: Egypt as one state; Palestine, Lebanon, and Transjordan forced into another state; Iraq; and the other countries in Arabia. Each state was to be independent in domestic matters but bound by cultural, economic, and political ties to the other states. Mutual help would be the basis of the unity. A league of Arab nations could avoid the mistakes of the old League of Nations, which was enslaved by the needs of one or two states. See "Arab Unity," *al-Thaqāfa,* August 5, 1941.

21. See 'Abd al-Nāsir's preface to Muhammad Mustafā 'Atā, *misr bayn thawratayn* (Cairo, 1956), series *ikhtarnā laka,* 16, p. 6.

22. El Ghonemy, "Investment Effects of the Land Reform in Egypt," *L'Égypte Contemporaine,* October 1954, p. 14.

23. El Daly, "Birth Rate and Fertility Trends in Egypt," *L'Égypte Contemporaine,* October 1953, pp. 1, 2, 11.

24. Vigneau, *op. cit.,* p. 455, quoted from a pamphlet of the Liberation Rally, *North Africa in Past, Present and Future* (Cairo, October 1954).

25. *Ibid.*

26. *al-Mu'tamar al-islāmī,* Cairo [1956], p. 14.

27. *Ibid.*

28. *Ibid.*

29. See 'Abd al-Nāsir's preface to Dr. Husayn Mu'nis, *misr wa-risālatuhā* (Cairo, 1956), p. 5.

30. *Ibid.,* p. 7.

31. Amīn Shākir, Sa'īd al-'Iryān, 'Alī Adham, *haqīqat al-shuyū-'iyya* (Cairo, 1956), series *ikhtarnā laka,* 11, pp. 170-77. A second edition, with slight changes, appeared in 1959, series *kutub siyāsiyya,* p. 102.

32. *Ibid.,* p. 7.

33. See Osgood Caruthers, *New York Times,* July 6, 1958; Jay Walz, *ibid.,* December 18, 1960.

34. See Muhammad Mustafā ʿAtā, *op. cit.*, p. 5.

35. See preface of ʿAbd al-Nāsir to Dr. ʿAbd al-ʿAzīz ʿAbd al-Majīd, *al-umma wa-ʾl-muwātin al-sālih* (Cairo, 1956), series *ikhtarnā laka*, 18, p. 7.

36. Osgood Caruthers, *New York Times*, December 6, 1957.

37. "A Declaration of Fundamental Principles," *The Egyptian Economic & Political Revue*, January, 1958.

38. "Pragmatic Socialism," *ibid.*, May–June, 1959.

39. Osgood Caruthers, *ibid.*

40. *New York Times*, February 23, 1958.

41. *Ibid.*, July 23, 1958.

42. The lesson of Iraq has caused a shift away from al-Baʿth. They served as a factor making for unity "where the only significant political elements are Arabs and where division tends to be more between Muslims and Christians." In Iraq, where there is a large non-Arab Muslim community, such as the Kurds, al-Baʿth tend to become a dividing factor. They tend to place political union of the Arabs above religious loyalty of Muslims. "Arabism in its purely political, linguistic and racial context, would only be another historical phenomenon in the rise and decline of political nationalism." See "Iraqi Defection," *The Egyptian Economic & Political Revue*, March–April, 1959.

The argument between Iraq and Egypt runs along the following lines:

Egyptian spokesmen maintain that Qāsim has "placed the political survival of his regime upon the armed forces, the Communist minorities and the wayward fantasies of the unreliable restless Kurds." See "*After Mosul*," *ibid.*

The writer Dhū al-Nūn Ayyūb, director general of guidance and broadcasting in Iraq, contends that ʿAbd al-Nāsir sought to "expand his hegemony" to Iraq, so as to find sources for industrial projects and markets for Egyptian capital. In the middle of the twentieth century he cherishes dreams of the Middle Ages. He sent arms to the rebels in Mosul. He extinguished democratic liberties in Egypt, suppressed the trade-unions and democratic parties, whereas Qāsim restored liberties to his people. People who assisted ʿAbd al-Nāsir in annexing Syria are traitors to the Arab cause. See *Orient*, No. 9, (1959), pp. 113-19.

NOTES TO CHAPTER SEVEN

1. On the rule of the National Bloc and Quwwatlī's policy, see *Memoirs of Muhammad Kurd 'Ali* (Washington, 1954), pp. 210-12, 214-17.

2. King 'Abdullah thought that the "blood of Shahbandar removed al-Quwwatlī from his seat and exiled Jamīl Mardam from his country." See *My Memoirs Completed (al-Takmilah)*, (Washington, 1954), p. 29.

3. "Shukri al-Quwwatlī and I did not see eye to eye, but when Husni al-Za'īm staged his coup I wrote to al-Quwwatlī inviting him to come to Amman and set up a government there. Thereupon Egypt suddenly began to show interest in Husni al-Za'īm; it . . . abandoned its former friend." *Ibid.*, p. 37.

4. According to "a person close to this party," al-Za'īm and Sa'āda met on May 27. The latter undertook to rouse the populace against the government in Lebanon, while al-Za'īm on his side pledged himself to support the party within "natural Syria," which in the opinion of both was a unit that should not be divided. Common points in their policies were: abolition of feudalism, separation of religion from the state, etc. Army lorries helped the party to bring arms to Lebanon. When al-Barāzī returned from Egypt, which sought to mediate in settling the economic dispute between Lebanon and Syria, Za'īm's attitude changed. See *Sa'āda wa-'l-hizb al-qawmī, 1933-1951*, pp. 173, 187, 188, 191.

5. In the trial of Hinnāwī's murderer, who was a cousin of al-Barāzī, the public prosecutor alleged that the *coup d'état* had taken place in the night, the Barāzī's case had been heard in the morning, and after it he had been executed. The defendant, however, asserted that al-Barāzī had been taken out of his house to the general staff building at three in the morning, that from there he had been immediately transferred to al-Mezze, and that five minutes later he had been put to death.

Barāzī's son gave evidence that at half-past two or three some drunken officers penetrated into their house. His father had been forced into an armored car with curses and blows. Near al-Mezze he saw officers shooting at al-Za'īm for five minutes. Soldiers trampled on his body. See *al-Hayāh*, Beirut, November 2, 1950; *al-Hātif*, Baghdad, December 21, 1950.

6. Another source attributes to him other qualities, some contradictory: fermeté de caractère, acharnement au combat, officer méditatif, au désintéressement évident, ennemi du panache et du faste, d'un abord très simple et parfois bourru. See Charentenay, "Où va la Syrie?," *L'Afrique et l'Asie*, 1949, 3e trim., pp. 48-57.

Kurd Ali, *op. cit.*, p. 213, praises the "hero of Damascus," a son of "the learned Sheikh Rida al-Za'im."

Special mention must be made of the instructive article by Alford Carleton, "The Syrian coups d'état," *MEJ*, IV (1950), 1-11.

7. On the fortieth day after his death a newspaper of Iraq mourned him in a special issue. See *al-Yaqza*, December 12, 1950.

8. *Ibid.*, November 12, December 6, 1950. On the techniques of such indictments see *My Memoirs Completed, op. cit.*, p. 28.

9. See the indictment of the military investigator, *al-Ayyām*, January 11, 18, 1951.

10. *al-Jarīda*, March 10, 1954, as quoted in Taysīr Jīfī, *al-thawrāt wa-'l-inqilābāt fī dhākirat al-'ālam al-'arabī* (Damascus, 1954), pp. 123-24.

11. See Georgio Chamy, "L'Énigme Syrienne," *Études Méditerranéennes*, 1957, No. 2, pp. 47-66; Bishr al-'Awf, *al-inqilāb al-sūrī*, Damascus, 1949; Saqqāl, *min dhikriyyāt hukūmat al-za'im Husnī al-Za'īm*, Cairo, 1952.

NOTES TO CHAPTER EIGHT

1. In his study "La langue française avant et après la révolution" (*Critiques littéraires*, [Paris, 1936], pp. 34-85, from *L'Ére Nouvelle*, 1894, pp. 24-46, 216-42), Lafargue tried to account for the changes in French in terms of social and cultural trends. As the Enlightenment movement gathered strength, the needs of expression multiplied and educated society began to borrow, carefully testing and weighing, elements from popular speech. Slowly, a smoothly constructed language came into being which assumed democratic features.

With the revolution, the center of public life shifted from the *salon* to the street. Political and social life grew tempestuous and changes in language followed suit: new nouns and verbs appeared, countless metaphors were coined, and old phrases were given new meanings. As the revolutionary urge died down, it subsided in language, also. The language of the bourgeoisie had crystallized.

The polemics between those who rejected innovations in language and those who favored them at that period are by no means dissimilar to the controversies which flared up after World War I. One school claimed that literature had been captured by the untalented, that inflated ideas had given rise to bombastic style, to dazzling but sterile phrases. Their opponents contended that the language was purified in the furnace of the revolution, that most of the innovations were remarkable images of the course of events.

For the controversy over purism in Germany from the seventeenth century onwards, see the fine résumé by Fr. Mehring, "Über Sprache und Stil," *Neue Zeit*, January 1913, pp. 456-69. Goethe "cursed all negative purism." Lessing and Schiller, too, made a stand against the "pedants."

2. *Fī awqāt al-farāgh* (Cairo, 1925?), pp. 368-69.

3. *Ibid.*, p. 369.

4. *Ibid.*, pp. 371-74.

5. *Ibid.*, p. 356. Cf. Ahad Ha'am's statement on Hebrew some fifty years ago: "If you wish to bring the language to life, you must attempt to revive literature. And if you wish to revive literature, you must infuse it with live thought. . . . Improve thought, and it will raise the standard of the language." ("The Language and Its Literature," *At the Crossroads* (in Hebrew), I (1921), 195-96.

6. *Mutāla'āt fī al-kutub wa-'l-hayāt* (Cairo, 1924), pp. 228, 230.

7. *Hāfiz wa-Shawqī* (Cairo, 1933), p. 71.

Ibn al-Muqaffa' was the translator of Kalīla wa-Dimna (d. ca. 142 A.H.) His direct and economical style marked a sharp deviation from the 'arabiyya.

Al-Jāhiz (d. ca. 256 A.H.) was the first polyhistor in the Arabic literature. His work on the position of Arabic in various social groups is most revealing.

It was an upsurge of human interests in the literature of the ninth and tenth centuries—with due reserve to be called humanism—that brought about these changes in Arabic.

In the eleventh century, traditionalism gained the day. A forceful prose, capable of serving exact thinking, was replaced by rhymed prose, which subsequently pervaded for many centuries nearly all branches of prose communication. See W. Marçais, "La Langue Arabe," *Bulletin des Études Arabes*, Alger, January–February, 1945, pp. 4-5.

Pre-Islamic Arabic already had a large foreign element drawn from Hebrew, Aramaic, and Persian. The conquests brought it in closer touch with them and with Coptic as well. The controversy over "old" and "new" could be traced to the first century A.H. From the beginning of Islam the terminology in law and grammar had been built up, by way of new derivations or modification of the meaning of existing words. The translations of scientific works from Greek, chiefly by the medium of Syriac, forced the language to respond with new terms—the philologists notwithstanding. Down to the fourteenth century, Arabic was in a tense state of growth and adaptation. And how many peoples, from Turkestan to Morocco, have left the imprint of their world outlook and of their imaginative power on this language! Cf. Charles Pellat, *Langue et littérature arabes* (Paris, 1952), pp. 41-45. See also a stimulating review of this book by Adolphe Faure, *Hespéris*, XL (1953), 265-68.

8. *Bayn al-jazr wa-'l-madd* (Cairo, 1924), pp. 155-56.

9. *Ibid.*, p. 42.

10. *Op. cit.*, pp. 79, 80.

11. *Ibid.*, pp. 83, 82.

12. Some of these factors are masterfully summarized by J. H. Kramers, "The Language of the Koran," *Analecta Orientalia* (Leiden, Brill), 1956, pp. 150-52.

13. al-Suyūtī, *al-Muzhir* (Cairo, 1325), pp. 18, 20, 126.

14. Abu 'Ubayd, *Fadā'il al-Qor'ān wa'ādābuh* (ms.), *Bāb i'rāb al-Qor'ān*. See Brockelmann, *Geschichte der Arabishen Literatur*, I, 106.

15. Goldziher, *Muhammedanische Studien*, I, 170, 212, 213.

16. G. E. von Grunebaum, "The Aesthetic Foundation of Arabic Literature," *Comparative Literature*, IV (1952), 331.

In the course of time, 'arabiyya, considered a subsidiary to theology, became an end in itself. Overindulgence in grammar was severely criticized. It deprives the heart of humility; study of 'arabiyya leads to contempt for people. See Goldziher, *Stellung der alten islamischen Orthodoxie zu den antiken Wissenschaften* (Berlin: kön. Akademie der Wissenschaften, 1916), p. 9.

17. J. Pedersen, "The Islamic Preacher," *Ignace Goldziher Memorial Volume*, I, 226-51.

A liberal exposition of rhetoric, stemming from an evolutionist approach to the language, is given by al-Zayyāt in *Difāʿ ʿan al-balāgha* (Cairo, 1945), p. 120. His concept of *balāgha* covers writers once considered modernists (Taha Husayn, Taymūr, al-Māzinī) as opposed to those who use a literary or market vernacular (*suqiyya* or *ʿāmmiyya adabiyya*). Unfortunately, in asserting that strong manhood is coextensive with rhetoric he throws into one pot, as examples of audacity of heart and tongue, ʿAli, al-Hajjāj, Tarīq, Alexander the Great, Caesar, Napoleon, Hitler, Churchill, Mustafā Kāmil.

18. *Mukhtārāt Salāma Mūsā* (Cairo, 1927), pp. 52, 6; see also "Arabic Language Problems," *Middle Eastern Affairs*, VI (1955), pp. 41-44.

The argument is indicative of the gradual change in literature itself, which becomes more and more a literature of the middle class, of the self-made man. Similar changes occurred in the third century A.H., during which the hegemony passed to the citizens of the large cities (Mez, *Die Renaissance des Islams*, p. 227). Curiously enough, some *laudatores temporis acti* of Egypt cleave to the *tempus actum* in Baghdad and other Arab capitals in the ʿAbbāssid period, while this literature actually proves the point of the innovators, not only because of the shift of stress to prose, to the multitude and matters of interest, but also because of the relation of its principal writer, al-Jāhiz, to foreign literature.

Owing to economic and social decline resulting from the disintegration of the ʿAbbāsid empire, the *ʿarabiyya* had been eliminated from the spoken language and "conservatives" prevailed for centuries.

J. Fück (*ʿArabiyya, Untersuchungen zur arabischen Sprach— und Stilgeschichte*, 1950) made a comprehensive contribution toward destroying the dogma of *ʿarabiyya* as a uniform and obligatory pattern. This was done, broadly speaking, in three ways:

1. By defining the stages in the development of Arabic in terms of historical periods.

2. By expounding the close relationship between the language and social stratification.

3. By emphasizing the change in standards of purism from period to period.

19. ʿAli ʿAbd al-Rāziq, one of the most daring among liberal

Muslims, writes in his essay on "The Quality of Speech in the Arabic Language":

"And with regard to the nature of the Arabs, this is doubtless among the most perfect thereof, the Arab souls being the purest of souls and their hearts of the most wakeful of hearts, and undoubtedly the Arabs possess some of the finest comprehensions among men, because of their purity of character and excellencies of temperament.

"And of the languages current in our age, Arabic is undoubtedly the most ancient, the firmest in its spirit, and most praiseworthy in its history" (*Ahsan ma katabtu*, ed. *al-Hilāl*, 1934, pp. 135-36).

Mansūr Fahmī, a prose lyricist, makes the pangs of expression a kind of inner worship:

"Let the writer struggle and toil and pass nights seeking one word out of many. Nay more: after a pearl wherein he houses a novel concept. Yes, more: for the mingling and combination of letters, which are as notes expressing the lofty and melodious sounds of concept. Aye, more: for the bonfire illuminating that which is concealed in the folds of the soul, so that it may be clear and light" (*Khatarāt nafs*, Cairo, 1930, pp. 93-98, 100).

This is not particular to Egypt. The late Dr. Shahbandar, an enlightened Syrian leader, praised King Faysal in the following terms: "He was courageous of soul and rich in intelligence; he lived for the sake of others: for his body grew thin that his brethren should grow fat. . . . So he ascended the ladder of glory, but on the skulls of the enemies of Arabism" (*Ahsan mā katabtu*, p. 9).

20. The basic element of a meaning in an Arabic root is frequently and often easily traceable in immediate and sensuous impressions of a primitive man in his contacts with nature. See Goldziher, *"Beiträge zur Geschichte der Sprachgelehrsamkeit bei den Arabern." Sitzungsberichte der phil.—hist. Classe der kais. Academie der Wissenschaften*, Wien, LXVII (1871), 215-16.

21. See Franz Rosenthal in his highly instructive *Humor in Early Islam* (Philadelphia, 1956), pp. 1-16; also Prof. Margoliouth, "Wit and Humour in Arabic Authors," *Islamic Culture*, I (1927), 522-34.

22. See Shouby, "The Influence of the Arab Language on the Psychology of the Arabs," *MEJ*, V (1951), 284-302. To him, the main factors which feed the conservatism of Arabic are: close

attachment to the literary heritage, and Arab nationalism which rests on the laurels of the past. Its main characteristics are: over-assertion and exaggeration; abundance of details in which the main issue is lost; stereotyped emotional expressions and other rhetorical devices. All this cannot but weaken the power of the thought and cause vagueness. The preoccupation with word-play, assonance, and a mild form of rhymed word-endings gives pleasure to author and reader alike. The literary language serves the *ideal ego* of the Arab, while the vernacular serves his every-day life. The antinomy in the process of expression is one of the main sources of the antinomies in the Arab individuality.

Shoubi's conclusions do not conflict with Ch. Issawi (*ibid.*, pp. 525-26) on the possibilities of Arabic as an instrument of ex-pression after it will have become the property of the whole of society and after the Arab mind will have been refined in the furnace of Western thought and modern science.

J. Lecerf (*L'Afrique et L'Asie*, No. 22, 1953, pp. 60-61) con-siders influence of a language on the mentality a "notion absolu-ment chimérique." And yet it is futile to deny the retarding effect of amassed clichés and all the stereotyped devices of ex-pression, which are absorbed in the memory and nurtured by ideological (religious, national) motives. Of course, being condi-tioned, it may be transitory.

Here one cannot overemphasize the aesthetic approach to Arabic. It is a criterion of *l'art pour l'art*, as Ch. Pellat put it. Curiously enough, it is combined mainly with service to the upper stratum of an authoritarian society.

L. Massignon ("*Mouvement intellectuel du Proche-Orient*," *Hesperia*, No. 10, 1953, pp. 71-79) seems to be concerned more with the moral individuality of Arabic and the forms of thinking enshrined in it, that is, *his* vision of Arabic: "solid like silex and, like it, capable of sparkling; sapient, more than philosophical, condensed, enemy of paraphrases," and which, unlike Hebrew and Aramaic, kept the "Semitic intellectual mission, certain sig-nificant and original values of religious life intact." He denounces intellectual conformity to Western capitalism and to communism alike, and discerns traces of renascence in efforts to find, some-times by the medium of foreign inspiration, the "ancient per-sonality of Semitic intellectuality" (the short stories of Taymūr, recovered through Maupassant; the metric novelties of Ma'lūf from Brasil that tied surrealism to the medieval poem *zajal*). Cf.

his paper: "Language," in *Mid-East: World-Center*, ed. by Ruth Nanda Anshen (New York, Harper, 1956), pp. 235-51. Recently ʿAbd al-Rahmān Badawī uncovered a native source for Arab existentialism in Sūfism.

H. A. R. Gibb stresses the immediacy of artistic speech upon the Arab mind: "The words, pressing through no filter of logic or reflection which might weaken or deaden their effect, go straight to the head"; and "the part that language plays in determining his psychological attitudes." See *Modern Trends in Islam* (Chicago, 1946), p. 5.

To ʿAdnān al-Atāsī (*Azamāt fī sūriya*, Damascus, 1954, pp. 79, 80), owing to inherited predilection for word and its sound, word overpowers sense and makes it seemingly easy to solve world and national problems by a "web of gleaming expressions."

Anīs Furayha (*Nahwa ʿarabiyya muyassara*, Beirut, 1955) complains about the duplicity of the "linguistic personality": a "flowing chain" in everyday life, and a "knotted" one in official capacity, as preacher, broadcaster, lawyer. This duplicity bars spontaneity, burdens the thought, and has its part in forming the Arab personality. Furayha speaks of the "tyranny of form over meaning." He himself, when writing, feels that he is an employee of the language. In the last thirty years, a common colloquial tongue of the educated in Arab lands is coming into being. It is formed in school, press, conferences, radio, and draws on the classical language and on the spoken alike. See also Sātiʿ al-Husrī, *Arāʾ wa-ahādīth fī al-lugha wa-ʾl-adab*, Beirut, 1958, pp. 42-48.

The deliberations at the Congress of Arab Academies (Mushkilāt al-lugha al-ʿarabiyya, *Majallat al-Majmaʿ al-ʿIlmī al-ʿArabī*, Damascus, XXXII [1957], 3-281) betray some helplessness in handling the problems of modern Arabic. The main difficulty is seen in the syntax, its stagnation, and vagueness. The time seems ripe to draw theoretical conclusions from the evolution of Arabic since World War I. Academies may decide on reducing or eliminating "basic principles," in accordance with the Qurʾān and other sources. But the psychological difficulties to remove such a fine work as Arabic syntax from its pedestal are not overcome easily.

Since knowledge of Arabic diminishes, idioms that have fine equivalents in Arabic are introduced by way of translation or adaptation. It is generally agreed that elements of Arab descent in the colloquialisms are to be transplanted into the written language.

Ahmad Hasan al-Zayyāt, once a staunch purist, likens, it seems simplifyingly, the differences between the schools of Beirut and of Cairo to those between the old Kūfa and Basra schools. The Lebanese, like the Kufans, were liberal in their use of Arabic. Theirs was a "practical progressive free" school, which "committed knowledge to deed and literature to life." Time lessened the differences between those schools, and the academy of language brings about a reconciliation between them. See *Majallat Majma' al-Lugha al-'Arabiyya*, VIII (1955), 36-42. [Hereafter *Majalla.*]

Abundant synonymic is no longer considered a merit. Ahmad Amīn carrries his argument to the extreme of simplification, the ideal being "one word one meaning, neither synonym, nor homonym" (*ibid,.* p. 211).

Nowadays problems of distilling, not of conserving, are considered the acutest. The "lexical inflation" in dictionaries is due not only to the inherent qualities of Arabic. Indiscriminate recording is one of the main reasons, and ignorance may have had a large part in it. The Arab dictionary became the receptacle of: tribal differences in pronunciation and other dialectal variations; addition, omission or misplacing of diacritical points; arbitrary vowelling; transposition of consonants or replacing them by others, augmentation, likewise rejection of middle or final consonants; mutation for the sake of rhyme or assonance; changes in Hebrew or Aramaic loan words; mistaken changes because of similarity of the letters; foreign accent of Muslim non-Arab scholars; ignorant use of technical or scientific terms. See Khalīl al-Sakākīnī, *Majalla, ibid.,* pp. 124-32; Ahmad Amīn, *ibid.,* IX (1957), 36-41; al-Shihābī, *Majallat al-Majma' al-'Ilmī al-'Arabī,* XXVII (1952), 369-82.

23. See also Schoonover: "Survey of the Best Modern Arabic Books," *The Muslim World,* XLII (1952), 50-55; "Some Observations on Modern Arabic Literature," *ibid.,* XLIV (1954), 20-30.

Taha Husayn came perhaps closest to a style representing a synthesis, such as envisaged by Haykal. Some of its characteristics seem to derive from French, or are conditioned by specific circumstances in his life.

24. For obvious reasons the adaptation of Hebrew took far less time.

Al-Māzinī demands that richness of vocabulary should no longer be one of the qualities of Arabic. Austerity in words does not prejudice the capacity for expression. "The four strings of the guitar can render an infinite number of melodies" (*al-Hilāl*, 1942, pp. 113-14).

25. Also: "The writers of our generation are victims of confusion; they are like soldiers of the vanguard who know they are going toward certain death. Today's Egyptian literature fights in order that on its ruins there will arise geniuses to build a new culture, and the efforts of present writers will be the invisible foundations of that lofty building (*al-Makshūf*, Beirut, March 16, 1942).

26. See Charles Pellat, *Langue et littérature arabes*, pp. 49-54; Schoonover, "Contemporary Egyptian Authors," I, *The Muslim World*, XLV (1955), 26-36; also J. Lecerf, "Littérature dialectale et renaissance arabe moderne," *Bulletin d'Études Orientales*, Institut Français de Damas, 1933, t. III, pp. 117-20; *ibid.*, "Esquisse d'une problématique de l'arabe actuel," *L'Afrique et L'Asie*, No. 26, 1954, pp. 31-46.

27. Al-Hakīm envisages an ideal stage at which, through mutual borrowing, the colloquial has been raised to the literary language, and this simplified, so as to reduce the difference between them to a minimum.

Taha Husayn contends that raising the colloquial to a status of literary idiom also necessitates disciplining it, like the literary language, by a set of rules.

Both stress the necessity to simplify the norms originally set up for a classical language. See al-Shanāwī, "al-sirā' bayn al-'arabiyya wa-'l-'āmmiyya," *al-Adīb*, March, 1955, pp. 71-73; also: al-Hakīm, *Majalla, ibid.*, X (1958), 186-88; al-'Aqqād, *ibid.*, XI (1959), 75-78; Taymūr, *ibid.*, IX (1957), 19-24.

The cause of the spoken tongue has recently been espoused by the extreme left-wing in Egypt.

28. Khalfallah, "Literary Life in Egypt," *The Muslim World*, XLIV (1954), pp. 98-100. Cf. the observations of Prof. Fathy as quoted by Eric F. F. Bishop, "The Case for the Colloquial," *The Moslem World*, XXXII (1942), 331-32, and of Nabih Amin Faris, "The Case Against the Colloquial," *ibid.*, XXXIII (1943), 217-20.

Apart from the above mentioned sources, I feel indebted to the thorough treatment of these problems in H. Wehr, "Entwicklung und traditionelle Pflege der arabischen Schriftsprache in der Gegenwart," *ZDMG*, 97 (1943), pp. 16-46, and in B. Farès, "Des difficultés d'ordre linguistique, culturel et social que rencontre un écrivain arabe moderne spécialement en Égypte," *REI*, X (1936), 221-42. Farès holds to "traditionalisme eclairé." See also J. Lecerf, "Renaissance de la langue et de la littérature arabes" in *Entretiens sur l'évolution des pays de civilisation arabe* (Paris, 1936), pp. 31-42. For the unifying and differentiating forces in a language, see Jespersen, *Mankind, Nation and Individual* (London, 1946), pp. 38-83.

NOTES TO CHAPTER NINE

1. Fritz Steppat, "Nationalism und Islam bei Mustafā Kāmil," *Die Welt des Islam*, n. s., IV (1956), 252.

In the "basic principles" of the National Party, adopted in 1907, no mention is made of Arabs or things Arabic (*ibid.*, pp. 338-39).

To M. Colombe ("l'Égypte et les origines du nationalisme arabe," *L'Afrique et l'Asie*, No. 14, 1951, p. 20), Ibrāhīm Pasha's "panarabism" was rather a diplomatic maneuver to make Europe receptive to his political and territorial ambitions.

2. *Fī awqāt al-farāgh*, p. 373.

3. *Hāfiz wa-Shawqī*, pp. 209-10.

4. After twenty years Taha Husayn could openly state that the sanctity of the caliphate and the authenticity of the pre-Islamic poetry were myths. See "Tendances religieuses de la littérature égyptienne d'aujourd'hui," *Les Cahiers du Sud*, 1947, p. 238.

5. *Thawrat al-adab* (Cairo, 1933).

6. Taha Husayn considered it a mistake on the part of the Egyptians that they attached themselves intellectually to the East. The culture of Egypt in our days, he held, is the culture of the West, and moreover, its ancient culture, which was co-extensive with that of the Mediterranean, was close to ancient Greece. Islam, even through its language, did not turn the Egyptians into Orientals, just as with the acceptance of Chris-

tianity Europe did not become oriental. See *Mustaqbal al-thaqāfa fī misr* (Cairo, 1938), pp. 6-11, 15, 21.

Actually, his work represents, even through his Arab style alone, a synthesis of East and West.

7. *Mukhtārāt Salāma Mūsā*, pp. 261-64.

8. In the variations in attitude toward East and West, and also to the past in its various periods, traces of rationalization may be seen. The changes of attitude among the writers also indicate the pressure of prevailing political concepts.

In the 1940's Taha Husayn placed more emphasis on Arabdom. To him, the more Egypt's freedom increases, the more keen is she on cooperation with her neighbors. See *al-Muqattam*, September 6, 1944.

9. "The French Enlightenment culminated in the Revolution of 1789. From the first it was marked by a revolutionary trend, wholly political, which was impatient to turn ideas into acts. Hence the publicist reformer is dominant in it.

"In the ultimate resort all its philosophical, religious and artistic criticism is merged in its critique of society" (S. Marck, *Das Jahrhundert der Aufklärung*, 1923, p. 37).

10. "Studies in Contemporary Arabic Literature," III, BSOS, V (1928-30), 466.

11. After twenty years H. A. R. Gibb saw fit to note: "c'est un phenomène remarquable que la littérature arabe de l'Égypte d'entre les deux guerres, très occidentaliste, n'a pas eu de suites, ou n'a trouve qu'un faible echo tout au plus" ("La réaction contre la culture occidentale dans le Proche Orient," *Cahiers de l'Orient Contemporain*, 1951, p. 10).

12. *Tendances religieuses . . .* , *op. cit.*, p. 239.

13. On the ups and downs of the official attitude, in the main politically colored, see A. G. Chejne, "Egyptian Attitudes Towards Pan-Arabism," *MEJ*, XI (1957), 253-68.

14. "Intellectual Currents in Egypt," *Middle Eastern Affairs*, II (1951), 270-72.

15. "Contemporary Egyptian Literature," *ibid.*, pp. 90-97.

16. K. Schoonover, "Some Observations on Modern Arabic Literature," *The Muslim World*, XLIV (1954), 28-29.

17. *Op. cit.*, p. 9.

On the other side, Gibb stresses the effect of "the cleavage between the moral and technical culture of the West" and "the disregard of Western political leaders for human and social interests." See *Near Eastern Culture and Society*, T. Cuyler Young, ed. (Princeton, 1951), pp. 230, 239.

18. At the congress of Arab writers, held in Cairo in 1957, Arab nationalism seemed an incontestable fact to all the Egyptian speakers. To Taha Husayn, it is to be fostered by a literature born of the artist's freedom. Political enmities may disappear, but national literature is to stay.

Mahmūd Taymūr sees in nationalism "the prophecy of our epoch." Arab writers have renounced abstract speculation and sentimental reveries. They are animated by a new spirit of vigilance, work and battle.

Bint al-Shātī' defends *l'art pour l'art* as the highest form; it brings about refinement of public taste. Peaceful co-existence and Arab nationalism are her twin themes to extol.

As for the leftists, "peoples' movements," not literature, produce nationalism. Poetry is national insofar as it expresses people's feelings (al-Sharqāwī). Arab nationalism is a step forward. The moment the fight against imperialism comes to an end, there will be a need for a new philosophy (Mandūr). See G. C. Anawati, "Le congrès des écrivains arabes," *La revue du Caire*, 1958, No. 215-16.

19. For the contact with European literature in the last two centuries see Henri Pérès, *La littérature arabe et l'Islam* (Algiers, 1949), pp. v-xiv. Also: M. Colombe, *L'Évolution de l'Égypte, 1924-1950* (Paris, 1951); "Cinquante ans de littérature égyptienne," *La revue du Caire*, XXXI (1953), especially M. M. Chawkat, "La fiction dans la littérature contemporaine d'É-gypte," pp. 134-35.

NOTES TO CHAPTER TEN

1. Gertrude C. Bell, *Review of the Civil Administration of Mesopotamia* (London, 1920), pp. 6, 7, 76.

2. Dowson, *An Inquiry into Land Tenure and Related Questions* (London, 1931), p. 16.

3. *Ibid.*, p. 17.

4. Bell, *op. cit.*, pp. 16n-17.

5. *Report . . . on the Administration of 'Iraq in the period April, 1923–December, 1924* (London, 1925), p. 138.

6. *Special Report . . . on the Progress of 'Iraq during the period 1920-1931* (London, 1931), pp. 203-4; Bell, pp. 17, 22, 85.

7. *Report . . . on the Administration of 'Iraq for the year 1929* (London, 1930), p. 47.

8. Bell, pp. 82-86.

9. *Report on 'Iraq Administration, October, 1920–March, 1922* (London, 1923), p. 18.

10. Art. 88 of the Constitution, passed in July 1924, provides for Special Courts or Committees to be set up when necessary "for settling criminal and civil cases relating to the tribes in accordance with tribal custom." The Tribes Criminal and Civil Disputes Regulations Amendment Law of 1924 transfers the powers conferred on the Civil Commissioner and other British officials to the Ministry of Interior, Mutasarifs and Qaimmaqams, respectively, to deal with offences committed by tribesmen without reference to the ordinary courts of the land.

11. *Report . . . for 1929*, p. 47.

12. *Report . . . 1923-1924*, pp. 6, 7, 21, 58, 68, 76, 139.

13. *Report . . . 1920-1922*, p. 21.

14. *Report on the 'Iraq Administration, April, 1922–March, 1923* (London, 1924), pp. 71-72.

15. *Ibid.*, p. 168.

16. *Report on the Administration of 'Iraq for the year 1928* (London, 1929), pp. 47-48; *Special Report . . . 1920-1931*, p. 125.

17. *Report . . . 1928*, p. 152.

18. *Report on the Administration of 'Iraq for the year 1927* (London, 1928), p. 174.

19. *Ibid.*, p. 126. The legislators were even more generous: Law No. 11 of 1928 granted to ex-King 'Alī ibn al-Husayn of Hijāz miri land not exceeding 22,000 donums without equivalent.

20. *Report on the Administration of 'Iraq for 1926* (London, 1927), p. 133.

21. *Report . . . 1927*, p. 173; *Report . . . 1928*, pp. 152-53; Dowson, *op. cit.*, p. 28.

22. *Report . . . 1929*, p. 165.

23. *Special Report . . . 1920-1931*, p. 125.

24. Dowson, pp. 10, 27.

25. Hassan Mohamed Ali, "Miri Sirf Land Development in Iraq," *International Social Science Bulletin*, V (1953), 713-17; Salāh al-Dīn al-Nāhī, Muqaddima fī al-iqtā' wa-nizām al-arādī fī al-'Irāq (Baghdad, 1955), pp. 25-9.

26. Majid Khadduri, *Independent Iraq* (London, 1951), pp. 51-53, 57-60, 115-18.

27. Yūsuf Ismā'īl, *Inqilāb tishrīn al-awwal* (Baghdad, 1936), pp. 9, 11, 49. On the other hand, al-Yāfī, *'Irāq bayna inqilābayn* (Beirut, 1948), states that Hikmat Sulaymān, one of the *coup d'état* men, owned 48,000 donum.

28. *Liwā al-Istiqlāl*, November 30, 1950.

29. Hasan Muhammad 'Alī, "al-mulkiyya al-saghīra fī tarīq numuwwihā fī al-'Irāq," *Majallat al-Zirā'a al-'Irāqiyya*, VIII (1953), 289.

30. Norman Burns, "The Dujaylah Land Settlement," *MEJ*, V (1951), 363; Hasan al-Thāmir, "mashrū' al-Dujayla," *'Alam al-Ghad*, August 1, 1946; Farīd Ahmar, "mashrū' al-Dujayla," *al-Watan*, August 24, 1945.

31. Farīd Ahmar, "mashrū' al-Hawīja," *al-Watan*, October 19, 1945.

32. The statistical data differ widely. According to Hassan Mohamed Ali, *Land Reclamation and Settlement* (Baghdad, 1955), p. 67, there were 290 leaseholds of which 13 between 10,000 and 35,000 donums, 10 between 5,000 and 10,000, and 95 between 1,000 and 5,000. Other versions: 29 holdings each more than 20,000 donums (Lord Salter, *The Development of 'Iraq*, London, 1955, p. 13).

33. Bell, *op. cit.*, p. 86; (y.), "al-nizām al-zirā'ī," *al-Watan*, January 15, February 2, 23, March 16, 1946; Eugen Wirth, "Landwirtschaft und Mensch im Binnendelta des unteren Tigris," *Mitteilungen der geographischen Gesellschaft in Hamburg*, LII (1955), 55-63; al-Shaykhlī, "min mashākil al-arādī fī al-'Amāra," *al-Watan*, September 28, 1945; *ibid.*, "arādī al-'Amāra tu'tā bi-'l-iltizām," *al-Watan*, June 21, 1946; Farīd al-Ahmar, "arādī liwā al-'Amāra," *al-Watan*, December 28, 1945; Edmonds, "The Marshmen of Southern 'Iraq," *The Geographical Journal*, CXXIV (1958), 92-94.

34. Hassan Mohamed Ali, *op. cit.*, p. 69.

35. al-Nāhī, *op. cit.*, pp. 48-55; Warriner, *Land Reform and Development in the Middle East*, pp. 150-54.

36. al-Zāhir, "hikāyat al-iqtā'," *al-Bilād*, February 1, 1946.

37. *Ibid.*, "hikāyat al-iqtā' fī liwā al-Hilla," *al-Bilād*, April 9, 1946.

38. *Ibid.*, "hikāyat al-iqtā' fī liwā Baghdad," *al-Bilād*, March 24, 1946. According to Hasan Muhammad 'Alī, *al-Islāh al-zirā'ī*

wa-'l-i'mār (Baghdad, 1956), there are 3,800 holdings, four more than 20,000 each, 606 less than 4 donums each.

39. al-Yāsirī, "arqām tatakallam," *al-Husūn*, December 14, 1945; al-Zāhir, "hikāyat al-iqtā' fī liwā Diyāla," *al-Bilād*, April 7, 1946.

40. al-Zāhir, "iqtā'iyyāt al-nakhīl fī liwā al-Basra," *al-Bilād*, March 11, 1946; Muzaffar Ahmad, "al-tumūr al-'irāqiyya wa-athruhā fī al-iqtisād al-watanī," *Majallat al-Zirā'a al-'Irāqiyya*, VIII (1953), 519-29; Barakāt, "al-mallāk wa-'l-ta'āb," *al-Bilād*, April 3, 1946; al-Dabbāgh, *al-Nakhīl wa-'l-tumūr fī al-'Irāq* (Baghdad, 1956), pp. 124-27; V. H. W. Dowson, "The Date Cultivation and the Date Cultivators of Basrah," *JRCAS*, XXVI (1939), 247-49.

41. al-Dabbāgh, *op. cit.*, pp. 48-50, 68.

42. 'Abbās al-'Azzāwī, *'ashā'ir al-'Irāq al-kurdiyya* (Baghdad, 1947), II, 237-38; Khadr, *"ba'd mashākil al-fallāh fī Tall 'Afar,"* *al-Watan*, October 12, 1945; E. R. Leach, *Social and Economic Organization of the Rowanduz Kurds* (London, 1940), pp. 15-16; Frederik Barth, *Principles of Social Organization in Southern Kurdistan* (Oslo, 1953), pp. 20-23; Ja'far Khayyāt, *al-qarya al-'irāqiyya* (Baghdad, 1950), pp. 22-23; 'Abd al-Razzāq al-Hilālī, *al-hijra min al-rīf ilā al-mudun* (Baghdad, 1958), pp. 14-17.

43. al-Dujaylī, *"hissat al-fallāh min al-intāj al-zirā'ī fī al-'Irāq,"* *'Alam al-Ghad*, October 7, 1945; *The Economic Development of Iraq* (Washington, 1952), pp. 142-44.

44. For the effects of this law, see Warriner, *op. cit.*, p. 156.

45. Hāshim Jawād, *muqaddima fī kiyān al-'Irāq al-ijtimā'ī* (Baghdad, 1946), pp. 43-48.

46. *Report . . . 1923-1924, op. cit.*, p. 138.

47. al-Uzrī, "The Council for Reconstruction" (in Arabic), *al-Abhāth*, VIII (1955), 44-55.

Other sources: C. J. Edmonds. "The Place of the Kurds in the Middle Eastern Scene," *JRCAS*, XLV (1958), 149-50; Carl Iversen, *A Report on Monetary Policy in Iraq* (Copenhagen, 1954); B. A. Keen, *The Agricultural Development of the Middle East* (London, 1946), pp. 5, 27-30, 85-87; *Statistical Abstract*, 1956 (Baghdad, 1957).

NOTES TO CHAPTER ELEVEN

1. The lower limit of a statistical large estate unit is 100 hectares. Before World War I large landownership in the vilayet of Damascus was estimated at 60 percent, medium at 15, and small at 25. See Louis Cardon, *Le régime de la propriété foncière en Syrie et au Liban* (Paris: Librairie du Recueil Sirey, 1932), pp. 57-58.

2. For a survey, especially until World War I, see Paul J. Klat, "The Origins of Land Ownership in Syria," *Middle East Economic Papers,* (Beirut, 1958), pp. 51-66; also, Joseph Chaoui, *Le régime foncier en Syrie,* (Aix-en-Provence, Roubaud, 1928), pp. 15-34.

3. K. Bazily, *Siria i Palestina pod turetzkim pravitel'stvom* (Odessa, 1862), I, 8-10; Laurence Oliphant, *The Land of Gilead* (Edinburgh, 1880), pp. 129, 320; George E. Post, "Essays on the Sects and Nationalities of Syria and Palestine," *Palestine Exploration Fund, Quarterly,* April 1891, pp. 106-7; Mohammed Sarrage, *La nécessité d'une réforme agraire en Syrie* (Toulouse, 1935), p. 19.

4. *Ibid.,* p. 20.

5. Norman N. Lewis, "The Frontier of Settlement in Syria, 1800-1950," *International Affairs,* XXXI (1955), 48-60.

6. Sarrage, *op. cit.,* p. 242; also J. Weulersse, *Régime agraire et vie agricole en Syrie,* Bulletin de L'Association de Géographes Français, No. 113, 1938, pp. 59-60.

7. "Notes sur la propriété foncière dans la Syrie Centrale," *L'Asie Française,* April 1933, pp. 132-34.

8. *Rapport à la Société des Nations sur la situation de la Syrie et du Liban* (1927), p. 130.

9. *Ibid.,* 1926, pp. 167-68.

10. 'Isām 'Ashūr, "Métayage in Syria, Lebanon and Palestine" (in Arabic), *al-Abhāth,* I (1948), 53.

11. According to Nafi Sayem El-Dahr, "Land Settlement in Syria," *International Journal of Agrarian Affairs,* January, 1955, pp. 70-71, the major part of the state domain, which originally covered up to 1,334,000 hectares, or about 23 percent of the cultivable (nondesert) area, "seems to have already been disposed of, mostly to large landowners."

Another estimate: 1,815,100 hectares, most of the areas cultivable but not cultivated. See Youssef Helbaoui, *La Syrie; mise en valeur d'un pays sous-développé* (Paris: Librairie générale de droit et de jurisprudence, 1956), p. 87. It is generally agreed that a part of the state domain is near-desert land.

12. J. Weulersse, *Paysans de Syrie et du Proche Orient* (Paris: Gallimard, 1946), pp. 99-108; Paul J. Klat, "Musha Holdings and Land Fragmentation in Syria," *Middle East Economic Papers*, 1957, pp. 12-23.

13. 'Isām 'Ashūr, *op. cit.*, pp. 65-67.

14. Doreen Warriner, *Land Reform and Development in the Middle East*, 1957, pp. 88-89.

15. 'Isām 'Ashūr, *op. cit.*, II (1949), 62.

16. Government of Syria, *Report on Jazira*, 1952; André Gibert et Maurice Févret, "La Djézireh syrienne et son réveil écono-mique," *Revue de Géographie de Lyon*, XXVIII (1953), 1-15, 83-99; Robert Montagne, *Quelques aspects du peuplement de la Haute-Djéziré*, Bulletin d'Études Orientales, Institut Français de Damas, t. II, 1932, pp. 52-66; J. Rowlands, "The Khabur Valley," *JRCAS*, XXXIV (1947), 144-49; J. S., "le Bec de Canard Syrien," *L'Asie Française* (March, 1929), pp. 52-66; R. Boghossian, "Une région particulière, la Djéziréh," *Mélanges proche-orientaux d'économie politique*, Beirut, pp. 241-89.

For the capitalist entrepreneurship, see Warriner, *op. cit.*, pp. 88-93. At the end of 1956, the area surveyed was 830,715 hectares out of a total of 2,217,000 hectares, all of it considered cultivable. See *Statistical Abstract of Syria*, 1956, p. 495.

17. H. Charles, *Tribus moutonnières du Moyen-Euphrate*, Documents d'Études Orientales, Institut Français de Damas, t. VIII, 1939; *ibid.*, *La sédentarisation entre Euphrate et Balikh*, Beirut, 1942; F. de Dainville, *Phénomènes de sédentarisation dans les tribus du Moyen-Euphrate*, Bulletin de L'Association de Géographes Français, Nos. 177-78, 1946, pp. 54-58.

18. André Gibert, L'Irrigation de la plaine de Homs et ses problèmes, *Revue de Géographie de Lyon*, XXIV (1949), 151-58; 'Abd al-Basīt al-Khatīb, The Ghāb Project (in Arabic), *al-Abhāth*, VIII (1955), 329-41; Norman N. Lewis, "Malaria, Irrigation and Soil Erosion in Central Syria," *The Geographical Revue*, XXXIX (1949), pp. 278-90; *ibid.*, "Selemiya, Three Years After," XL (1950), pp. 479-81; Anwar Naaman, *Précisions sur la structure agraire dans la région de Homs—Hama* (Syrie), Bulletin de L'Association de Géographes Français, Nos. 208-9, 1950, pp. 53-59.

19. J. Weulersse, *Pays des Alaouites* (Tours, 1940), pp. 218-24; Deane R. Hinton, "Latakia Tobacco," *Foreign Agriculture,* February, 1949, pp. 44-45.

20. George Hakim, "Land Tenure Reform," *Middle East Economic Papers,* 1954, pp. 75-90; Notes . . . , *op. cit.,* pp. 135-36; Sa'd Himadeh, "Effect of Land Tenure on Land Use and Production in the Middle East" (in Arabic), *al-Abhāth,* IX (1956), 3-20.

21. *Statistical Abstract of Syria, 1953,* pp. 214-15. Since approximately the same figure is given for 1943, it could be assumed that the discontinuation of the settlement work enabled enterprising landowners and operators to get hold of unregistered land. See also Warriner, *op. cit.,* p. 101.

22. *Statistical Abstract of Syria,* 1956, p. 494. The survey in Jabal al-Durūz has not yet been started, obviously for political reasons, and the area covered in the Euphrates province was 8,641 hectares.

23. According to the ministry for agrarian reform, 3,260 owners are to be affected by this law. A total of 1,700,000 hectares are due to be expropriated (*The Middle East Economist and Financial Service,* November 1959, p. 157).

Law No. 252 of 1959 provides for alienation of state domain. A total of 800,000 hectares are to be dissolved and assigned for distribution.

A decree-law of June 1959 provides for assigning lots of three hectares of adjacent mountainous desert land to residents of forest land or of nearby villages.

Other sources: Albert Khuri, "Land Tenure," *Economic Organization of Syria,* ed. by S. B. Himadeh (Beirut, 1936), pp. 51-69; Sa'd B. Himadeh, Second Social Welfare Seminar for Arab States of the Middle East (Cairo, 1950), pp. 429-32; Nazim Moussly, *Le problème de l'eau en Syrie* (Lyon, 1951); Akram El-Ricaby, "Land Tenure in Syria," *Proceedings of the international conference on land tenure and selected problems in world agriculture* (University of Wisconsin Press, 1956), pp. 84-95; Victor Sonum, "Aperçu historico-économique, sommaire de la structure de la Syrie, *Tijdschrift voor economische en sociale geographie,* June–July, 1955, pp. 139-40; Adnan Mahhouk, "Recent Agricultural Development and Bedouin Settlement in Syria," *MEJ,* X (1956), 167-76; Doreen Warriner, *Land and Poverty in the Middle East* (London, 1948).

NOTES TO CONCLUSION

1. Kurdish tribes had an important part in the suppression of the Mosul revolt in March, 1959. See Munīr Razūq, *Mu'āmarat 'Abd al-Nāsir*, Baghdad, April, 1959.

2. *Ibid.*

3. Rashīd al-Badrī, *Majzarat al-Mawsil*, kutub qawmiyya, No. 40 (Cairo, January, 1960).

4. See *Economic Development in the Middle East, 1957-1958.*

5. See "Oil and Social Changes," *The Economist*, July 2, 1955.

6. The recent Kurdish revolt in Iraq, after employment of Kurdish tribes in suppressing the Mosul revolt, and the secession of Syria from the U. A. R. speak for themselves.

Index